EXPERIENCING
and
COUNSELING
MULTICULTURAL
and
DIVERSE
POPULATIONS
Second Edition

Nicholas A. Vacc, Ed.D.
Professor and Chairperson
Department of Counseling and
Specialized Educational Development
University of North Carolina
Greensboro, North Carolina

Joe Wittmer, Ph.D.
Professor and Chairperson
Department of Counselor Education
University of Florida
Gainesville, Florida

Susan B. DeVaney, M.Ed.
Doctoral Student
Department of Counseling and
Specialized Educational Development
University of North Carolina
Greensboro, North Carolina

ACCELERATED DEVELOPMENT INC.
Publishers
Muncie   Indiana

EXPERIENCING and COUNSELING MULTICULTURAL and DIVERSE POPULATIONS

© Copyright 1988 by Accelerated Development Inc.

4 5 6 7 8 9 10

Printed in the United States of America

Technical Development: Tanya Dalton
                        Delores Kellogg
                        Marguerite Mader
                        Sheila Sheward

Library of Congress Cataloging-in-Publication Data

Experiencing and counseling multicultural and diverse populations.

Rev. ed. of: Let me be me. 1980.
Includes bibliographies and index.
1. Social work with minorities--United States.
2. Minorities--Counseling of--United States. I. Vacc, Nicholas A. II. Wittmer, Joe. III. DeVaney, Susan B., 1947-   . IV. Let me be me.
HV3176.E96 1988   362'.973   88-70008
ISBN 0-915202-78-6

LCN: 88-70008

ACCELERATED DEVELOPMENT INC.
PUBLISHERS
3808 West Kilgore Avenue
Muncie, Indiana 47304-4896
Toll Free Order Number 1-800-222-1166

DEDICATION

To
Our
Colleagues

TABLE OF CONTENTS

4   GAY AND LESBIAN POPULATIONS
Joseph L. Norton **61**

1

INTRODUCTION

NICHOLAS A. VACC, Ed.D.

JOE WITTMER, Ph.D.

SUSAN B. DE VANEY, M.Ed.

INTRODUCTION

This book presents an overview of twelve diverse populations. Published originally as *Let Me Be Me: Special Populations and the Helping Professional,* this edition has an increased number of populations represented, been revised and updated in content, and been stylistically improved. Although this edition is by no means all inclusive, those needs, experiences, and characteristics of the groups presented are representative of divergent, unique, or ethnic subgroups in American society; thus the term "diverse populations."

PURPOSE OF THE BOOK

The purpose of this book is to expose practitioners such as counselors, teachers, college professors, mental-health workers, and social workers to the unique and genuine characteristics of several of United States' subgroups and to effectively assist these same professionals as they work with clients and/or students from these populations. We believe that knowledge and awareness of those factors which influence the behavior of individuals from these subgroups will assist helpers to be more effective in their work. The fundamental assumption is that helpers can improve their effectiveness if appropriate attitudes, information, and self-understanding exist.

This book also was written to partially fill the existing gap in the lack of relevant educational materials and satisfy a growing consciousness that action is needed in order to make school, work, and personal experiences more meaningful for those individuals whose racial, social, religious, and/or cultural backgrounds; sex; physical abilities; or language differ from those of mainstream society.

THE EDITORS' PHILOSOPHY FOR
WRITING THE BOOK

Our belief is that the helping professional may hold the key to the process of reducing, if not eliminating, the social and emotional barriers which prevent many of the members of America's subgroups from becoming secure citizens. To do this, helping professionals must make a concerted effort to approach the different subgroup members among their clientele, with a cognitive understanding over and above the affectual. Love and empathy are not enough! We cannot and do not refute the abundance of research findings which indicate that to be effective as a helper one must communicate warmly, empathetically, and genuinely with clients. However, if helping professionals are inexperienced in the values and conduct of special populations, these professionals will be less effective than they would be when operating with an accurate, cognitive understanding of the total milieu of these individuals.

Acute disparities are compounded when a helper with a lack of cognitive knowledge about a special subgroup interacts with a confused and bewildered group member. Functioning in a congenial, familiar cultural situation, the helper may be prone to impose idealized values on the client. A lack of cognitive understanding makes one more prone to impose one's own values. In contrast, knowledgeable helping professionals can be catalysts in the process of helping others develop an appreciation of the different subgroups found in America as well as facilitating improved individual functioning within the groups themselves.

Why is a lack of true understanding of the many different subgroups still found in United States today? Our feeling is that much of the misunderstanding stems from American standards determined by college graduates who often believe that everyone is like them or should be like them. This phenomenon of assumed similarity causes a lack of desire to understand accurately those who are different socially and culturally. For example, can the Amish truly not want television? As you read Wittmer's chapter concerning this subgroup, you will find that they really do not want TV in their homes. Helpers with a sound cognitive knowledge of their clients' cultural background will more easily understand the source and reasons for the behaviors which may appear odd or peculiar at times.

As you read the subsequent chapters, you will learn that the participants of most of the special groups included in the book do not want to be mainstreamed, to develop middle-class values, or be robbed of their individuality and dignity. They want their difficulties and differences to be understood rather than interpreted and evaluated. They desire to be appreciated for what they are— members of a particular subgroup who have a right to exist in the United States as long as they are unoffending and tax-paying citizens. Many of the special population groups addressed in this book are still sadly misunderstood; their experiences in today's schools and in society in general are a long way from being positive and productive.

Most experiences and perceptions are relevant to the group in which one was reared. Likewise, what is considered peculiar behavior in one cultural setting may be viewed as proper and necessary in another culture. Helpers should realize that clients or students who are members of a special population may never be completely at ease with them. However, these clients or students will communicate if accepted on an affective level as fellow human beings and on a cognitive level as possessing a unique cultural background. Thus, we urge readers to work hard to preserve their own self-respect and the self-respect of all persons with whom they come in contact. In conclusion, the helping professional is not to stamp out mistakes nor to institutionalize, but rather to help each client or student become a productive and worthwhile individual within society, regardless of race, social beliefs, sex, age, religion, or cultural background.

HISTORICAL INFLUENCES

Special population groups frequently have been politicized and influenced by the social mood of the times. The dominant thought until the 1960s was that America was a melting pot of cultures. Its social institutions, schools, and industries reflected the democratic ideal of providing opportunity to all and upward mobility to the deserving. An assumption basic to this thought was that cultural homogeneity (assimilation) was success and cultural heterogeneity was failure. Assimilation connoted the unacceptability of minority populations' culture, language, and folkways in the United States. Today, a new interpretation relative to special populations is being viewed with increasing favor; that the democratic ideal, imposed by the majority on individuals through education, serves to stamp out much that is good in society simply because it is different. Ravitch (1976) stated:

> For a variety of reasons, the despair which followed the political assassinations of the Kennedy brothers and Martin Luther King, the anger which flowed from urban riots and the Vietnam War, and the cynicism which followed the Watergate disclosures—the failure theory of the radical revisionists—is strongly in the ascendancy. (p.214)

The discernable interest of American minorities for recognition and preservation of their uniqueness, for whatever reasons, has added impetus for greater understanding of America's special populations.

United States, unfortunately, has a long history of oppression of minority groups. A case in point is the native American. The process of assimilation was actually funded by Congress in the early 1800s to "promote civilization among the aborigines" (Ravitch, 1976). Not until the 1930s did the government's Bureau of Indian Affairs relax its efforts for "Americanization," and then it was only for a brief period of time.

Assimilation was basic to the American system, particularly during and after World War I. Many an immigrant's children were made to feel ashamed of their family's speech, customs, and cultural values (Ravitch, 1976). During World War II, heightened patriotism and fear of subversion caused the relocation of thousands of Japanese Americans. Many Germans changed their names for fear of reprisal. Many Americans once again took note of the negative value of being different.

Not until the late 1940s, after World War II, did some significant events occur that moved society toward accepting differences. In 1947, President Truman created the president's Committee on Employment of the Handicapped to promote, on a voluntary basis, more jobs for handicapped people. In 1954, the landmark Supreme Court decision in the case of Oliver Brown brought an end to existing patterns of segregated schools. Starting with the Kennedy years in the 1960s, and more decisively during President Johnson's term of office, public policies and political forces gave impetus to the movement for individual rights. The Economic Opportunity Act and the Civil Rights Act of 1964, as well as the Elementary and Secondary Education Act of 1965, helped foster the rights of minority persons. No one act of legislation granted all "rights," but each contributed to a ripple effect for minority populations. Legislation affecting Blacks or Native Americans, for example, also affected the handicapped and refugees. Pathways were established for all special groups. Coalitions among members of special populations grew; quiet organizations became active lobbyists at all levels of government and demonstrators took to the streets

Historical influences relative to special populations can be easily oversimplified and explained by simplistic slogans or by topographical historical counts. But, to do so is to mock what is explicitly being sought by these groups—individuality and recognition of uniqueness.

This brief attempt to synthesize some of the influences affecting special populations has been included to generate in the reader a sense of the complexity of the situational and political factors which bring us to this point in history. As stated by Ravitch (1976):

> Until late in the nineteenth century, this nation was considered by its majority to be a white protestant country; at some time near the turn of the century, it became a white christian country; after World War II, it was a white man's country. During the past several years it has become a multi-ethnic, multi-racial country intensely aware of differences of every kind...(p. 228)

The emerging sense of worth of members of special populations, then, can no longer be neglected. Learning about their different values, attitudes, desires, aspirations, and beliefs affects every citizen's life.

USERS OF THE BOOK

We urge teachers, professional counselors, and others, as they work with members of special populations, to seek out naturally existing characteristics that will aid the "different" students or clients as they learn. In other words, rather than bending the student to match the curriculum, we suggest cultivating the talents and unique cultural characteristics that already exist within that individual.

Authors of chapters in this book are writing from a particular perspective. In most cases, they either have been members of the respective subgroup or are members of that group today. We caution you not to stereotype each individual within a population strictly by the characteristics outlined within the respective chapter. For example, after reading the chapter concerning the Southeast Asian refugee, one might conclude that all such persons are reserved and shy when receiving assistance. This is not necessarily the case. You also could encounter, for example a Vietnamese client or student who is highly extroverted and wishes to shed any vestiges of the Asian culture. Thus, we urge you to avoid stereotypic generalizations of particular groups as you work with respective members.

Basic to working with individuals in a given population group are a number of assumptions which are woven into the succeeding chapters:

1. Individuals rather than mass methods of working with individuals are important.

2. The individual, not the subgroup, is the unit of consideration. The individual is a person primarily and a Black, Mexican-American, or single parent, for example, secondarily.

3. The social aspects of an individual's life, including relationships at home, work, and school, are as important as that person's body and mind.

4. Accurate information is necessary as a foundation for providing services for the individual.

5. Staffing of services by adequately trained professionals via preservice and inservice programs of preparation and skill development is essential.

The process of assisting the helper to gain an understanding and awareness of the variations among individuals is a basic goal of a helping professional's instruction or training. In our opinion counselor educators, sociology and psychology professors, and teacher educators will find this book useful as a text for courses that are now being developed at the college level to train individuals to work with America's subgroups. The book also can be useful in inservice consultation activities with professional counselors, teachers, para-professionals, and social workers. Although the book is aimed at helping professionals, we are convinced that it also is a worthwhile reference and text for high school teachers preparing units on United States' subgroups. The informative nature and authenticity of the book, we think, will greatly enhance the interest level of high school students. Helping children and adults to understand the diversity of United States' population is basic to fostering a healthy American society and developing a greater understanding of and appreciation for the different societies of the world.

We recommend responding to the awareness index as you read each chapter, then thoroughly reading Loesch's epilogue. In that final chapter, Loesch provides a variety of helpful suggestions and exercises to enhance counselor preparation programs (helping professionals) with regard to special populations.

REFERENCE

Ravitch, D. (1976). On the history of minority group education in the United States. *Teacher College Record, 78*, 213-228.

2

A COUNSELOR in a MULTICULTURAL WORLD

JANET J. LARSEN, Ed.D.
Professor Emeritus
Counselor Education Department
University of Florida

and

RICHARD D. DOWNIE, Ph.D.
Assistant Dean and Director
International Student Services
Affiliate Assistant Professor
Counselor Education Department
University of Florida

JANET J. LARSEN, Ed.D.

Janet J. Larsen is Professor Emeritus, Counselor Education Department, at the University of Florida. A reading specialist, licensed school psychologist, and consultant to schools both nationally and internationally, she has studied problems of communication in communist and non-communist countries, participated in numerous international conferences, taught graduate courses in measurement and in multicultural counseling, and chaired many doctoral students' programs in which research was related to cross-cultural problems. Her B.A. was earned at the University of Iowa and her M.Ed., Ed.S., and Ed.D. from the University of Florida.

RICHARD D. DOWNIE, Ph.D.

Richard D. Downie is currently Assistant Dean and Director for International Student Services at the University of Florida. He also is Affiliate Assistant Professor in the Counselor Education Department. Dr. Downie held the office of President, National Association for Foreign Student Affairs (NAFSA) in 1986-87 and is active in many other national and international professional associations. He has been the recipient of Fulbright awards for international educators and administrators to West Germany and Japan and lived in India when employed as the Director of Pupil Services for the American International School in New Delhi. Dr. Downie began his counseling career in California after completing his B.A. degree at the University of California, Davis. He later completed his M.A. at the University of Michigan and Ph.D. at the Michigan State University.

A COUNSELOR IN A MULTICULTURAL WORLD

AWARENESS INDEX

Directions: Mark each answer agree, disagree, or don't know. Compare your answers with the scoring guide at the end of the test.

1. Counseling theory and practice today are still adequate for cross-cultural and multicultural counseling.

2. The events in history such as war and famine seldom influence the basic customs and values of a society.

3. All persons have the same basic needs regardless of the society in which they live.

4. In meeting psychological and physical needs, people in all cultures show remarkable diversity.

5. Stereotyping always has a negative impact.

6. Persons experience less anxiety and alienation when their daily lives are predictable.

7. Persons who have lived in several cultures experience the same problems as those who have lived in only one culture.

8. The question of identity (who am I?) becomes a special concern for persons in rapidly changing social and cultural relationships.

9. Fortunately, commonalities across cultures provide a strong foundation for establishing positive relationships with persons from other cultures.

Scoring Guide for Awareness Index

1. Disagree	4. Agree	7. Disagree
2. Disagree	5. Disagree	8. Agree
3. Agree	6. Agree	9. Agree

"Know then thyself, presume not God to scan
The proper study of mankind is Man
Placed on this isthmus of a middle state
A being darkly wise and rudely great."

Alexander Pope

How many times have you heard it said, "The world is changing;" "The world is a global village;" "The world is interdependent;" or "The world is growing smaller?" No matter how it is expressed, the general idea is simple yet profound. How has the world changed? It seems to be a result of a combination of forces that at times are overwhelming to assimilate. As counselors in today's world, we must understand how these changes affect our profession (Wrenn, 1962). How do we avoid being culturally encapsulated in our role of counselor?

The nature of the world in which we live is forcing persons in the helping profession to become aware of cultural configurations within and without the United States that affect the manner in which people interact. Emerging social patterns based on the expansion of relationships across previous barriers place a special responsibility on us. Brislin et al.(1986), in his explanation of our tendency to have a one-culture outlook, has indicated that a monocultural set of assumptions results in professional encapsulation. When reality is defined in terms of only our own views, one can easily develop an insensitivity to cultural variations among other individuals. Ponterott and Casas (1987) said, "Counseling programs are still operating from a culturally encapsulated framework; however, given the changing social and ethnic demographics in this country, such encapsulation is no longer feasible or ethically acceptable" (p. 434).

Although the United States has made major strides in many areas, the counseling and mental health profession has yet to become seriously concerned with relevant issues for culturally diverse groups. A need exists to develop a professional awareness of complexities that are a part of a multicultural society (Axelson, 1986).

FORCES OF CHANGE

In the past, physical borders tended to divide societies, isolating people by preventing access to those who were different.

As we moved rapidly into an interdependent world, boundaries changed and multiculturalism (pluralism, internationalism) became a fact of life. As McLuhan (1968) said, "The electronic culture of the global village confronts us with a situation in which entire societies inter-communicate by a sort of macroscopic gesticulation" (p.11). With advances in technology, mobility has expanded. A vast increase in planes, railways, and highways has made almost any place in the world accessible within a few hours or days. Foreign travel is not reserved for the wealthy or the adventurous but is within the grasp of the average citizen.

Persons have been mobile in other centuries before our own; however, the rate and number moving from one society to another is phenomenal by comparison. Because of the magnitude of the movement, cultural contacts have become extensive at all levels in all societies. The massive movement of persons between societies and the inter-mingling of their cultures have become a reality (McNeil, 1963).

Another factor contributing to the change is the availability of radio, TV, transistors and satellite transmission at fairly low cost. People in remote villages are able to receive news from almost anywhere on the globe. People are learning about one another through visual and auditory means. No longer are they dependent upon books, letters, and an occasional visitor for information. Closely related to the advances in communication systems is the increased demand to learn other languages, including a greater dependence on English as a second language. Persons can see, hear, taste, smell, and feel almost every variety of human experience through new-found technologies. They are the "toys" for culture contact.

Following technological innovation has come accelerated contact through the exchange of goods, products, and services. As third world nations develop their economics, the prospect for trade increases. Rarely are we aware of how much other cultures affect our buying habits. Are there many homes in the Unites States today without a product from another country, another society?

Ideas also spread through out the world as communication processes increase. Although political and language differences continue to be barriers and gross misunderstandings abound, the velocity of new paths of transmission is heartening (McNeil 1963). The most influential factor and the most difficult to measure is the exchange of ideas. Whether it be philosophy, music, art, politics, or religion, now is a time when all cultures are contributing to the knowledge of others through the interchange of ideas.

Powerful forces are causing the world to shrink in our perceptions. Communication systems, technological development, international trade, second-language emphasis, and opportunities for the exchange of ideas are affecting our cultural orientation. In the United States the time has come for counselors to re-evaluate basic theories, techniques, and practices that have traditionally been oriented to a monocultural world view.

We are in an awakening period as we discover the wide variety of customs and values within and without our borders. Counselors can not assume that clients come from a fairly homogeneous background. No longer can we feel secure in our familiarity with customs and values. As Axelson (1986) reminded us, "the goal of a culturally pluralist society is unity in diversity. The dominant culture benefits from co-existence and interaction with the cultures of adjunct groups" (p. 13). A new view of the population we serve is forming.

FACTORS AFFECTING CULTURAL CHARACTERISTICS

Every culture is molded by environmental conditions and historic events that contribute to the uniqueness of persons sustained in the society. What must be remembered is that human society does not exist without culture and culture cannot exist without a society (Kupferer & Fitzgerald, 1971).

A major determinant of the value system associated with a culture is the physical environment in which people live (Brislin 1981). Perceptions of persons are colored by the physical dimensions of their life space. Rainfall, snow, temperature range, and weather hazards affect the daily affairs of individuals. The external factors of geography place further limits on choices. Living in mountainous regions, grasslands, coastal plains, or deserts will determine growth processes. For instance, Egypt has built its culture along the banks of the River Nile; populations have clustered around the water supply in that desert country. The varied coastline of Greece and its abundance of shipping lanes throughout the Mediteranean region have stimulated a different form of culture. Iceland and Hawaii have other characteristics related to their physical environment. The relationship of the environment to human experience is an important aspect of cultural diversity.

The history of a society may explain the reason why certain customs and values have been maintained or are in a period of change. For instance, the history of the United States, with its disengagement from England, unification of the States, westward movement into new territories, and development of scientific knowledge tended to promote the idea of independence and self-sufficiency. Values associated with competition, personal development and upward mobility in the social order are values directly related to past history.

Similarly, in Chinese society, respect for elderly parents is a strong value. Historically, the nuclear family has been the central control system for many generations. Creel (1953) in describing Chinese society said, "We have seen that the importance of the family in China goes back to a time before our knowledge of Chinese history begins. Three thousand years ago the principle was already established that a child's first loyalty was due its parents" (p. 190). Public support of older persons was not implemented through government channels because it was not needed. In keeping with custom, children cared for aging parents; the respect accorded the elderly was an expression of responsibility. With the profound changes in Chinese society in this century, undoubtedly the strength of this custom is waning. Thus, the environment and history of any society determine the conditions under which persons live and grow. Customs and habits develop within the context of reality and the need for survival.

COMMON CHARACTERISTICS
ACROSS CULTURES

"Every man is like all other men in certain respects, like some other men, and like no other man" (Kluckhohn & Stodtbeck, 1961). In attempting to understand other societies and their cultural patterns, differences and similarities must be recognized. One method is to take a "culture-general" approach to the study of cultures. With this system, common experiences of all cultures are identified and main areas of differences are categorized. With a culture-general background, any combination of cultures may be studied under the umbrella of general characteristics that apply to all cultures. Then fairly easily one can apply a "culture-specific" approach in which unique factors related to two societies can be compared and the varying values and customs of each society are highlighted.

Some culture-free phenomena apply to all human beings regardless of environment or history. Probably of major importance is knowing that people around the world have similar physical and psychological needs. According to Maslow (1959), all persons have a hierarchy of needs, and basic to the human condition is the need to survive. Safety, shelter, and food are necessary before higher needs can be met.

> Individuals, regardless of their genetic makeup, ethnic heritage, or geographical location on earth are in the same predicament. They confront the same basic survival problems. Housed in a frail, soft, naked body, humans exist in arid, frozen, rocky, fertile and tropical environments cluttered with a multiplicity of potentially destructive forces. (Vontress, 1979, p. 117)

A society in which food production barely meets nutritional requirements of its members must solve the problem through economic planning and educational information before other conditions adding to the quality of life can be considered. On the other hand, the needs of persons in an affluent society in which loneliness, alienation, and anxiety are widespread are very different.

Regardless of an individual's place in the hierarchy of needs, certain emotions in human experience are shared by everyone. A bond of happiness prevails at a wedding, even though customs and behaviors vary. Such a bond is related to the continuity of life and a concern for future generations through the union of marriage. Also, another universality is the emotion associated with the death of a child or loss of a mate. All persons have hopes, dreams, expectations, and beliefs that give special meaning to life.

The counselor in today's multicultural world needs to develop a special sensitivity to central themes in a client's report of self. In the area of common feelings associated with major events, empathy can be evident. The counselor can say with true emotion, "Yes, I know. I have felt it too." This commonality may be the first step to a meaningful relationship.

Areas of difference are grounded in the historical roots and environment of the culture. Each of us is a product of personal experiences and incorporates beliefs and values of the society in which nurturing occurred. Conflicts between cultures arise from the fact that values are ordered differently (Brislin, et al., 1986). For instance, cultural views on central issues such as aesthetics, politics, religion, and economics are reflected in social customs and behaviors, which vary among cultures.

Differences among persons and their value systems are often expressed in child-rearing practices. They are specific within every society and ensure the continuity of certain customs and beliefs. Traditional patterns regarding birth processes, feeding, discipline, sexual identity, and self-worth are modeled for children as they live and grow in the home environment under the jurisdiction of parents. As children are seldom able to evaluate parenting attitudes during their younger years, they tend to grow into maturity following the pattern of that socialization process. Therefore, customs and attitudes are continued into the next generation unless a new force is introduced. The power of child-rearing practices in continuing traditional ideas and limiting the incorporation of new information should be recognized by every counselor. At the same time a recognition needs to be made that any change in the social order will influence the manner in which children are raised (Berger & Luckman, 1968).

Another factor that directly affects individuals is the basic religious orientation and its relationship to the political structure of a society. Every religion has a model for how persons should behave and what attitudes they should hold. A definition of justice is stated in most religious philosophies. Beliefs concerning whether people are born good or evil, or whether nature is controlling or to be controlled are often based on the foundations of religion. For example, according to Pederson (1976), the Protestant ethic in America has been a major influence in placing persons into categories of good or bad, sick or healthy.

Closely related to religion is the structure of government. Cooperative, authoritarian, or individualistic forms of government foster group cohesion, dependency, and self-determination, respectively, ideas deeply embedded in various value systems.. No counselor in a multicultural setting can ignore the power of the religious and political background of a client fostered within the context of socialization processes.

The dynamic relation between culture and environment may be clarified with the outline in Figure 2.1 which is a modification of Kluckhohn and Strodtbeck's (1961) model.

Choices in Cultures

Human Nature:	Born Evil	Born Neutral	Born Good
Relation to Nature:	Submits to Nature	Harmonizes with Nature	Masters Nature
Sense of time:	Past Tradition	Present is Important	Focus on Future Goals
Social Relationship:	Authoritarian	Cooperative	Individualistic

Possible Variations in Cultures

Eye Contact	Space between Persons	Discipline
Attitude toward Aging	Custom of Touching	Non-verbal Cues
Need for Privacy	Display of Affection	Male/Female Roles

Figure 2.1. Outline of choices and possible variations in cultures. (Based on Kluckhohn and Strodtbeck's 1961 model.)

The issues of time perspective and orientation to space are culturally determined early in life (Brislin 1981). Frequently, misunderstanding between counselor and client is based on body language, voice intonation, emotional cues, or situational behaviors. The proximity of seating is important for counselors to explore since persons have a sense of space that is appropriate between persons. The sole of a shoe extended toward the client indicates rejection in many cultures. Waving of hands might be acceptable in one society but indicate a lack of control in another. Looking directly into a client's eyes might be considered invasive and overly familiar. Knowledge of gestures, customs, and personal protocol may be necessary for a counselor if rapport is to be established (Morris, et al., 1980; Hall, 1959).

PERCEPTIONS IN COMMUNICATION: STEREOTYPING AND PREJUDICE

Stereotyping is a factor in all forms of communication and often is an efficient way of describing different groups. By combining elements of differences into categories, statements can be made about a group as a whole. It is easy to say, "They are conservative;" "They are friendly;" "They are lazy." Usually these statements refer to behaviors or beliefs that are different from the dominant group. According to Brislin (1981), "Stereotypes are forms of categorization and are always used since people cannot respond to every individual piece of information" (p. 69). However, stereotyping might limit true understanding of a person from an "out-group." Therefore, counselors must be careful to gather information rather than make an assumption coinciding with a stereotypical view of the client's society. Awareness of the influence of stereotyping is important for all professional relationships in order for counselors to reach beyond general categories to true understanding.

Counselors who plan to work with the culturally different should avoid stereotyping clients from any given subgroup of the general population. In working with these groups, counselors will find that the basic qualities of empathy, respect, genuineness, and understanding are as fundamental to establishing a relationship with a culturally different client as they are in any counseling relationship...However, counselors must be cognizant of the differences that exist in working with culturally different clients. (George & Christiana, 1986, p. 170)

SPECIAL PROBLEMS WHEN COUNSELING THE MULTICULTURAL CLIENT

For the counselor today, and especially for the counselor of the future, the pluralistic nature of our own society and the increased international mobility of people everywhere present special problems. The range and type of culture mobility and culture contacts necessitate that counselors be aware of the most common personal problems that their clients are likely to exhibit (Taft, 1977).

Problems presented by people in this new kaleidoscope of cultures may well tend to cluster around ambiguity, alienation, anxiety, rootlessness, and identity formation. People have a strong need for a predictable universe, one in which an assurance exists that beliefs and values are known and behaviors are accepted by others. They want to know they will not be rejected. To feel a sense of belonging—a sameness with the group—is vital to maintaining a sense of predictability. When persons enter a new or strange society with its own ready-made rules for behavior, new and more appropriate behaviors must be learned. Most often a strong desire exists to regain that sense of belonging by fitting into the new group (Axelson, 1986).

People who remain in a familiar cultural milieu become socialized and comfortable with certain behavior patterns and develop a sense of belonging. In moving across cultures where old learned behaviors may present problems in adaptation and new patterns have to be learned, insecurity may develop. In changing patterns of cultural contact, the once secure basis for behaving becomes less certain. Those rules and ready made patterns which were learned and accepted as correct may no longer be accepted and indeed may not work (Schutz, 1971).

Not everyone is successful in making adaptations to new social and cultural situations. A person may need time to learn ways to cope with the new environment. For persons who move into another culture as immigrants, refugees, or sojourners, some adaptation may occur, but it may never be complete. In such cases, they often express a sense of being both a part of and apart from the new group (Adler, 1974). Such situations can contribute to ambiguous feelings toward self, the new society, and the group left behind. This sense of marginality to the dominant new culture, expressed by many minority and immigrant groups, increases feeling of insecurity (Park, 1963; Gist & Wright, 1973). As belief systems are challenged and undergo shifts, persons may become detached, isolated, and alienated from both cultures.

Frequently when social and cultural disruptions occur an individual attempts to re-create the old culture in the new context or to create new cultural patterns. For example, refugee and immigrant populations or displaced, disrupted minority groups carry with them cultural roles from their former lives that may clash with the host culture. In time they might adjust. On the other hand, the cultural discrepancy may stimulate disruptive behavior and violence. Considerable tension, sometimes called "culture shock," may occur for individuals, thus promoting anxiety, alienation, and mild paranoia. As Brislin, et al., (1986) stated:

> One consequence is that sojourners will spend a great deal of time brooding over their feelings, often coming up with both inexact and incorrect conclusions concerning their plight. One incorrect conclusion is that sojourners come to believe that hosts are plotting against them. Frequent thoughts include, "These people are always talking about me. They are purposely trying to make me unhappy" (p.243).

Along with feelings of anxiety and alienation, a sense of rootlessness often develops. It is as if a person cannot describe "home" in a precise or physical sense. The nature of home and roots become abstractions. Normally, a person does not need to be physically at home as long as one can remember it (Soddy, 1962). Rapid change due to social and cultural disruption or geographical relocation, however, may disrupt the reality of home and contribute to a sense of rootlessness (Berger et al., 1974).

When experiencing alienation and/or rootlessness, a question of identity may develop. Who am I? becomes a pressing problem with elusive answers. For people undergoing major social and cultural upheavals such as those in modern and developing societies, no satisfactory answer may be available. In relatively stable societies—those with longstanding traditions, customs, beliefs, and values—the reason to raise the question, Who am I? is minimal if at all. Identity has been established so firmly that the question need not be asked. However, in a multicultural world learning to manage one's identity becomes a vital skill (Soddy, 1962; Berger & Luckman, 1966; Erikson, 1959).

Resolving the question of identity is a necessary step for human beings, especially when the question reemerges for the person. Part of achieving identity is to be recognized by a group, to recognize the group, and to feel a part of it. Identity is the quality of self, a sense of belonging, of being "at one with," feeling rooted, and being at home (Erikson, 1975). According to Axelson (1980), "The split from another larger culture and immediate group relations drives the search for identity and ideals and the quest to find a group (family substitute?)" (p. 9).

Counselors must be alert to the broad dimensions of a personal search for identity in a fluid social and cultural world. The problem is not confined to the United States or to Western societies but may appear as a growing phenomenon for humankind into the twenty-first century. Faced with a diverse clientele from a vast array of cultural origins, the counselor will be hard pressed but challenged by the knowledge that the "helping relationship" can be made available to everyone.

LEGAL PRINCIPLES

A desire to be sensitive to the cultural dimensions of the client's background may be motivation enough for counselors to expand their horizons; however, in the United States we are moved to action by legal decisions. For example, **Brown versus Board of Education** advanced the cause of equal opportunity for all races. The decision stated that "Racial segregation generates feelings of inferiority as to status in the community that may affect their hearts and minds in a way unlikely ever to be undone.....Separate educational facilities are inherently unequal" (347 U.S. 483, 1954). Likewise, in the 1974 case, **Lau versus Nickels,** the Supreme Court held that to deny English language instruction or other services in San Francisco schools was a violation of the Civil Rights Act of 1964 (414 U.S. 563, 1974). More recently, the Supreme Court held in **Pyler versus Doe** (457 U.S. 202, 1982), that the state of Texas could not deny children of illegal aliens access to public education. To do so would render them illiterate, prevent them from advancement based on individual merits, and inhibit their growth as useful members of society.

Helping professionals and especially counselors, therefore, not only have a mandate of conscience but of legal precedent supporting the view that we serve all persons, regardless of race, creed, beliefs, or national origin. Now is time to expand our services from the confines of a monocultural perspective to a multicultural world view.

CONCLUSIONS

Many of the basic assumptions of counseling reflect the social, political, and economic beliefs of western cultures as well as imply the universal applicability of these assumptions in non-Western cultures (Pederson, 1976). We have an urgent need to abandon this attitude of isolationism by rethinking our priorities and evaluating our skills, techniques, and attitudes. At present, eclectic approaches in counseling seem to be favored for lack of a clear multicultural statement based on acceptable learning theory. "Counselors need to be cautious about taking rigid positions on the likeness versus difference dichotomy. We human beings are alike and we are different. The complexity of human beings does not always give us the luxury of taking an either-or position" (Parker, 1987, p. 33).

Whatever the method, a good counselor in a multicultural world will avoid statements of evaluation as much as possible as it is very difficult to determine what should or should not be done. What is right for one person might be totally inappropriate, even harmful, for another. However, facilitation of the process of exploration for the client can contribute to the possibility of discovering a solution.

The process of interpretation must be initiated carefully. Reflective listening may help to clarify, and restating a problem could improve the counselor's ability to identify issues correctly. However, words have different meanings within different cultural contexts. The complexity of translation and the emotional impact of words must be recognized during any session in which two persons are trying to communicate across cultures.

The client in a pluralistic society needs to feel a sense of unconditional acceptance and an affirmation of worthiness. Confidence in the client's ability to make good decisions within the context of cultural guidelines should be established by the counselor as soon as possible. Counselors must be careful not to impose their world views on clients without regard for the legitimacy of other values and ideas; to do so would be to propagate a form of cultural oppression (Sue, 1978).

In order to accept a larger view of the world and its variabilities, counselors must become aware of the forces of change brought about by technology and increased cultural contact. Factors that affect cultural characteristics and determine customs, beliefs, and values need to be firmly established in their repertoire of working knowledge. The identification of common experiences which cut across cultural boundaries will enhance the counselor's potential for success in counseling the client from another society. Knowing areas of major differences will prevent counselors from making major mistakes, causing misunderstanding, and fostering hostility.

Many counselors are and will be engaged in helping clients solve problems within a cross-cultural or multicultural context. New educational guidelines addressing the issues of alienation, rootlessness, and identity management need to be made available for counselors. Legal, ethical, and moral obligations related directly to professional stature promote expansion of the world of counseling. With this expansion the goals of the profession are advanced and its clientele better served.

REFERENCES

Adler, P. S. (1974). Beyond cultural identity: Reflections on cultural and multi-cultural man. *Topics in Culture Learning.* (Vol. 2) Honolulu: East-West Center Culture Learning Institute.

Axelson, J. (1985). *Counseling and development in a multicultural world.* New York: Brooks Cole.

Berger, P.L., & Luckman, T. (1966). *The social reconstruction of reality.* Garden City, NY: Doubleday.

Berger, F., Berger, B., & Kellner, H. (1974). *The homeless mind.* New York: Vantage.

Brislin, R.W. (1981). *Cross-Cultural encounters.* New York: Pergamon Press.

Brislin, R.W., Cushner, K., Cherrie, C., & Yong, M. (1986). *Intercultural interactions.* London: Sage.

Creel, H.G. (1953). *Chinese thought from Confucius to Mao Tse-Tung.* Chicago: University of Chicago Press.

Erickson, E. H. (1959). *Identity and the Life Cycle.* New York: International Universities Press.

Erickson, E. H. (1975). *Life history and the historical moment.* New York: W.W. Norton.

George, R. L., & Cristiana, T. (1986). *Counseling: Theory and practice.* Englewood Cliffs: Prentice Hall.

Gist, N. P., & Wright, R. D. (1973). *Marginality and identity: Anglo-Indians as a racially mixed minority in India.* London: Brill.

Hall, E. T. (1959). *The silent language.* Greenwich, CT: Fawcett.

Kluckhohn, F., & Strodtbeck, F. (1961). *Variations in value orientation.* Evanston, IL: Row, Peterson.

Kupferer, H.J., & Fitzgerald, T.J. (1971). *Culture, society and guidance.* Boston: Houghton-Mifflin.

Maslow, A. (Ed.). (1959). *New knowledge in human values.* Chicago: Henry Regnery.

McLuhan, M. (1968). *War and peace in the global village.* New York: McGraw Hill.

McNeil, W. (1963). *The rise of the west.* Chicago: University of Chicago.

Morris, D., Collett, P., & O'Shaughnessy, M. (1980). *Gestures.* New York: Stein and Day.

Park, R. E. (1963). Human migration and the marginal man. *American Journal of Sociology* 33: 881-893.

Parker, W. M. (1987). Flexibility: A primer for multicultural counseling. *Counselor Education and Supervision, 26,*(3) 176-180.

Pederson, P. B. (1976). The cultural inclusiveness of counseling. In P. Pederson, J. Draguns, W. Lonner, & J. Trimble (Eds.), *Counseling Across Culture.* Honolulu: University of Hawaii.

Ponterott, J, & Casas N. (1987). In search of multicultural competence within counselor education programs. *Journal of Counseling and Development, 65,* (8) 430-434.

Pyler versus Doe (1982), Case 457 United States, Code 202.

Schutz, A. (1971). Collected Papers II. In A. Brodersons & M. Nijhoff (Eds.), *Studies in social theory.* The Hague, Netherlands.

Soddy, K. (1962). *Identity, mental health and value systems: Cross-Cultural studies in mental health.* Chicago: Quadrange.

Sue, D. W. (1978). World views and counseling. *Personnel and Guidance Journal,* 458-462.

Taft, R. (1977). Coping with unfamiliar cultures. In N. Warren (Ed.), *Studies in cross-cultural psychology* (pp. 121-153). New York: Academic Press.

Wrenn, C.G. (1962, Fall). The culturally encapsulated counselor. *Harvard Educational Review*, Vol. 32, No. 4, 444-449.

Vontress, C. E. (1979). Cross-cultural counseling: An existential approach. *Personnel and Guidance Journal*, 117-121.

3

OLDER ORDER AMISH:

Culturally Different By Religion

JOE WITTMER, Ph.D.
Professor and Chairperson
Department of Counselor Education
University of Florida

THE OLDER ORDER AMISH:

CULTURALLY DIFFERENT BY RELIGION

AWARENESS INDEX

Directions: Please test your knowledge by responding to the following questions before proceeding to the text in this chapter.

Compare your score with the scoring guide at the end of this Awareness Index.

Select the best response for each item.

1. Approximately how many Old Order horse-and-buggy Amish are in America today?

_____ a. 10,000
_____ b. 20,000
_____ c. 40,000
_____ d. 60,000

2. When Amish parents have a marriage-age daughter they do which of the following?

_____ a. paint the barnyard gate blue.
_____ b. move the hex signs off the barn onto the house.
_____ c. put an ad in the Amish newspaper.
_____ d. behave similarly to most American parents.

3. Today, the Amish are located

_____ a. basically in Pennsylvania.
_____ b. throughout 20 states, Canada, and several South American countries.
_____ c. a. and b. above, plus Europe.
_____ d. none of the above

4. Another common name for the Amish is

    ———   a. the Amana.
    ———   b. the Mennonites.
    ———   c. the Plain People.
    ———   d. all of the above

5. The Amish left Europe for America

    ———   a. to escape religious persecution.
    ———   b. at the invitation of William Penn.
    ———   c. in search of religious freedom.
    ———   d. all of the above.

6. Amish parents forbid their children to

    ———   a. salute the flag.
    ———   b. pledge allegiance to the flag.
    ———   c. attend educational movies at school.
    ———   d. all of the above.

For each item mark true or false.

T F 7. The Old Order Amish are growing in numbers.

T F 8. The Amish family organization is strictly patriarchal.

T F 9. Divorce is non-existent among the Amish.

T F 10. The first language of all Amish is German.

T F 11. The Amish are offshoots of the Mennonites.

T F 12. The problems with high school education caused several thousand Amish to migrate to South America during the late sixties and early seventies.

T F 13. Hex signs on barns are popular among the Amish.

T F 14. Amish farmers are exempt from social security payments.

T F 15. Tourism offers no monetary benefits to the Amish by their own choice.

T F 16. A 1972 Supreme Court decision exempted the Amish from compulsory high school education.

T F 17. The Amish produce and market a popular brand-name refrigerator.

T F 18. Upon marriage, Amish men grow a chin-beard.

Scoring Guide For Awareness Index

1. d	7. T	13. F
2. d	8. T	14. T
3. b	9. T	15. T
4. c	10. T	16. T
5. d	11. T	17. F
6. d	12. T	18. T

INTRODUCTION

I think they are beautiful people. They are so sober. The way they think, the way they feel, the way they dress—it is all one unit. They mind their own business and live their own life and I think this is beautiful.

These words are from Mauricio Lasansky, the artist of the famous intaglio portrait, "Amish Boy," in his description of the more than 60,000 Old Order Amish people scattered throughout twenty states, Canada, and more recently, Central and South America. Americans often confuse the Old Order Amish with the Mennonites, Amana, House of David, Hutterites, Beachy's and other such religious sects in America that are culturally different because of religion and dress. As an illustrative example of these special populations, this section concerns the Old Order, German speaking, no electricity, horse-and-buggy-driving Amish often referred to as the "Plain People."

ABOUT THE WRITER[1]

I am often asked what being Amish is like. Most Americans know them only by newspaper reports as a simple, virtuous people who live on farms, use no electricity, automobiles, trucks, tractors, radios, television or other such "necessities" of modern life. Their broad-brimmed black hats, black buggies, and past tussles with educational authorities all have further stereotyped the Amish as anachronisms in the space age.

Religion on our Indiana farm was a seven-day-a-week affair. The way we dressed, the way we farmed, the German we spoke—our whole lifestyle was a daily reminder of our religion, as it is for all Amish.

The fourth of six children, I learned the Amish way by a gradual process of kindly indoctrination. At five I was given a corner of the garden to plant and care for as my own and a small pig and calf to raise. Amishmen are either farmers or in related occupations such as blacksmithing and buggy-making. My father had no doubt that I would someday be a God-fearing farmer like himself, and my mother often added in her German dialect, "and a nice black beard like your father's, you will have yet."

Because Amish parochial schools were not yet in existence, I entered the strange world of public schools at age eight. My parents deliberately planned this late entry into school so that I would be sixteen, minimum age for quitting, in the eighth grade. High school to the Amish is a "contaminating" influence that challenges the Biblical admonition to be a "peculiar people." Old Order Amish children are not permitted more than eight years of formal education. The Amish also resist education below the eighth grade if it originates in modern consolidated schools. America was at war with Germany when I entered the first grade. Without radios and newspapers or relatives fighting (all Amish are conscientious objectors), I had little opportunity at home to keep up with its progress. School was another matter.

---

[1]From "Good Guys Wear White Hats" by J. Wittmer, *Liberty*, 1972, 67,(2) 12-17. Reprinted by permission.

Boys played war games and talked constantly about the war and the branch of service they someday would join. Often I was asked where I would serve. I knew that as a conscientious objector I would never go to war.

I often wished that I could help the non-Amish children gather sacks of milkweed pods, used to make parachutes for American flyers. However, I was taught to engage in activities that would further the war effort was sinful. Because I did not participate, I was often the object of derision.

The ordeal of Amish students reached its cruel peak during the daily pledge to the flag, which for religious reasons, our parents taught us not to salute or to pledge allegiance. The jabs of the students and the disappointed looks of the teacher as we remained seated cut me deeply. How could I explain that the Amish believe in praying for all governments, which, they hold, are ordained by God? How could I explain that hate is not in the Amish vocabulary? Explain it, moreover, in a German accent, for German was the first language of all Amish youth, the church requiring it to be spoken at home.

In retrospect, I can understand all too well the feelings of the non-Amish students. I can understand also why the Amish have established their own schools. What was at stake was not the feelings of Amish youth, but a way of life.

The average person often has difficulty understanding the pressures on a nonconformist in the public school system. Many activities are strictly off limits to the Amish youth, not only dancing and other "worldly entertainments," but also class pictures and educational movies. When such activities were scheduled, we Amish children were herded into another room usually to the chiding and laughter of our classmates.

My most vivid memories of boyhood days concern hostility and harassment endured by my parents and others in the Amish community because of our non-resistance stance to the war. Often "outsiders" attacked us when we rode in our buggies. They threw firecrackers, eggs, tomatoes, even rocks. Soldiers home on leave burned our fodder shocks, overturned our outdoor toilets. broke windows, and stole buggies. A favorite tactic was to sit in a car trunk and hold onto a buggy while the car sped down the road. The buggy was turned loose to smash into bits against a road bank. After witnessing many such acts of vandalism I became terrified of non-Amishmen. Because the Bible admonished them to be "defenseless Christians," my father and the other elders of the community refused to summon law officials to their defense. By Scripture they lived and by Scripture they would die if necessary. They turned the other cheek.

Although turmoil and conflict occurred outside the Amish community, peace was the watchword within its borders. We worked hard and we played hard, though without the competition of the outside world. Thrashing days, barn raisings, and public auctions were a more than adequate substitute for radios, comic books, and organized sports.

Amish families are close-knit. We worked as a unit for ourselves and for the Amish community. We played together. We ate together—no meal was started until all members were present, and dinner was never interrupted by Walter Cronkite. Security and love abounds within the Amish way of life.

Why, then, did I, at sixteen, make the decision to continue in school—the first step away from Amish origins? The answer is not simple. It includes (1) a passion for knowledge and (2) a growing resentment toward my Amish heritage, sparked by the years of derision and scorn in public schools. Somewhere on my way to a Ph.D. I fulfilled the one and outgrew the other, leaving still some unanswered questions with which the psychiatrists wrestle.

Perhaps my Amish kinsmen community claimed me. And, indeed, the campus on which I teach is a far cry from my father's farm. And "a nice black beard like your father's" I do not have. But there is no animosity, no shame, among the Amish that I have left. And though I live within mainstream society, I am also vice-chairman of the **National Committee for Amish Religious Freedom,** the organization which defended the Amish right not to attend high school all the way to the Supreme Court and won (May 15, 1972) a unanimous decision.

ABOUT THE AMISH

The Amish are unique, picturesque, and strive to follow the biblical dictate to be a "peculiar people." They want no part of the values and ways that exist in the modern world about them; they wish to be left alone to live their life away from the mainstream of the secular society.

The Old Order Amish strive continually to remain different from the "other people," the "outsider" or the "English" as non-Amish are called. They shun the use of television, radio, telephone, most other modern technological luxuries, and travel via horse-drawn carriages. Their homes are extremely plain and lack running water, electricity, refrigerators, and most other conveniences that are found in the modern American home. Their within-group conversation is in a German dialect and they wear home sewn garb reminiscent of the 18th century.

> ...I know why we don't have TV like the outsiders do. We are different like God wants. The outsiders can have their TV because it's not good for you. Mom and me were in Sears one day and I saw TV a bit. Mom said they use bad words and dance on TV. We didn't watch any more. I don't want TV ever in our house...Amos, 4th grade[2]

Values of peace, total nonviolence, and humility are in evidence in any Amish community. They do not teach the skills of violence and technology. An Amishman realizes early in life that he is totally non-resistant and that he will never go to war. These values, lived by the Amish adults, gain the allegiance of the Amish youth, as less than five percent leave the sect. Further, no indigence, divorce, or unemployment exists. There is very little delinquency and no record of an Old Order Amishman ever being arrested for a felony and none has appeared on a welfare roll. The Amish also value calmness and tranquility—it is difficult to be in a hurry while driving a horse and buggy!

---

[2]These excerpts as well as others which follow, were taken from essays written by Amish elementary school children in response to an assignment; *What It's Like to be Amish.* Appreciation is extended to the Amish school teacher for sending me the essays. She wishes to remain anonymous.

...Our horse is almost red. He is a nice horse and he takes us where we want to go. Some horses kick, but ole Jamie doesn't. I sit in the back of the buggy and I get scared when the cars come. They get close and make dust. Once Uncle John's got hit and the driver died. I was sad. Uncle John was hurt ...Rebecca, 3rd grade.

Mainstream society's emphasis on high-powered cars, computers, and contraceptive devices is conspicuously absent from the horse-and-buggy Amish world. The Amish constantly live by the scriptural admonitions to "Come out from among them, and be ye separate," and "Be ye a peculiar people." They live in isolated communities attempting to stay apart from the secular influences of the "outsider's" world. However, the Amish feel the pressing-in of America's emphasis on technology, violence, and twentieth century progress.

All Amishmen are oriented toward one goal—that of eternal life, and they equate their personal pursuance of this ultimate goal with present methods of attaining it. Industry, careful stewardship, the sweat of the brow, and beards on married men, are all means to an end—eternal life.

Uniforms of any type are taboo among the Amish but dress is uniform. Youngsters are attired as miniature adults. No change in style is to be considered and status is not attributed to type of clothing worn. This alleviates coveting and self-pride while building group cohesion. Thus, a deviate is highly conspicuous and the similarity serves as a boundary-maintaining device.

...We wear plain clothes because the Bible says we should. Sometimes the outsiders stare at you but they never have said anything to me about my clothes. We can be a witness for others by being plain...But, just wearing plain clothes doesn't make you a Christian. I think sometimes we forget that...Elizabeth, 7th grade.

An Amish man begins growing a chin beard the week before his marriage, but the upper lip and neck are kept clean shaven. This custom is in keeping with their non-conformity to "worldly" values and ways; an "outsider" with a moustache is often in evidence. A straight line is shaved across the back of his neck and his hair is bobbed in a "crockline" appearance. An Amishman doesn't part his hair and it is never "tapered" on the sides. The men wear large broad-brimmed black hats, suspenders, homesewn shirts without buttons or pockets, homesewn pants without hip pockets or zippers, and homesewn underwear without stripes. All shirts are sewn in such a manner so as to necessitate being put on and removed by slipping over the head.

> ...My dad said when he was little one time he was with my grandpa and some outsider boys called them "bushhogs." Then the boys said baa-baa like a goat. I think that is funny. Dad has whiskers but nobody went baa-baa yet...Noah, 4th grade.

Amish women do not wear make-up of any sort nor shave any part of their body. They wear dresses that are full-blown and not adorned with buttons, hooks and eyes, press buttons, or zippers. The only means of keeping their dresses intact is straight pins. They do not wear lacy under clothing and bras are prohibited. The female's hair is never cut and is always parted in the middle.

To an Amishman the "world"begins at the last Amish farmhouse. He has not acquired the "worldly" need for a tractor with which to farm. He may rely on a tractor for belt power, but it will be mounted on a steel-wheeled wagon and pulled from job to job by horses. He also uses horses to plow his fields and to pull his black buggy. Work is a moral directive. Labor saving devices are mere temptations and "something new." Something new or different is of the Devil while tradition is sacred. Although these customs may seem stern from the outside looking in, the Amish are healthy and happy. They have not acquired the methods of the "world" to attain their happiness or to fulfill their needs.

As a former Amishman, it is difficult to explain the feeling of being truly different from the dominant, surrounding society. Amish youngsters are reared very carefully and various methods are employed to protect them from the contaminating influences of the "outsider." The fact that one is different and peculiar is a continuous indoctrinating process for the young. They develop a strong conscience. Once indoctrinated, a person indeed finds difficulty in altering oneself to accept the values and ways of others without experiencing extreme psychic pain.

...Being Amish means not doing what the world does. It means living a plain life for God on earth. It means being happy without the things outsiders have...Elam, 5th grade.

ABOUT THE FAMILY

The family system is the primary unit which organizes the dominant patterns of value orientation in the Old Order Amish culture. Older members of the family funnel the cultural heritage to the younger offspring. Within the Amish family setting the child first learns to respond to authority, to play roles in the cooperative structure, and to obey the norms of the sect.

Rank differences are not extreme within the Amish sect nor within the family structure. However, father commands the highest rank with mother being second. Sibling rank is based according to age. The older siblings' roles include disciplining the younger children.

Amish married couples do not reveal overt affection for one another in public. An Amish husband refers to his wife as "her" and she makes reference to "him." However, there is mutual respect and seldom does arguing occur in presence of children.

The Amish family organization is strictly patriarchal. The father rears his son in the exact same manner he was reared by his father. The father-son relationship is excellent and the generation gap seldom exists.

Women of the family take a back seat to the men in most endeavors and the Amish male rarely does the tasks of a female, although women are expected to help with most all male tasks. Only on special occasions such as butchering, cooking apple butter, and weddings, does the husband participate in household tasks. However, women and adolescent girls frequently help with the harvest of crops, especially during cornhusking.

Although varying degrees of cooperation are present between the husband and wife in the fulfillment of their roles, the Amish generally adhere to the biblical tradition in which the husband is in direct charge over both his wife and children. Male and female roles clearly are differentiated and the woman's place is perhaps best typified by the biblical admonition: "The head of the woman is the man."

Divorce is non-existent and no written or unwritten provisions exist for securing either divorce or separation. Marriage is supported by kinship and religious sanction. As mentioned previously, Amish couples do not reveal any overt signs of affection for one another. And, although procreation may be upper-most in their minds, it is the opinion of the writer that Amish couples permit themselves to enjoy sex.

Most Amish couples have several children and realize that as they grow older the children will care for them. The older one becomes, the wiser one becomes. The Amish never use nursing homes; it's nice to grow old. The youngest son brings his bride to his parents' farm upon his marriage. At this time, a second residence—**grossdawdy haus**—is built for the parents, often adjacent. The old folks get the new homes in the Amish community! The management of the farm is then turned over to the son, and the parents retire. Relationships between the two families are cordial, and even the mother-in-law/daughter-in-law relationship, which is so troublesome for other cultures with patriarchal family customs, appears amicable.

ABOUT CHILDREN AND GROWING UP

Amish couples do not practice birth control of any type and pray for children. It is indeed a happy occasion when a child is born to Amish parents. A new baby is showered with love and neighbors come from miles around for **sees koffee**—"sweet coffee." Sweet coffee is the custom of visiting and eating at the home of the proud Amish parents. Neighbors provide the food. There are no Godfather ceremonies or gifts.

The birth of a child is a welcomed event in the Amish community. A baby means another corn husker, another cow-milker, but, most of all, another God-fearing Amishman. The birth is always seen as a blessing of the Lord. Thus, Amish parents feel that their children really don't belong to them; they belong to God.

Few Amish couples are without offspring. Families usually range from eight to ten children; two Amish families in my former community had sixteen children. My Old Order sister has fifteen. Couples without children almost always adopt, often from outsiders.

People marvel at the attention, the love, and the affection given to the newborn Amish infant. Even when asleep the baby will be in someone's arms. For the first several months of life he or she will be held constantly by some member of the family. The baby goes where the parents go, even to the fields to work, and also will attend the long and tiresome church services when just a few weeks old. The Amish baby is a pleasure, a gift from God and is too precious to be left in a nursery or with a baby sitter. A baby is an integral part of the family from the moment of birth.

They may spoil babies, but Amish parents seldom refer to an infant as being spoiled. Infants can do no wrong; they remain blameless. If they have adjustment problems, the parents and community erred. An Amish baby is always diapered on someone's lap, usually the mother's or an older sister's. Amish parents do not read books on child rearing and do not stick to strict time schedules; if babies cry, something is wrong and if hungry, they are fed regardless of the hour.

Every Amish baby, if physically possible, is breast fed. No turmoil ever occurs concerning whether to breast feed or not. It is simply the only thing to do. Breasts are not viewed as sex symbols and nursing may occur whenever Amish are gathered socially, in church, and so forth. Breast feeding is done without any apparent shame, but never in the presence of an outsider.

Food from the table is shared with the baby at a very early age. It is not unusual to see a four month old baby being fed mashed potatoes directly from the table while sitting in the mother's lap. Eating time is an important time and activity for an Amish family. The believe that one always eats better in a group, including the new baby.

To others the Amish mother may appear to be hiding her infant from the eyes of the world when in public as the baby is entirely covered with a blanket. An Amish woman always wears a black shawl over her shoulders, and a mother carefully tucks the baby away under her shawl, often making the child unnoticeable to the public. The Amish child is to be protected, even at an early age, from the "world."

The new baby sleeps with the parents for the first few months of life. Along with the security this practice affords, it also is convenient for breast feeding and provides warmth in the poorly heated homes. Psychologically, this practice may contribute more to the Amish youths' apparent security than any other factor. It is difficult to pinpoint the age at which weaning occurs, but usually around age two.

Toilet training usually begins around age two with no apparent harshness or anxiety attached to the endeavor. As previously stated, Amish babies are held constantly, and of course, in the absence of rubber pants (which are considered "worldly") they often leave their "mark" on the holder's lap. Although this may draw a snicker from an "outside" observer, the wet spot warrants no attention or concern from the Amish people present. In the absence of modern, closed-in bathrooms, waste containers for human elimination are evident in all Amish bedrooms. To the Amish, human elimination is simply a natural activity and thus toilet training is facilitated by the process of imitation and observation. This activity should not be construed to mean that there is no privacy; however, much less concern over privacy is associated with toilet activity than in the "outsider" culture. Bedroom doors are not fitted with locks.

Amish parents believe that one of their basic duties is to transmit the Amish cultural heritage to their children. They are not alone in this high priority activity as the total Amish community is highly involved in the rearing of all its participants.

ABOUT AMISH ORIGIN

The Amish sect was born out of the religious turmoil of the Anabaptist movement in 16th Century Europe. To say the least, the sect's emergence was turbulent.

The Anabaptists refused to baptize their offspring before the age of reason and also refused to bear arms. They were a unique group during that time in history. They were not directly involved in the fierce fighting (in the name of religion) that surrounded them and were in total disagreement and disfavor with the Catholics, Martin Luther, and the whole Reformed movement. The Anabaptists yearned to return to a primitive, earlier brand of Christianity. To bring back this primitive Christianity, the Anabaptists literally accepted the Bible as their dictate. They made it clear to both church and State that they would stop taking oaths, would not baptize their offspring before the age of reason, would not drink, and would never again pick up a sword. Further, this return to primitive religion brought the wrath of the Reformers, the Catholics, and several Protestant groups upon the Anabaptists. The Anabaptists were denounced as being heretics and were subjected to the death penalty when caught.

Despite much suffering and death, the Anabaptists prevailed. They migrated throughout Europe in their attempts to avoid persecution. Mennonites were in Holland and North Germany, the Hutterian Brethren in Moravia, and the Swiss Brethren in Switzerland.

In the early 1600s a division occurred among the above mentioned Mennonite Anabaptists in Holland. In 1632 Mennonite ministers from several different areas in Europe met in Holland in an attempt to heal this breach within their church. Menno Simon, a former Catholic priest, was the leader of the Anabaptists in Holland and his followers became known as "Mennists." The name "Mennonite" was later applied to them. The rift came about regarding the practice of shunning or *Meidung*—total avoidance, both physically and spiritually of the excommunicated member. The ruling bishop of the Mennonite group did not enforce shunning. A deep split developed within the Church and the leader of the emerging group which enforced the *Meidung* was an aggressive young man named Jacob Amman. Amman, a Swiss Brethern bishop who lived in Canton of Bern, Switzerland, took it upon himself to excommunicate all those Mennonite bishops and ministers not enforcing the *Meidung*. Amman's followers became known as "Amish."

History records that thousands of Amish and members of other Anabaptist sects were martyred for their religious con- victions during the 15th and 16th centuries throughout Europe.

As mentioned previously, the Anabaptists were especially persecuted for their rejection of infant baptism. Also, their refusal to bear arms was considered treason. The **Martyrs' Mirror,** a 1,582-page book found in most Amish homes today, contains a careful account of hundreds of Amish martyrs with details of how they met their deaths. Accounts are recorded of the severing of hands, tongues, ears, and feet plus many eyewitness accounts of drownings, crucifixions, live burials, stake-burnings, and suffocations. These accounts are related over and over again to Amish children by their parents and elders. This past persecution has been an important element in Amish historical memories, has helped to keep alive their present sense of distinctiveness, and has definitely contributed to their group cohesiveness.

One historical event alone saved the Amish from extinction—William Penn's tour of Europe offering Pennsylvania as a haven from religious persecution. The Amish accepted the invitation to take part in Penn's religious experiment and came to America in the early 1720s and settled in Pennsylvania. No Amish are left in Europe today.

ABOUT THE AMISH AND PROGRESS

...Sometimes I wonder what the world is coming to. Everybody in the outsider community seems to be in a hurry when you meet them. I read in the Budget that this is why they have so many heart attacks. They are no longer satisfied with cars and airplanes as they are building rockets to ride in. Will they ever be satisfied? For me the buggy is quick enough...Esther, 7th grade.

How long will civilization go along with the Amish? How long can the Amish with their closed society housed within a highly progressive secular society survive? My opinion is that the Amish will survive and maintain their distinctiveness so long as they can keep the figurative wall between themselves and the secular society. Although the Amish are growing in numbers, failure to maintain this wall brought about their disappearance in Europe which also could occur in America.

Urbanization is threatening the Amish way of life, particularly as farming becomes more mechanized and real estate developments increase the price of land. Economic problems of a people committed to a primitive technology, but embedded in a highly technological society with which they must make exchanges, are immeasurable. For example, one of the Amish farmers' largest economic supplements is the selling of fluid milk to the local dairies. However, the new laws and demands of milk inspectors have made it almost impossible for an Amishman to continue to sell milk to these dairies. Indiana passed a law in the late 70s drastically lowering the required temperature of milk which would have eliminated the 3000 non-mechanized Amish milk producers had an interested group not intervened on their behalf. The law was later changed to the Amish milkers' benefit.

Many Old Order Amish members have gone along with the new type milk parlors and gasoline engine operated cooling systems, but the notion of milking machines is not compatable with the Amishman's belief in non-conformity. However, the milk buyers no longer wish to buy milk that has been produced by hand. Further, the amish continually have refused to allow their milk to be picked up on Sunday and dairies require the Amishmen milk seven days a week or not at all. Many more examples could be cited.

The Amish settlements most threatened by urbanization are those located near metropolitan areas. In central Ohio (Madison County) an Amish community is faced with the spread of urban life from the state capital of Columbus. Many Amish farms are selling for as much as $3,000 per acre. And, if they are close to large metropolitan areas, they often bring up to $5,000 per acre. Amish farmers have always supported one another financially and used to outbid their non-Amish neighbors for land within the settlement. However, the going prices are more than they can afford to pay. Also, more and more farm auctions are being held on Sunday to eliminate the sabbath-keeping Amish bidder. Thus, many Amish people have found themselves dividing their acreage into much smaller plots and taking jobs in industry on the side. Others are moving to Central and South America in search of "new lands." As a matter of fact, several Central and South American countries are successfully recruiting the Amish today, offering them inexpensive land, no military inscription, and total religious freedom.

Almost half of the Amish people in Starke County, Ohio, one of the larger Amish settlements in America, have given up farming during the past fifteen years. Some have maintained a small farm for cattle and pasture to graze their driving horses while turning to traditionally approved occupations of masonry and carpentry. However, many are now pursuing work in church-approved factories, which in the past were strictly taboo, while many other families are moving to other states and/or to Central or South America.

I'm confident that factory work, in time, will erode many of the values the Amish have so long treasured. Industrial work is a departure from tradition made necessary by the changing economy. Factory hours are shorter and pay checks are higher but factory work is especially detrimental to the Amish farm family organization. Also, joining the Union is strictly forbidden by the Amish church. During 1980 a group of Amishmen lost their factory jobs in Ohio because of the closed-shop situation in that state. Some Amish churches that recently permitted factory work have now reversed that decision. And, many outsider factory owners are perplexed when, because of a new rule made on Sunday, not one of their hard-working Amishmen shows up for work the following Monday morning.

In the past the Amish farmer has had lower overhead than his non-Amish neighbor simply because he used horses and had more "hands" around to help. The horse drawn equipment used to cost much less than the mechanical type. However, with inflation and scarcity, this type of equipment is increasing in price every day. Also, an Amish farmer never accepts a subsidy of any type from the government. Observing his outsider neighbor accepting government subsidy for not growing a particular crop, for example, is personally stressful and difficult to understand.

Not only has urbanization and progress brought about a change for many Amishmen, but also it is changing the lifestyles of many Amish females. A few young men always have been leaving the Amish church for the more liberal Mennonite way of life or even to join an outsider church, but now some young women are following suit. In the past, a woman leaving the Amish church was unheard of. Why this sudden shift? Most Amish elders blame it on "working out" in modern outsiders' homes. When young women work as maids for another Amish family they earn between $15 to $20 per week. However, they learn quickly that they can earn the same amount in one day by doing housework in town for outsiders. Also, some young Amish women, much to the disdain of the elders, are taking jobs in factories. However, many Amish women are still keeping with tradition—my mother, at age 80, gave up her job as maid among the outsiders.

America's emphasis on education threatens the Old Order Amish sect's way of life. They teach their young that formal education is worthwhile up to a point, but that too much is un-Christian and only for the foolish. If a fear exists among Amish parents, it is that of losing their children through too much formal education. The parents yearn for complete jurisdiction over their children's activity and have it everywhere except in the public school classroom.

Against formal education beyond the eighth grade (and sometimes below that level if it requires attending a modern consolidated school), they are especially opposed to the "godless" science, the competitive atmosphere, and the alien teachers found in the modern school. They prefer the old-fashioned one-room school with its limited facilities, since this type is more in keeping with their simple domestic life. The Amish want to train their youth at home in the care and operation of farms and, to them, this requires no more than eight years of reading, writing, and arithmetic. This view has caused tremendous conflict for them because most states require that a child attend school until 16 years of age. To meet this requirement, the Amish initiated a vocational plan of their own for all students beyond the eighth grade not of legal quitting age. The vocational plan came under repeated legal attack by state and local school authorities across the country.

These school battles were fought in communities in Michigan, Ohio, Iowa, Pennsylvania, Kansas, and several other states. In Iowa, in 1966, deputy sheriffs chased Amish children through cornfields in an attempt to bus them to a public school after school officials had demanded that the Amish comply with the state's attendance laws. The jailing of many Amish parents with fines totaling nearly $10,000 failed to alter their beliefs.

Literally dozens of documented legal encounters could be cited. One of the most publicized took place in Kansas in a 1967 test case.

An Amish farmer, convicted for sending his fifteen year old daughter to the sect's vocational school instead of to the local high school, disregarded a centuries-old stricture against litigation and permitted the then recently formed National Committee of Amish Religious Freedom to take his case to the State Supreme Court. By a four to three vote, the court refused to hear the case. This ruling created a precedent; many subsequent cases were lost as lower courts continuously ruled against the Amish. However, the troublesome predicament ended on May 15, 1972 when the previously mentioned committee won a unanimous U.S. Supreme Court decision exempting the Amish from state laws compelling their children to continue schooling beyond the eighth grade. In essence, the Court indicated that compulsory, formal education beyond the eighth grade would greatly endanger, if not destroy, free exercise of the Amish religious beliefs. The ruling affirmed a 1971 judgment by the Wisconsin Supreme Court. Legal scholars indicate that this case was the first time in the history of America that compulsory education laws had been challenged successfully. In simple terms, the ruling meant that the Amish cannot be forced by any state authorities to continue the schooling of their offspring beyond the eighth grade.

Although the school controversy, as summarized previously, was the basic reason for the emigration of several thousand Amish to Central and South America in the late 60s and early 70s, there are currently more eminent ones. Impingement, persecution, and harassment come from several different sources. Local, state, and national legislators often pass new laws without the consent, knowledge, or consideration of different minority groups. A case in point was a law passed in Indiana requiring a triangular shaped reflectorized emblem to be affixed to the back of all slow moving vehicles. The Amish viewed this three-cornered emblem as a hex symbol, or "the mark of the beast" as described in the Bible, and refused to affix it to their buggies (contrary to popular belief the Amish do not affix HEX signs to their barns!). They further felt that the gaudy emblem would glorify man rather than God. The Amish offered to use neutral color reflector tape in an attempt to compromise but failed and several served 20 days in jail. Finally a compromise was reached. The Indiana Amish farmers placed in local jails for following their religious scruples never raised their voices and served their jail sentences without any apparent feelings of animosity.

However, the slow moving vehicle (SMV) sign controversy is currently very much in the news in three states. Several Amish men recently spent 15 days in jail in upstate New York for refusing to pay $10 fines for substituting reflective gray tape on their buggies instead of the standard orange. And, the previously mentioned National Committee for Amish Religious Freedom recently filed (April 6, 1987) in a Michigan Court of Appeals on behalf of an Amish man arrested and jailed for a similar violation of this controversial SMV law. Current Minnesota law also requires that all animal-drawn vehicles display the bright orange triangle to alert faster moving traffic and prevent accidents. Many Amish men there have been fined and jailed for using a different color reflective tape on the backs of their buggies.

The SMV law, therefore, has forced the Amish into a no-win dilemma: they must abandon their religious beliefs to the mandates of the state, stop using the public roads and highways or disobey the law and amass burdensome fines or go to jail. Refusing to compromise their convictions and finding it economically impossible to avoid traveling the public roadways, they have disobeyed the law; many are spending a lot of time in jail.

In general, Americans seem to think that Social Security is a good idea. However, it has caused immeasurable problems for the Amish, who view it as a form of insurance which is religiously taboo. Many an Amish farmer lost good cattle and horses confiscated by the Internal Revenue men during the middle sixties for failure to pay social security even though they would never collect one cent. Many documented stories are told about this problem. When the IRS men came to an Amish farm to confiscate livestock, the non-aggressive Amish unselfishly assisted them in choosing the livestock they felt would best make up for their lack of paying social security. They were extremely kind to the IRS men and local newspapers carried stories about them being taken to the house, given coffee, and fed. In one case they loaded the livestock and went fishing with the Amishman in the farm pond. Other news accounts revealed how the government men left (with the confiscated livestock) with tears in their eyes. However, unlike many other controversies involving the Amish, this one had a happy ending— President Johnson attached a rider to the Medicare Bill exempting all Amish farmers from paying social security.

But the problem keeps coming up. In a recent case, the courts ruled against an Amish farmer for not withholding social security payments from Amish employees on his farm. Thus, in a strange interpretation of the Medicare Bill rider, an Amish farmer does not himself have to pay social security, but must pay it on behalf of his Amish employees!

One of the Amish counties being most threatened by urbanization and progress today is Lancaster County, Pennsylvania, the county first offered as a sanctuary to the Amish by William Penn. Civilization is refusing to go along with the Amish in this county and many are leaving it. Lancaster County is the Amish heartland. The more than 12,000 Amish in this beautiful area of Pennsylvania are the target of more than 3,000,000 tourists per year. The tourists go through the county's back roads in tour buses or sometimes rent buggies and are a nuisance to the Amish. Several Amish have written me about this problem telling of the tourists' rudeness. Recently a scribe wrote to the Budget, the weekly Amish newspaper, describing how a busload of tourists trampled his garden in pursuit of a glimpse of him and his family as they worked in the garden.

Traveling through Lancaster County, Pennsylvania, one finds an endless string of supposedly Amish motels, Amish food, Amish restaurants, Amish gift shops, Amish museums, Amish amusement parks, and so forth. This exploitation of the Amish is growing at an alarming pace. A Lancaster County newspaper indicated recently that the director of the tourist bureau stated that tourism in this one Amish community was now a 100 million dollar a year business!

In the winter time, one can travel through Lancaster County, going through such tiny Amish villages as Paradise and Intercourse, which have been left undisturbed for 100 years. One sees the horse and buggy driving Amish, water, wheels, windmills, and other sights reminiscent of a century ago. But, in the summertime the mood changes to a carnival atmosphere as bumper to bumper traffic and billboards indicate the "it's real—it's genuine, you're here. Visit the house and farm occupied by the German-speaking Amish. Stop and talk to these genuine Amish people." Their inquisitiveness has become a nuisance to Amish who strive to avoid publicity as well as photographs, which are strictly forbidden by the church.

...the tourists often bother us. They have cameras and we don't want pictures. The other night dad was milking and the man kept trying to take dad's picture. He kept hiding his face...Esther, 5th grade.

Tourism in Lancaster began only some 14 years ago but is now a bonanza for the owners. They succeeded well beyond their wildest dreams, and today Pennsylvania Dutch county is the seventh largest tourist attraction in the United States. As many as 10,000 visitors a day in season swarm down over the amish back roads. Tourists seldom ask permission to take pictures. They snap pictures from their car windows and burst uninvited into the easily accessible, quaint, inviting Old Order school houses.

...I don't know what the tourists want at school. They just want to look at us maybe. I wish they would leave us alone...Esther, 5th grade.

The recent movie "Witness," an intriguing suspense/love story set in the Amish community of Lancaster County, Pennsylvania, may have heightened many viewers' understanding of the centrality of religion in the Amish lifestyle. However, the filming marked a new high in symbolic and real life intrusion and harassment for the Amish. Filming the movie set off a furor among Amish and non-Amish alike. The Amish were strongly opposed, but most kept their views to themselves. One can only imagine the turmoil created among the Amish in Lancaster County when the sound trucks and taboo movie cameras arrived. The National Committee for Amish Religious Freedom tried to stop the filming but to no avail. However, as one Amish bishop explained to the writer, "Fortunately, no Amish person will ever see the movie!" Unfortunately, tourism has increased dramatically because of the movie.

Tourism offers no monetary benefits to the Amish by their own choice. They are not in the selling business, nor the hotel and motel business. One of the most damaging aspects of tourism is that Lancaster County has now been "discovered" and recently married Amish farmers cannot find land to purchase. People who are benefiting the most from the Amish leaving the farms are the local industry owners. Amish men have been groomed to awaken at 4:00

AM, and work is a moral directive whether on the farm or in a factory. They make excellent factory workers, but, as previously mentioned, usually unhappy ones.

Most material written about the Amish, although often filled with myths, is favorable, but frequently an unfavorable article is written. In July, 1979, the **TV Guide** contained an editorial type article titled "The Amish Hadn't Changed Much Since 1693—And Then Came TV" in which the author wrote some damaging untruths, printing that volumptuous Amish maidens flirt with the young men of the city while at the market and that Amish men relish TV shows with half-clothed girls, are girl-crazy, and have low morals. He also further exploited the myth that Amish fathers paint their barnyard gate blue when a daughter reaches marriageable age. A cartoon, accompanying the article, depicted an Old Order Amish man admonishing the cow he was milking to be quiet as he secretly watched a TV hidden under a blanket in the corner of his barn.

The total effects that America's progress has on a people such as the Amish are difficult to measure. However, the Amish are a tenacious people and are intent on maintaining their way of life since the family and closeness to one another is everything to them. With such ties they have survived for over 300 years. Now, the land offered them as a haven from religious persecution is causing them difficulty in refraining from becoming "modern man."

ABOUT COUNSELING THE OLD ORDER AMISH CHILD[3]

What role does public education play in the threat to the Amish way of life? In the past, most Amish communities were content to send their children to the local public elementary schools. Approximately 10,000 still attend today. However, the emphasis on science and evolution, the apparent increase of violence and drug usage, and educational TV have contributed to a sudden increase in the number of Amish parochial elementary schools.

---

[3]Parts of this section are from "Counseling the Old Order Amish Child" by J. Wittmer and A. Moser, *Elementary School Guidance and Counseling*, 1974, 8(4), 263-271. Reprinted by permission.

Public school personnel who come into daily contact with Amish children can lessen the Amish people's perceived threat. This lessening of threat is especially so with elementary school counselors, since many varied methods or approaches can be used effectively when working with these "peculiar" children. Some common counselor functions, however, might be ineffective with Amish children.

Rebecca is a young child who attends a public elementary school. In her broken English, she says, "It makes me wonder why outsider kids make fun when a movie is on by the teacher and we make quick to leave the room."

Amos, a young boy attending the same school and who, like Rebecca, speaks German as a first language, also wonders about his relationships at school. "The Englisher boys are mad with me for not pledging the flag. Dad says a graven image it is. Why do they git me, already?"

And Elam, another child in the same school, says, "The coach he says that shorts I must wear next PE class. What should I tell him, yet?"

How would you respond to these children? Would you tell little Rebecca that she might enjoy the movie if she stayed in the room? Would you suggest that Amos should be patriotic and join in the pledge of allegiance? And Elam? Would you tell him that he should put on the PE shorts because physical education is good for his health? Would you respond differently if you knew that these children are Amish and that pledging allegiance to the flag, attending any type of movie, and wearing shorts are contrary to their religious beliefs?

Are Amish children different from other non-Amish children? Because the Amish are suspicious of "outsider" investigations, very few studies have been completed concerning their personalities, but of the few available studies, all but one study has been about Amish children. The research indicates that Amish youth are significantly more introverted and submissive than non-Amish youth (Engle, 1945; Engle & Engle, 1943; Hostetler & Huntington, 1972; Lembright & Yamamota, 1965; Loomis & Jantzen, 1962; Smith, 1958; Stuffle, 1955). These studies also describe the Amish personality as being quiet, responsible, and conscientious. The first and only research concerning the personality of Amish adults (Wittmer, 1970) suggested that the adult Amish personality parallels that of Amish elementary school children.

An uniqueness exists about the Amish personality which is unlike any other American group. Its elements are common to all members of the sect. This model personality or psychic unity among the Amish people is largely due to common childhood experiences and child-rearing practices.

Hostetler and Huntington (1972) administered the Myers-Briggs Type Indicator (Myers, 1962) to 251 Amish elementary children. Further evidence of homogeneity was found when more than 60 percent of the total Amish population fell within two personality types: (ISFJ) Introversion, sensing, feeling, judgment, and (ESFJ) extraversion, sensing, feeling, judgment. One of the most interesting findings in the Hostetler—Huntington (1972) study dealt with the "happy time drawings" of Amish children. Amish and non-Amish children exhibited striking differences in their happy time drawings. The Amish drawings always included work-related activities, whereas non-Amish drawings frequently showed competitive activity and some hostility; neither of these factors was found in any of the Amish drawings. Further, the drawings revealed that regulation and conformity, rather than spontaneity, were dominant Amish characteristics. One important finding for teachers and counselors was the de-emphasis of the self and the person and the importance of the group. The family, the church, and the community are seen as having more significance than the individual.

About the Effective Counselor

The counselor who is effective with Amish children will be genuine and empathic, but also will follow the guidelines presented.

De-emphasize the concept of self. The Amish child is taught to be cooperative rather than competitive, innovative, or aggressive. To the Amish, a child is not a unique individual. He or she is simply one member of a God-fearing group and should be treated as such. Individual resolution is undesirable. Humility is a virtue, and pride, especially self-pride, is a cardinal sin. Amish children do not show pride in dress or appearance (no mirrors are in the home) or self-accomplishments (e.g., they never recite memorized prayers aloud as this would show pride in one's ability to memorize). Yet, Amish children, like other children, have basic psychological and developmental needs. They desire to be wanted, to be needed, and to gain acceptance from peers and authority figures. If Rebecca seems aloof to your praise for a task well done, don't confuse her reactions with indifference. Her reactions most likely coincide with her culture's sanctioned behavior.

Amish youth seek academic achievement and most teachers report that Amish children are good students. This fact may appear contrary to denial of self-accomplishment. However, work is a moral directive within the culture. The Amish child works hard in school and achieves but does not talk about these accomplishments and does not expect praise for doing those things that are expected. For example, when an Amish boy does an excellent job of cleaning the barn, his father simply states, "The barn is now clean."

Any attempt on the part of educators to introduce competitive activities in order to achieve educational goals could only mean, in Amish terms, the loss of humility, simply living, and God's love!

Recognize the limitations of tests. Can you imagine the frustration of taking a test that requires you to identify a gas tank correctly being removed from a car, a well-known cartoon character, or a particular control dial on an electrical appliance when you've never seen them before? Amos, for example, sees school as a bewildering environment, and most of his experiences that are new. The Amish child will most likely never have heard of the Michael Jackson, Sesame Street, or the Miami Dolphins. When using the school's restroom for the first time, the child will not understand how a commode functions. For Amos, it is likely to be a perplexing experience.

Speed is rarely stressed in the Amish culture and children are admonished by their elders to do careful, accurate work. Amish children are told to work steadily and to do well what one does, rather than do a great deal and make careless mistakes. Children are taught never to skip anything that they do not understand. They are to ponder it, to work at it, until they have mastered it.

Thus, a teacher or counselor who administers a speed test to an Amish child could increase unnecessary psychological stress and fail to gain a true picture of the child's skill.

Amish children are at a disadvantage when taking any standardized test, especially if they are being compared to non-Amish children. The Amish see no purpose in formal schooling beyond the elementary grades. Performing well on a standardized test in order to gain a better job or enter high school or college has no special meaning and is useless as a motivational scheme. In addition, testing is often taboo within an Amish community, and educators should seek the consent of Amish parents before administering any test. Educators also will find that Amish parents are not interested in knowing their children's achievement test scores or a comparison of their child's scores with those of other children in the United States, or for that matter, even in the classroom.

Understand culturally different groups' varied "worlds of work." The world of work of Amish children is rather limited. Both children and parents are uninterested in career exploration. The vocational preferences of Amish children, for example, tend toward service occupations and manual work. These children emulate the work roles of Amish adults and want to be farmers or farmers' wives. Studies reveal (Hostetler & Huntington, 1972) that Amish boys prefer farming or farm related work, whereas girls prefer housekeeping, gardening, cooking, cleaning, and caring for children. These vocational aspirations and dreams are realistic and attainable within the limits of Amish culture. One should note that the feminist movement has not brought about any changes in the Amish life style. The Amish interpret the King James Bible literally, especially those sections concerning the submissive role of women.

Respect the need for social distance that Amish children have with non-Amish children. A very real concern among Amish parents today is the possibility that their child will form close, personal friendships with non-Amish children and become too comfortable with the ways of the outside world before they totally understand their own Amishness. Any attempt on the counselor's part to have Amish children form friendships (such as mixed group counseling) with non-Amish children will be contrary to the wishes of Amish parents.

Avoid probing into home or Amish community problems. Because institutions such as the home and the church are held in high esteem, Amish children enjoy participation within these institutions. The possibility of bringing shame on their family will inhibit talking about family or cultural problems. For example, even though an Amish child may be overwrought concerning an excommunicated family member, it would be even more shameful to discuss it with a non-Amish person.

Realize that a caring relationship is not enough. Affective understanding alone is not sufficient when counseling Amish children. The effective counselor also will be knowledgeable of the customs, traditions, and the values existing in the Amish child's unique environment. The acute disparities in culture will most certainly be compounded if a counselor lacks knowledge and then interacts with a confused and bewildered Amish student.

Accept the fact that an Amish child's parents may have asked him or her to avoid counselors. Amish parents are responsible for training their children and are morally accountable to God for doing it correctly. Thus, your counseling or talking with them concerning values or morals may appear disrespectful and even belittling to an Amish parent. If the home is responsible and obligated for moral and religious training, then you may appear as a meddler.

Amish adults do not seek counseling from professional counselors. At times, however, an adult Amish person will seek the "advice" of others within the commune, especially ministers. Thus, school counselors and teachers should realize that Amish parents are extremely leery of any outsider with advice for them or their children. They will quietly listen to these suggestions, but will definitely not incorporate them until after they have sought council with at least three additional Amish adults. Using three adults to solve problems and/or make decisions is a common Amish practice. For example, if a dispute develops between two Amish farmers, three men are selected to arbitrate and decide the solution. Their decision is final.

In summary, to be an effective counselor with an Amish child in a public school setting you will need to learn about the values and ways of the Amish culture. It often will be necessary to keep your own cultural biases in check. Be genuine and empathic. Don't bend the child to match the curriculum. Let the curriculum meet the Amish child's needs.

The Amish are only one distinct religious minority group found in public schools. They are easily recognized, but other such groups are not. Mennonites, Hutterites, Christian Scientists, and many other groups may, in appearance, blend into a school's population. But their values, beliefs, and attitudes, like those of the Amish, play a significant part in attitudes toward school and the way in which they learn.

REFERENCES

Engle, T.L. (1945) Personality adjustments of children belonging to two minority groups. *Journal of Educational Psychology, 36,* 543-560.

Engle, T.L., & Engle, E. (1943). Attitude differences between Amish and non-Amish children attending the same schools. *Journal of Educational Psychology, 34,* 206-214.

Hostetler, J., & Huntington, G. (1972). *Children in Amish society.* New York: Holt, Rinehart & Winston.

Lembright, M.L., & Yamamoto, K. (1965). Subcultures and creative thinking: An exploratory comparison between Amish and urban American school children. *Merrill-Palmer Quarterly of Behavior Development, 2,* 49-64.

Loomis, C., & Jantzen, C. (1962). Boundary maintenance vs. systematic linkage in school integration: The case of the Amish in the United States. *Journal of Pakistan Academy of Rural Development,* 59-83.

Myers, I. (1962). *The Myers Briggs type indicator.* Princeton, N.J.: Educational Testing Service.

Smith, E.L. (1958). Personality differences between Amish and non-Amish children. *Rural Sociology, 23,* 371-376.

Stuffle, C.R.(1955). A comparison of the adjustment of Amish and non-Amish children in Van Buren Township Schools. Unpublished master's thesis, Indiana State Teachers College, Terre Haute.

Van Bracht, T.J. (1938). *Martrys' mirror.* Scottdale, PA: Mennonite Publishing House.

Wittmer, J. (1970). Homogeneity of personality characteristics: A comparison between Old Order Amish and non-Amish. *American Anthropologist, 72,* 1063-1068.

Wittmer, J. (1972). Good guys wear white hats. *Liberty, 67,* 12-17.

Wittmer, J., & Moser, A. (1974). Counseling the Old Order Amish child. *Elementary School Guidance & Counseling, 8,* 263-271.

4

GAY AND LESBIAN POPULATIONS

JOSEPH L. NORTON, Ph.D.
Professor Emeritus, Education
State University of New York—Albany

JOSEPH L. NORTON, Ph.D.

Joseph L. Norton, Professor Emeritus of Education at the State University of New York at Albany, has been a counselor and counselor educator since 1949. He has been active in the New York State Association for Counseling and Development, serving as president 1970-71, and has served in governance of the American Association for Counseling and Development and the SUNY State wide Faculty Senate. He founded the Association for Gay and Lesbian Issues in Counseling and has served on the steering committee of the Association of Lesbian and Gay Psychologists. Co-founder of the Gay, Lesbian and Bisexual Interest Groups of the American Association of Sex Educators, Counselors, and Therapists and of a similar group in the Society for the Scientific Study of Sex, he has transferred much of his efforts in sex education and work with professional groups to the support of gay/lesbian counseling and liberation. Since retirement in 1983, he has devoted much time to volunteer work with the local AIDS Council and to his favorite recreation, skiing.

GAY AND LESBIAN POPULATIONS

AWARENESS INDEX

Directions: Mark each answer true, false, or don't know. Compare your answers with the scoring guide at the end of the test.

T F   1. Lesbians have not been studied with real research until very recently.

T F   2. Lesbians comprise a lower proportion of the population than do gay males.

T F   3. Homosexuals engage in child molestation proportionately more than heterosexuals.

T F   4. The gay militant is highly susceptible to blackmail.

T F   5. Those with same-sex behaviors are easily changed by therapy to heterosexual feelings and behaviors.

T F   6. Administering male hormones make gay males more active homosexually.

T F   7. You can be sure a person is not a lesbian or gay male if the person is legally married.

T F   8. Lesbians may be married to each other legally in at least 5 states in the U.S.

T F   9. Evidence shows that open lesbians and gay males are as well adjusted as non-gays.

T F 10. The civil rights of gays have never been taken away by law or popular vote.

T F 11. Most homosexuals have a choice of being "straight" or gay.

T F 12. Most transsexuals and transvestites are heterosexual.

T F 13. Indicating work with a local gay alliance (on job applications) is a good way to show you are a productive person.

T F 14. Gays and lesbians moving to a new city can usually find "the gay scene" by buying a guide to gay bars, baths and groups.

Scoring Guide for Awareness Index

1. T	6. T	11. F
2. T	7. F	12. T
3. F	8. F	13. F
4. F	9. T	14. T
5. F	10. F	

FIVE CASES

Three young men and a woman came to this counselor's office last month. Peter was a tall, all-American boy who had decided he was gay. He had told his mother, who accepted it openly, but Peter had little notion of how to go about meeting other gays. He believed he was gay because he fantasized about males while having sex with his girlfriend. He had talked with her about his inclinations toward males but had never had the "typical adolescent homosexual experiences" and had never had gay sex. He sought ways to get to know other gays.

Anthony was less attractive physically, a bit overweight, and, like Peter, a college student. He had been having sex with males for three years, had a lover with whom he was having some hassles, and was bothered about how to tell his parents (if at all) and still have their support through his last year of college and graduate school. Unlike Peter, Anthony had told no one he had homosexual feelings (except those with whom he had sex), but had found his way into the gay scene through overhearing gossip of his (presumed) non-gay acquaintances who mentioned a gay bar.

Ed's was another situation. Somewhat older, late 20s, Ed was married and had a two-year old son. His work as a salesman took him on the road and through a chance out-of-town acquaintance he discovered that he enjoyed sex with men as much, maybe more, than with his wife. He did not want to lose his son, whom he loved dearly, nor hurt his wife, but he found himself increasingly seeking out gay locales on his travels. Ed had found a gay guide book which contained information helping him find gays in a new city. Ed wondered if he was likely to bring sexually transmitted disease, especially AIDS, home to his wife, and whether he could or should continue to keep his gay leanings from his wife.

A fourth young man did **not** come to the counselor. Knowing he was gay from the earliest teens, he fought the feelings and married early to prove he was "straight." Three children later, he found himself increasingly turned off sexually by his wife, and finally turned again to clandestine, impersonal gay contacts in the local bus station and other public places. Caught by the police, he was unable to face the public humiliation and took his own life. The latter is a true report. However, happy endings **have** occurred even in similar situations where divorce followed and continued happy contacts with their children.

Jane, too, came for counseling. Forty-six, having trouble both with her lover and her small private business, she sought both vocational and relationship counseling. Her lesbianism was not the problem, but she needed to see someone who would not make it the problem.

These cases are, as in any illustrative cases, only five of hundreds who brought, or should have brought, problems to a counselor. For every Peter, Anthony, or Ed, there are myriad variations, and some of these stories have ended up in print and will help the counselor get a broader picture of the needs of lesbians and gay men. Lesbians appear less often among these cases, reflecting the finding that they often are not thought of when the words homosexual or gay are used (Adler, Hendrick, & Hendrick, 1986; Biemiller, 1985; *Lambda Update,* 1987; Norton, 1982; Rickgarn, 1984; Spees, 1987; Wilensky & Myers, 1987).

One of these cases is, in one sense, insoluble: Ed can hardly avoid hurting **someone** sooner or later. Some decisions can sometimes only be about how to lessen the hurt, or how long to postpone it, or how best to balance the counselee's needs with others' needs. With increased public attention, however, help is more available. Now even support groups exist for gay fathers, bisexual married men and wives of these men (Wilson-Glover, 1987).

Different counselors will experience different levels of difficulty in dealing with gay clients depending on their own attitudes and knowledge. Is the counselor's first reaction, "Certainly Peter is best off, the easiest to help," or, "I wonder if I can help Peter enjoy women more?" Is the first inclination to refer Peter and Anthony and Ed **all** to the local psychiatrist to see if they can be "cured"? Or does such a response fly in the face of current research? Would it be easier to find out about the local gay scene to help Peter find his way than it would be to discover whether Anthony's dad is homophobic enough to cut off his son's support? How can the counselor facilitate a decision in Ed's dilemma of "hiding unhappiness in the closet" or "coming out in the open to be freely himself"? And isn't Jane's problem a long-term one of improving relationships as well as resolving financial problems?

DEFINITIONS

Varying definitions of homosexuality have been presented (Kennedy, 1977; West, 1977). The simplest is "one who has an affectional and sexual orientation to a person of the same sex." This definition seems simple, but, is an individual with **no** same-sex experiences but regular fantasies, gay to all counselors? Or do some opt for the requirement that two people of the same sex establish achieving climax as a mutual goal? Enough males respond sexually to pressure on the genitals or to other external stimulation that it almost seems as if **intent,** or at least **feelings,** should be part of the definition. Evidence clearly shows that a single or a few same-sex acts do not necessarily make one gay. In fact, persons with similar sexual histories may label themselves heterosexual, homosexual, or bisexual, depending on environmental factors (Blumenstein & Schwartz, 1977).

As Father Paul Shanley stated, a same-sex act neither defines nor causes a person's sexual orientation. Many youth have same-sex experiences and grow to be adult heterosexuals. For others this experience is not "just a phase," and the orientation persists for life. Although for some, extensive behavior leaves no doubt as to the label, for others it seems to have to be a matter of self-definition. This very self-labeling, however, has been devastating to hordes of youth in the past. In this chapter, homosexuality means having a strong affectional or erotic attraction to members of the same sex.

One can question if a sexual label, noun or adjective, should be used at all since one's sexuality is not the only aspect of life. Perhaps someday society will acknowledge simply that humans are sexual beings who can develop a wide range of related behaviors, depending on a myriad of complex factors. But whatever the terminology, the gay/lesbian person does develop a homosexual entity. Many males who have identified themselves as homosexuals use the term "gay" as a self-chosen, non-clinical term; most homosexual females prefer to be called "lesbians," although a few prefer "gay women." Their point is that the other labels tend to ignore the female. The term "gay," not involving "a feigned happiness in spite of it all," came out of the backstage parlance of the theatre; the gays say they prefer the term to the outsiders' terms: homo, faggot, dyke, queer, pansy.

Use of the term "same-sex orientation" is better than "same-sex preference" used by some writers earlier, as the word "preference" implies to some a **choice.** The vast majority of lesbians and gay males simply "found themselves" or "discovered" they were wishing for love and affection from members of their own gender. They did not choose to be gay or lesbian; the only choice was whether to act in accordance with their own feelings.

Another problem in definition stems from the presence of increasingly visible bisexuals, who respond sexually and affectionately to both genders. Although some gay males have never been able to respond to women, the majority have had successful experiences, thus dispelling the myth that all gay males hate women and have a revulsion toward the female genitals. Many lesbians are mothers, and many gays are fathers.

HOMOPHOBIA

A term used by George Weinberg (1972), homophobia is the state of excessive fear of contact with homosexuals. Since most people with homophobia do not view it as a disease, counselors usually do not work with such counselees. Occasionally a gay or lesbian counselee will get her or his homophobic parent(s) to come in for counseling. Should that happen, the informed counselor will respond as did one psychiatrist who asked the parents in after talking with their gay son and said, "You have the problem, not he." But counselors should know that negative attitudes toward gays and lesbians are functional in the dynamics of maintaining traditional sex roles. Fear of being labeled homosexual keeps both men and women within the confines of what society has traditionally defined as sex-role appropriate behavior (Morin & Garfinkle, 1978). Another important aspect to note is that many gay men and women have internalized a lot of society's homophobia and hate themselves.

DIFFERENCES

Identifying differences between homosexuals and the population in general is helpful, as these differences are not usually visible. One ironic difference is that members of the gay and lesbian population can be members of any of the other populations discussed in this book. They may be disabled, Black, Hispanic, American Indian, all of whom are doubly special since counselors must not think of heterosexuality alone as the norm for their clientele, although one can note that sexuality itself has been pretty much ignored for the retarded and disabled in general until just recently.

The most crucial difference, which really defines this group, is the strong affection and/or sexual attraction toward people of the same gender, which, as stated earlier, they **discover.** Some counselees are distressed at the discovery, while some find the problem to not be the orientation, but, as in Jane's case to be other concerns.

Another difference is that the other populations do not fear for, or usually suffer, the lack of family support. While most blacks have the "black is beautiful" atmosphere, many gays and lesbians are very fearful. If your counselee watched parents chortling with glee when the news reported voter repeal of a gay rights ordinance, that counselee is unlikely to turn to those parents for support.

One other difference is that the homosexual *can* hide. This population is an invisible minority, and many have fought their societally labeled "affliction" all alone for years with some even taking it to the grave.

NUMBERS

With such amorphous definitions and with a condition readily kept invisible, one finds difficulty in finding precise figures on the gay and lesbian population. Kinsey's old figures stand unchallenged; 37 percent of males and 33 percent of females have had a climax with another of the same sex after the age of 18, or 8 percent have a primarily homosexual life for a period of three years. These data show fewer lesbians than gay males. Estimates of 4 to 10 percent of the U.S. population (i.e., over 20,000,000 Americans) have general support. Considering that each gay male and lesbian has parents, siblings, and/or children, some 50,000,000 Americans or more have intimate contact with homosexuality. Yet this topic has been virtually ignored in all of the counselor education programs in the country.

FURTHER DESCRIPTION OF
THE POPULATION

Altogether, generalizing about the gay and lesbian population is difficult. Lesbians have been virtually invisible in the research partially because they are fewer in actual numbers; and studies of gay men are spotty, although both are slowly increasing. Some of the studies have been surprising. One study by Saghir and Robins (1973) showed that gay men had heterosexual experiences earlier than a comparison group of heterosexual men. Riddle and Morin (1977) reported the average ages when selected events occurred in the lives of 63 lesbian and 138 gay male psychologists. These selected events and the average ages for the lesbians and gay males, respectively, were as follows: aware of homosexual feelings—14, 13; first same-sex sexual experience—20, 15; understood the term "homosexual"—16, 17; first homosexual relationships—23, 22; considered self homosexual—23, 21; disclosed identity to parent—30, 28; and disclosed identity professionally—32, 31. Interesting to note is that in the area of awareness of same-sex feelings, males were a year ahead of females, although women usually mature two years ahead of men. Males were active sexually five years ahead of females. Either gay males mature earlier than men in general, as suggested by Tripp (1975), or for the women more of a time span occurs between puberty and awareness of lesbian feelings.

One cultural stereotype is that gays and lesbians pervade the arts and literature, but no actual research shows gays to be more creative, although they have been shown to be more intelligent (Bonnel, 1976). More interesting is that the increasing research on personality characteristics and even sexual responsiveness reflect *few* differences between hetero- and homosexual people (Masters & Johnson, 1979; Bell, Weinberg, & Hammersmith, 1981; Sakheim, Barlow, Beck, & Abrahamson, 1985).

Despite the fact that gays are much like non-gays in many aspects of life—career development, intellectual development and even sexual development—in this society they do have some special problems, which are elucidated in the following sections.

CURRENT PROBLEMS

The question of how lesbians and gays are being treated in schools has one main answer: for the most part they are ignored. If they are open or happen to be part of the visible, so-called "effeminate" or "butch" groups, however, they are reviled. One gay was forced to take classes with females only (because he wanted to be one? (the myth) or because he was not a threat to them and was to straight males?). In addition, he was forced to eat lunch alone for a year. "Faggot" has not ceased to be the favorite put-down word from fifth grade up. If one is non-gay, such peer put-down can be handled as is any other, but for the gay it is likely to arouse the fearful unspoken response, Does he really know? So far the schools' sex education of youth has not been very helpful in overcoming hostility, if local young men scream "faggot" out of the school bus window at the writer, as has happened. Coaches still brag of heterosexual success but malign the same-sex successes of others. And in a few schools, counselors can still be heard telling and laughing at "faggot" jokes. Do as many counselors refuse to put up with anti-gay jokes and reject anti-semitic ones?

Myths

Probably the best generalization is that counselors are often uncomfortable with the topic, out of fear of hostility. One can hope that the first response to a youngster who comes in to talk about sexual orientation is not, "Well, I'll have to call your father so he can take you to a psychiatrist." While some counselors are "pretty cool" about homosexuality, many are still misled by the myths, and truly believe the following falsehoods:

1. Gays want to be of the opposite gender.

2. Gay men are primarily hairdressers, antique dealers, and interior decorators.

3. All gays are promiscuous.

4. Gay males are weak, introspective, and inactive physically.

5. Removing laws against homosexuality will increase its frequency.

6. Gays and lesbians hate those of the opposite sex.

7. Gays are a menace to children.

8. Just give a gay male some male hormones and he will want women.

Special counseling may be needed to dispel the myths that tend to limit the lesbian or gay male. Take, for instance, the stereotype that gay men are effeminate. Brown (1976), Kopay and Young (1977), and many others say they "knew" they could not be homosexual, despite their strong affection and sexual attraction to other males, because they did not swish, flip their wrists, and cross-dress like the few visible gays they saw. Actually, most transvestites (cross dressers) are heterosexual. Only 10 to 20% of gay males are "drag queens," and considerably fewer lesbians dress like men to an extent that would distinguish them from heterosexual women. Also, the fact is that many lesbians are very dainty and feminine, quite unlike the "bull-dyke" stereotype.

Another misconception is that gays and lesbians want to be of the opposite sex. Ironically another myth listed above is just the opposite, that gays and lesbians *hate* the opposite sex; how can we have such contradictory generalizations? People who wish to be of the opposite sex are properly called transsexuals. Lesbians and gay men are delighted to be the gender they are; they simply love others of the same gender and prefer them as sex partners.

Public clamor such as Anita Bryant's "Save the Children" campaign finally and clearly brought out the facts: gay men do not molest children even in proportion to their numbers. Child molestation is primarily a heterosexual phenomenon, a couple of notorious mass murderers notwithstanding. One of them may have been homophobic, since he killed young men who would sell themselves to men for money. Gay teachers do not molest their students. The *New York Times* estimate of the number of gay teachers in the U.S. was 120,000 to 240,000 (Macroff, 1977). Although the New York City school system has numerous records of heterosexual child molestations, no recorded incident exists of homosexual child molestation despite a membership of over 200 in the Gay Teachers Association. Further research on role modeling does not support the fear that gays and lesbians, either as parent or other role models, would create gay and lesbian children (Kirkpatrick, Roy, & Smith, 1976; Riddle, 1978). Another study has shown that gay/lesbian teachers are often "super-teachers" (Smith, 1985).

Another falsehood is that lesbian and gay couples take on "husband and wife" roles. While this arrangement has occasionally occurred, and such couples may appear on television talk shows, the research results clearly have been that *most* couples just don't take on such roles. (Jay & Young, 1979; Oberstone & Sukoneck, 1976).

Besides being faced with these stereotypes and myths, gay males and lesbians bring other orientation-related problems to the counselor. For instance, the fear of a lonesome old age is a specter held before gay males, who also are led to believe that the gay male subculture is totally youth oriented. In fact, many older gays have lovers or a circle of friends for companionship or sex. While some older gay males have accepted this much-repeated stereotype, others find it inappropriate (Kelly, 1977). Some research reports that the gay male, who is already isolated from his family, is **better** able to cope with old age than his heterosexual peers (Francher & Henkin, 1973).

Finding Others of Like Mind

As pointed out in Peter's case, gay/lesbian invisibility poses another problem for some who are coming out: finding others of like mind. Gay/lesbian rights groups exists in many college communities and in many cities are active adult groups and a few with special youth groups for those 21 and under. Unfortunately, for too many years the gay or lesbian bar was the only meeting place, but now in addition to the community centers, church groups also exist: Dignity (Catholic), Integrity (Episcopalian) and the Metropolitan Community Church, a primarily gay and lesbian church which has grown in just a few years to over 100 congregations and 30 affiliated groups. The Unitarian Universalist Association has an Office of Lesbian and Gay Concerns in denominational headquarters in Boston. Counselors can acquire or help their counselees acquire published guides to groups and meeting places, accommodations and social organizations (Gaia's Guide, 1987; Gay Yellow Pages, 1987). Large cities have groups like New York City's Institute for the Protection of Lesbian and Gay Youth and Senior Action in a Gay Environment (SAGE).

Some newly self-recognizing gays need help in realizing that not all gays fall in love the instant they meet another gay of the same sex. Discrimination, pickiness, and selectivity occur in the homosexual as well as the heterosexual world. Neither gay life nor gay sex is necessarily more idyllic than heterosexual life or sex; the situation is that for this population, gay lifestyles are better, more satisfying, and more fulfilling.

"I'm Afraid I'm Homosexual."

While fewer come to counseling these days saying, "I'm afraid I'm homosexual," their orientation is still a question for some. A good counselor query is, "What makes you think you might be?" As indicated in the discussion of definitions, being gay or lesbian is mostly a matter of perception; a few same-sex acts do not make one a gay or lesbian (and apparently for lesbians, most do not act until they are sure of the feeling of identity). Sexual orientation includes fantasy and affection as **well** as sexual attraction; if the person masturbates, any fantasy at that time can give clues. A review of the person's whole developing sexuality may still not give a clear answer, in which case keeping all options open seems advisable.

"How Did I Get This Way?"

Most of the research into this question seems to have been done with an eye to preventing this "sickness" in others. And, although for someone currently same-sex oriented the question seems superfluous, many still ask, perhaps to relieve guilt or to satisfy a parent. The answer has to be that no one knows. All the experts currently agree that to know is impossible. Hormonal influences, family influences, environmental or genetic, childhood sexual experiences—any or all of these may be involved. Some know from earliest memories that they are different from their peers, while others do not recognize their orientation until after years of heterosexual marriage. The whys of being gay and the timing of recognizing it simply do not have answers. Not one of the many theories proposed stands up to careful scrutiny (Bell, Weinberg, & Hammersmith, 1981; DeCecco, 1987).

"Can I Get Over It?"

This question has no absolute answer, although most generally the answer is no. Most counselors concede the easiest help is to make the person content with the same-sex orientation, but some psychoanalysts, behavior therapists, and Aesthetic Realists and other fundamentalist religions claim "cures." Much criticism from militant gays indicates that these cures make clients asexual, not heterosexual. Some behavior therapists now question whether or not trying to change the person is proper even if asked to do so (Davidson, 1976), but others forge ahead with their aversion therapy (Adams & Sturgis, 1977). [**Most** lesbians and gay males are happy with themselves and their lives (Jay & Young, 1979), even though some at first had wanted to change.] Some therapists report 20 to 50% success in changing those with a very strong motivation **to** change (Marmor, 1976; Masters & Johnson, 1979). Yet counselors should remember that such motivation is the result of an oppressive society, which formerly recommended clitorectomies for women who thought it bad to feel sexual. While some therapists have recommended hormone treatments, giving male hormones makes gay men more active with men; it does not make them turn to having sex with women.

One point counselors should make very clear to anyone who seems to have a same-sex orientation is that a heterosexual marriage does **not** create a cure or prove heterosexuality. It is dishonest to enter into a heterosexual marriage expecting it will cure, although this is another myth held by many non-gays. Unfortunately, what is often heard is, "All you need is a good—the right—man (or woman, for the male) and you'll get over your lesbian (gay) feelings." Ed is a case in point: what heterosexual responsiveness he had died out before long. Actually, some wives are relieved to learn a husband is gay; they had thought themselves to blame for a poor sex life and marriage (Gochros, 1978). But the notion that gays and lesbians do not marry heterosexually is wrong; note the 100 men in the gay fathers group in the Albany area. One estimate is that 50% of gays and lesbians are hetero-sexually married (Blair, 1979). On the other hand, although many same-sex couples are monogamous, in no state in the United States may two same-sexed people be legally married.

"Should I 'Come Out' to Others?"

Researchers say yes, but counselors need to counsel about, rather than give answer to, this question. That is, the open gay or lesbian has been found to be better adjusted than the "closeted" one, and even better adjusted than some non-gays (Freedman, 1975). This is understandable because the open gay has overcome the dissimulation involved in changing pronouns when talking about the weekend or having no picture of one's lover on the desk. The open gay can be true to self.

But circumstances vary. Anthony's father might refuse to pay his tuition. Both sides of the question of coming out to family and other non-gays need to be explored. How likely is it to slip out accidentally, or to be discovered from some other source? If Anthony has decided to tell is unwise and has managed his double life without pain, what counselor wants to override his decision? Many parents **must** actually know but appear to want not to bring it out in the open. Resources are available for use with one's parents (Silverstein, 1977; Clark, 1977; Fairchild & Hayward, 1979). Many an upset, disappointed, fearful, or hostile parent has been won over with patience, by reading relevant materials, or by a loved one's lover. And too, there are the **not** apocryphal stories of the parents who respond, "How nice, so am I." Some fathers, gay themselves, feel guilty that they "caused" a son's orientation, although research does not support such an anxiety.

This issue of remaining invisible, "suffering in silence," "carrying this burden" and never fully expressing one's self has no universal solution. Many have lived their entire lives hating themselves. The counselor cannot tell the counselee what to do but can discuss the pros and cons, helping the client weigh the alternatives. Helpful pamphlets by DeBaugh (1978), and the National Gay and Lesbian Task Force (1978); *Reflections of a Rock Lobster* (Fricke, 1981); *A Way of Love, A Way of Life* (Henckel & Cunningham, 1979); and *Young, Gay and Proud* (Anonymous, 1980) are also useful. For the gay father, see Bozett (1985).

Sometimes openness leads to hassles from a hostile society; a "swishy" gay beat up at a local shopping center, "fag" painted on a garage door, urine poured under a dorm room door. Often, openness is met with a shrug: "I couldn't care less." Sometimes the response is "I'm glad you shared this with me; it makes us closer." Studies do show that both men and women attribute fewer positive traits to research subjects presented as gay than to other subjects (Thompson & Fishburn, 1977). With such a range of responses to know what to do is difficult. However, more gays and lesbians than not say, "They really were more understanding and accepting than I expected."

"Will I Be Blackmailed?"

In the past blackmail was a more prevalent concern. One benefit of gay liberation is that the openly gay or lesbian individual is not subject to such threats. However, the left-over idea that all homosexuals have to hide from society does still let some disreputable people prey on others more readily than they might in the non-gay world. For example, theft after sex is a minor problem in the gay world, and almost unheard of in the lesbian, but it is one thing about which the gay males might benefit from some warning (Boggan, Haft, Lister, & Rupp, 1975).

Pair Bonding or Not?

Since most gay males and lesbians have been brought up at first with heterosexual expectations, most also have absorbed society's dictate of pair-bonding in monogamous relationships. Without the strictures of a legal marriage, however, many gays find it easy to stray from monogamy. Whether to stick with heterosexual patterns or venture into freer patterns of relationships and sex is a problem often facing this population. Research shows this decision is less of a problem for lesbians. Most of them are at least serially monogamous (Peplau, Cochran, Rook & Padesky, 1978; Peplau, Rubin, & Hill, 1977). Obviously, no one has to be promiscuous, but without question the opportunity is more available for gay males than for the rest of society. Some gay male couples are monogamous for thirty years or more, but the higher incidence of sexually transmitted diseases in the gay male population attests to a fairly extensive exchanging of partners.

"How Can I Avoid AIDS?"

Acquired Immune Deficiency Syndrome is transmitted by unsafe sexual activity and sharing of contaminated needles, so the counselor can take on the teacher's role and urge gay males to use condoms. While this word would never have been used in most schools before the late 1980s, essential information for gay males is to know that they should never let semen enter their bodies.

The spectre of AIDS has raised much panic and misinformation in the community at large. While anything written about AIDS is out of date by the time it is in print, the first thing a counselor must know is that to counsel a client who has AIDS prevents *no* danger of the counselor becoming infected. AIDS is spread only by blood to blood or semen to blood, and any such close contact is contrary to professional ethical principles. Aside from that, the primary factor involved is stigma. Both groups that were first affected by AIDS—drug abusers and homosexuals—are already stigmatized, and the counselor must examine his or her attitudes toward these groups. Then the counselor needs to become informed; resources are available to help overcome the hysteria and panic that now abounds. The media talk about "always fatal disease" is not accurate—AIDS is a condition that allows other diseases to run rampant. And it has not always proved fatal, although the survival rate has not been over 10%. But as of this writing, there have been exciting developments such as an aerosol spray that prevents the recurrence of the dreaded type of pneumonia that has been prevalent, a food extract (active lipids #721) that enhances growth of T-cells (the white blood cells needed for immunity, which are the target of the virus thought to cause AIDS), and combinations of anti-viral and T-cell facilitative medicines that offer hope. So a counselor should offer support, help the client find other support systems, and deal with the person with AIDS as one would anyone with a potentially fatal condition. Depending on the person's current status, this may involve coping with inability to work, loss of family support, need for contact with the welfare and Supplemental Security Income staff, or general psychological distress.

One worry that may come up with a gay male is fear of sexual activity. The hope is that enough safe-sex education will make its way into the school curriculum so that the counselor will only need to reinforce the importance of the protection of condoms rather than the unrealistic (for many teenagers) option of celibacy. Nowadays, this bit of education is appropriate for every group, not just multicultural and diverse populations.

How to combat societally dictated sex roles is an issue for some of the population, especially for the women. Lesbians defy society by asserting they will not be dependent on a male for life or by opting out of motherhood. Such defiance of sex role stereotypes creates some hazards for women. Gay males who are "macho" fit externally into the expected sex role, but internally their affectional and sexual needs are met differently from those of most men. Because most hostility seems to come from those with very narrow stereotypes of what being a man or a woman is, and from those with rigid attitudes about sex, some counselees may need help in sticking with their own feelings instead of letting the world dictate to them.

FURTHER PERSONAL COUNSELING NEEDS

As indicated earlier, a unique problem faced by this group in contrast to the other special populations is lack of security, even in the family. Black children are not rejected by parents because they are black. Some disabled children are rejected for their status, but then the parents feel guilty. Anecdotal reports seem to indicate that parents who reject gay or lesbian children appear to be more often self-righteous than guilty. Thus, these counselees may be more in need of finding support groups than others.

Most personal problems concerned with relationships, loneliness, bashfulness, and so forth are much the same as those of heterosexuals. Unrequited love is unrequited love; yet, falling in love with a straight roommate does pose special problems since most heterosexuals are not as closely exposed to their non-responding loved one, nor quite as likely to be met with hostility if the feelings are exposed.

Because of the prospect of hostility, special counseling on the legal aspects of living may be needed. Bernstein (1977) pointed out the need for clear and indisputable contacts on joint ownership, wills, and so forth, that will stand up to hostile family reaction in case of legal action or death.

The lesbian or gay male who comes out will have to deal with the fears of the non-gay community. Parents fear the child will have a tortured, promiscuous, or unhappy life, ending up lonely and abandoned. The straight roommate fears that somehow he might be tainted: "What made him think I might be that way?" Others fear that teachers will turn pupils (their children) gay. The counselor can help the counselee see that these fears stem from misinformation and myths and that the task is one of education. New York City gays and lesbians took 15 years to educate the City Council to overcome the shrill, narrowly moralistic cries of outrage. A counselee may need help in finding the resources and strength to carry on this educational process. See Green (1978), Kelly (1977), and Weinberg and Williams (1975).

CAREER NEEDS

As a group, homosexuals are as disparate as heterosexuals. Gays and lesbians are found in all occupations and all walks of life, although proportionally they number greater among the college educated. The gay caucuses in many professions attest to this variety: The American Psychiatric Association; American Psychological Association; American Association for Counseling and Development; the American Nurses Association; Modern Language

Association; National Council of Teachers of English; American Association of Sex Educators, Counselors and Therapists; American Public Health Association; social workers; lawyers; and New York City's Gay Teachers Association. Thus, career counseling needs should not differ much from those of the heterosexual client. Important factors to consider when making career choices, some of which have been pointed out by Canon (1973) and Norton (1976) are the following:

1. Probably a large city is the best location for most, since it provides, per the individual's need, either greater anonymity or greater opportunity to find support groups. Also, in the large city the personal behavior of employees is of less concern to employers.

2. Students should not put school or college gay alliance activity on a vita.

3. Be reasonably discreet; sexual orientation should be irrelevant to job hiring.

4. Make use of the National Gay and Lesbian Task Force's list of industries which state they do not discriminate against gays (National Gay and Lesbian Task Force, 1982). Having the list of communities protecting gay and lesbian civil rights is also reassuring, but very little, if any, encouragement can be offered to the counselee to ask for affirmative action!

5. While in the past a gay personnel manager has sometimes been harder on open gays than non-gays since it threatened his own exposure, nowadays some business gays are looking for like-minded personnel. One issue of a gay bi-weekly listed 26 openings (The Advocate, 1979), another weekly listed 19 (New York Native, Apr. 13, 1987).

SOCIETY'S UNDERSTANDING

The youth who reported that friends and family "really were more understanding than I expected" may well reflect the state of American society today. Yet one cannot forget the high school students in Tucson who went downtown to "beat up a queer" and killed a visitor from out of state, but were back on the Student Council within six months. Or the three youths who threw an openly gay male off a bridge to drown in Bangor, Maine. Hostility is countrywide, not just in San Francisco and New York City. More than one-half of the population, when polled, said they were for civil rights of homosexuals, although only in Seattle has a majority voted to retain such civil rights, and several jurisdictions have voted to retain such civil rights, and several jurisdictions have voted to rescind them (Dade County, FL; St. Paul, MN; Boulder, in the U.S. Constitution to prevent states from forbidding homosexual behavior. On the other hand, decisions are beginning to come in favor of the lesbian mother, and of gay fathers' visitation rights. Support for civil rights comes from many church groups, including the National Council of Bishops of the Roman Catholic Church and the Central Conference of the American Rabbis of the Reform Movement in Judaism. But not many groups actually condone same-sex behavior and orientation. While the majority seem to favor a "live and let live" policy, seemingly the majority do not understand and accept same-sex orientation (Leo, 1979). And a vocal minority actively oppose it.

HISTORY OF SERVICES TO GAYS

The history of services to gays and lesbians has been one of oppression; at first punishment, then treatment to cure the "illness." Such treatment has included isolation, incarceration, psychoanalysis, aversive therapy, electric shock, lobotomies, and castration. Many a youth was forced into an insane asylum by parents hostile to same-sex orientation. Not until 1974 did the American Psychiatric Association remove homosexuality from its list of illnesses, and only in 1986 did the word vanish completely with the removal of "Ego dystonic homosexuality" from the *Diagnostic and Statistical Manual III-R.*

Laws have forbidden homosexual acts throughout the United States, although since 1971 some 26 states have decriminalized sex between consenting adults. But in 24 states the law still invades the bedroom and labels 10% of the population as criminal. The history of court decisions until recently has been one of either direct punishment or depriving gay males and lesbians of their children, often depriving them of visiting rights especially if the gay or lesbian had a partner in the home. A reversal has begun, and the

American Psychological Association has taken the position that affectional and sexual orientation should not be the primary consideration in determining child custody. Despite this stand, four years later Garfinkle and Morin (1978) found that therapists rate the same hypothetical client differently when the client is presented as homosexual rather than heterosexual, the former being rated less healthy.

Change in the 26 states and in some public and professional attitudes has followed a surge of gay liberation sparked by the drag queens who refused to be docile any longer during a routine raid in 1969 of the Stonewall bar in New York City. Quiet efforts at reform had been progressing since the 1850s (Lauritsen & Thorstad, 1974), and quiet acceptance exists for the most part in some areas such as San Francisco, a comfortable home for many. But after 1969 the Gay Liberation Front, the Gay Activists Alliance, Street Transvestite Action Revolutionaries (STAR), and then, nationwide, gay and lesbian groups rapidly sprung up. Annual marches to celebrate the Stonewall riot have spread to major cities throughout America. As indicated, over 60 jurisdictions, including the State of Wisconsin, have passed gay civil rights ordinances; and, as mentioned, the professional caucuses have pressed education concerning gay and lesbian issues on their colleagues.

At local, state and national levels, organizations are at work on the reeducation needed to continue the improved state of lesbians and gay males and to counteract the added hostility brought about by the AIDS crisis. The National Gay and Lesbian Task Force (NGLTF), besides pushing for the removal of "homosexuality" for the DSM, has moved the Civil Service Commission, the Peace Corps, the Bureau of Prisons, the IRS and other government agencies to lift restrictions on gays and lesbians. This Task Force also publishes support packets for gay parents, sodomy repeal, and gay teachers and has published a book, *Our Right to Love,* to help end lesbian invisibility. The National Gay Rights Advocates and the Lambda Legal Defense and Education Fund (666 Broadway, New York, NY 10012) are both national organizations promoting legislation and education, including court decisions, supportive of lesbians and gay males (Human Rights Foundation, Inc., 1984; Lambda Update, 1987).

Counselors should be aware, however, that just because progress has been made does not mean that all professionals have been won over by the education of their gay militant members. The American Psychiatric Association decision to declassify homosexuality as a disease was opposed in 1974 by some members. Enough signatures were collected to require a vote, and one third of the members voting still felt that homosexuality should be retained on the list. This thinking is not surprising when one realizes that most of the early writing on the subject was based on homosexuals who came into treatment and that a very gloomy picture of the condition was the only one presented. Not until Hooker's 1957 study did the first data on well-adjusted gays appear, and only in 1969 did her National Institute for Mental Health study committee recommend nomenclature changes and legalizing consensual same-sex acts. Counselors who feel they must make a referral should recall that one-third of the APA voted against "curing by referendum" and should make sure they know of the attitude of anyone to whom counselees are referred.

THE HELPING PROFESSIONAL'S ROLE

Because most counselors were reared in our heterosexually oriented society, the vast majority have absorbed the misinformation and myths about or even the hostility towards lesbians and gay men. The first responsibility is for counselors to reeducate themselves. The quickest way is by meeting and talking to same-sex oriented people, to discover that they are people, not devils. Reading can take the place of personal meetings if the latter cannot be arranged (Martin & Lyon, 1972; Moses & Hawkins, 1982; Norton, 1982a.,b.) and can supplement such meetings as do occur. *Our Right to Love* (Vida, 1978), *The Homosexual Matrix* (Tripp, 1975) and *Loving Someone Gay* (Clark, 1977) would be a good beginning. The books for parents were previously referred to and included ones by Fairchild and Hayward, 1979; and Silverstein, 1977. Also previously referred were materials on coming out and included Anonymous, 1980; DeBaugh, 1977; and NGLTF, 1978. Once counselors have confronted any of their own personal hostility, doubts or uncertainties so as to be better able to keep personal values out of counseling as much as possible, they can go ahead and counsel with the gay male or lesbian just as they would with anyone else. Counselors must remember that not all gays and lesbians go to a counselor because they are gay; they go because they have other problems. Actually, many avoid personal problem counseling just because they are afraid of the reaction they will get.

In the past, many have gone to counselors with another problem, but the counselor made sexual orientation the problem.

Counselors have the responsibility to let it be known that they will listen to gays and lesbians as well as to non-gays. They can reject anti-gay jokes; they can put articles about gay civil rights or gay leaders on bulletin boards or in school papers; they can make clear that they have discarded, if they ever had, the stereotypes about gay males being "effeminate" and lesbians "butch."

Once the gay or lesbian is in the office, library, or wherever counselors counsel, the responsibility is to counsel as well as possible, keeping in mind the myths and the hostilities the counselee may have incorporated into her or his self-concept or met in the world outside. As with any counseling situation generating a feeling of acceptance and understanding is crucial, and can be genuine if the counselor has rid herself or himself of the myths. Correcting misperceptions, giving appropriate reas-surance, evaluating pros and cons of coming out—all regular counseling activities—will come into play while working with this population.

Specific suggestions have been scattered throughout the discussion of special problems. Yet the counselor cannot expect to have answers to all problems. Ed's dilemma has a variety of possible outcomes. Some wives truly want to make accommodations and maintain the marriage. Some husbands feel a need to be free but have contact with children. Some heterosexual husbands are happy to be rid of both the lesbian wife **and** the children and go off to seek greener pastures. Others can accept a wife's outside interests with equanimity, as long as it is not another male. Some gay husbands feel they **have** to lead a double life (Miller, 1978) and continue to have illicit sex on the side. Some handle this well, others with great guilt. As mentioned, some wives feel so relieved that they are not the cause of the marital problem that, although upset, they can move quickly to making rational decisions about the future. The helping professional's role in this, as in all cases, is to know that knowledge of others' behavior does not solve Ed's problem, and he alone can decide. Exploration of all his needs is crucial, as is true of all counseling. This can be done only in a warm, permissive, non-judgmental situation. A well-informed, self-aware counselor is what all lesbians and gay males need.

REFERENCES

Adams, E., & Sturgis, T. (1977). Status of behavioral reorientation techniques in the modification of homosexuality: A review. *Psychological Bulletin, 84* (6), 1121-1188.

Adler, N.L., Hendrick, S. & Hendrick, C. (1986). Male sexual preference and attitudes toward love and sexuality. *Journal of Sex Education & Therapy, 12* (2), 27-30.

Anonymous. (1980). *Young, Gay & Proud.* Boston: Alyson Publications.

The Advocate (1979, March 22). 6922 Hollywood Blvd., 10th floor, Los Angeles, CA 90028.

Bell, A.P., Weinberg, M.S., & Hammersmith, S.K. (1981). *Sexual preference: Its development in men and women.* Bloomington, IN: Indiana University Press.

Bernstein, B.E. (1977) Legal and social interface in counseling homosexual clients. *Social Casework, 58* (1), 36-40.

Biemiler, L., (1985, October 2). AIDS on campus. *Chronicle of Higher Education,* p.1.

Blair, R. (1979) Personal communication.

Blumenstein, F.W., & Schwartz, P. (1977). Bisexuality: Some social psychological issues. *Journal of Social Issues, 33* (2), 30-45.

Boggan, E.C., Haft, M.G., Lister, C., & Rupp, J.P. (1975). *The rights of gay people: The basic ACLU guide to a gay person's rights.* New York: Avon.

Bonnel, C. (1976). Heterosexuality, an enlightened view. *Christopher Street, 1,* 26-27.

Bozett, F.N. (1985). Gay men as fathers, in Hanson, S.H. & Bozett, F.W. (Eds.). *Dimensions of fathering.* Beverly Hills, CA: Sage.

Brown, H. (1976). *Familiar faces, hidden lives: The story of homosexual men in America today.* New York: Harcourt, Brace & Jovanovich.

Canon, H.J. (1973). Gay students. *Vocational Guidance Quarterly.*

Clark, D. (1977). *Loving someone gay.* Millbrae, CA: Celestial Arts.

Davison, G.C. (1976). Homosexuality: The ethical challenge. *Journal of Consulting Clinical Psychology, 44,* 157-162.

DeBaugh, A. (1977). *Coming Out!* Washington, D.C.: Universal Fellowship of Metropolitan Community Churches.

DeCecco, J.P. (1987). Homosexuality's brief recovery: From sickness to health and back again. *Journal of Sex Research, 23* (1), 106-114.

Fairchild, B., & Hayward, N. (1979). *Now that you know.* New York: Harcourt, Brace & Jovanovich.

Francher, S., & Henkin, J. (1973). The menopausal queen: Adjustment to aging and the male homosexual. *American Journal of Orthopsychiatry, 43* (4), 670-674.

Freedman, M. (1975). Homosexuals may be healthier than straights. *Psychology Today, 8* (10), 28-32.

Fricke, A. (1981). *Reflections of a rock lobster: A story about growing up gay.* Boston: Alyson Publications.

Gaia's Guide. (1987). Giovanni's Room, 345 South 12th St. NE, Philadelphia, PA 19107.

Garfinkle, E.M., & Morin, S.F. (1978). Psychotherapists' attitudes toward homosexual psychotherapy clients. *Journal of Social Issues, 34* (3), 101-112.

Gay Yellow Pages. (1987). New York: Renaissance House.

Gochros, H.L. (1978). Counseling gay husbands. *Journal of Sex Education and Therapy, 3* (2), 6-10.

Green, R. (1978). Sexual identity of 37 children raised by homosexual or transsexual parents. *American Journal of Psychiatry, 135* (6), 692-697.

Henckel, F., & Cunningham, J., (1979). *A way of love, a way of life: A young person's introduction to what it means to be gay.* New York: Lothrup, Lee & Shepard.

Hooker, E. (1957). The adjustment of the male overt homosexual. *Journal of Projective Techniques, 21,* 18-31.

Human Rights Foundation, Inc. (1984). *Demystifying homosexuality: A teaching guide about lesbians and gay men.* New York: Irvington Publishers Inc.

Jay, K., & Young, A. (1979). *The gay report.* New York: Simon & Schuster.

Kelly, J. (1977). The aging male homosexual: Myth and reality. *The Gerontologist, 17* (4), 329-332.

Kennedy, E. (1977). *Sexual counseling.* New York: Seabury Press.

Kirkpatrick, M., Roy, R., & Smith, K. (1976). A new look at lesbian mothers. *Human Behavior,* August, 60-61.

Kopay, D., & Young, P.D. (1977). *The David Kopay story.* New York: Arbor House.

Lambda Update. (1987, Winter). New York: Lambda Legal Defense and Education Fund.

Lauritson, J., & Thorstad, D. (1974). *The early homosexual movement.* Albion, CA: Times Change Press.

Leo, J. (1979) Homosexuality: Tolerance vs. approval. *Time, 113* (2), 48-51.

Macroff, G.J. (1977, June 24). Should professional homosexuals be permitted to teach? *New York Times,*

Marmor, J. (1976). Homosexuality and sexual orientation disturbance. In B.J. Saddock, H.I. Kaplan, & A.M. Freedman, (Eds.), *The sexual experience.* Baltimore: The Williams and Wilkins Co.

Martin, D. & Lyon, P. (1972). *Lesbian/Woman.* New York: Bantam Press.

Masters, W., & Johnson, V. (1979). *Homosexuality in perspective.* Boston: Little, Brown & Co.

Miller, B. (1978). Adult sexual resocialization: Adjustments toward a stigmatized identity. *Alternate Lifestyles, 1* (2), 207-234.

Morin, S.F., & Garfinkle, E.M. (1978). Male homophobia. *Journal of Social Issues, 34* (1), 29-47.

Moses, A.E., & Hawkins, R.O. (1982). *Counseling lesbian women and gay men.* St. Louis: C.V. Mosby Co.

National Gay and Lesbian Task Force. (1982). *Corporate survey results.* Author: (1517 U St., N.W., Washington, D.C. 20009)

National Gay and Lesbian Task Force (1978). *About coming out.* Author.

National Gay Rights Advocates. (540 Castro Street, San Francisco, CA 94114).

National Institute of Mental Health. (1969). *Report of commission on homosexuality.* Washington, D.C.: Author.

New York Native. (1987, April 13). P.O. Box 1475, New York, NY 10008.

Norton, J.L. (1976). The homosexual and counseling. *Personnel and Guidance Journal, 54,* 374-377.

Norton, J.L. (1982a). Integrating gay issues into counselor education. *Counselor Education and Supervision. 21* (3), 208-212.

Norton, J.L. (1982b). *Survey of lesbian and gay counseling centers.* Author Mimeo.

Oberstone, A.K., & Sukoneck, H. (1976). Psychological adjustment and life style of single lesbian and single heterosexual women. *Psychology of Women Quarterly, 1* (2), 172-188.

Peplau, L.A., Cochran, S., Rook, K., & Padesky, C. (1978). Loving women: Attachment and autonomy of lesbian relationships. *Journal of Social Issues, 34* (3), 7-27.

Peplau, L.A., Rubin, Z., & Hill, C.T. (1977). Sexual intimacy in dating couples. *Journal of Social Issues, 33* (2), 86-109.

Rickgarn, R.L. (1984). Developing support systems for gay and lesbian staff members. *Journal of College & University Student Housing, 14,* 32-36.

Riddle, D.I. (1978). Relating to children: Gays as role models. *Journal of Social Issues, 34* (3), 38-58.

Riddle, D.I., & Morin, S.F. (1977, November). Removing the stigma: Data from individuals. *APA Monitor,* pp. 16; 28.

Sakheim, D.K., Barlow, D.H., Beck, J.G., & Abrahamson, D.J. (1985). A comparison of male heterosexual and male homosexual patterns of sexual arousal. *Journal of Sex Research, 21* (2), 183-198.

Saghir, M.T., & Robins, E. (1973). *Male and female homosexuality: A comprehensive investigation.* Baltimore: Williams and Wilkins.

Silverstein, C. (1977). *A family matter.* New York: McGraw-Hill.

Smith, D. (1985). An ethnographic interview study of homosexual teachers' perspectives. Unpublished doctoral dissertation, SUNY at Albany, NY.

Spees, E. (1987). College students' sexual attitudes and behaviors, 1974-85: A review of the literature. *Journal of College Student Personnel, 28* (2), 135-140.

Thompson, G.H., & Fishburn, W.F. (1977). Attitudes toward homosexuality among graduate counseling students. *Counselor Education and Supervision, 17,* 121-130.

Tripp, C.A. (1975). *The homosexual matrix.* New York: McGraw-Hill.

Vida, G. (Ed.). (1978). *Our right to love: A lesbian resource book.* New York: Prentice-Hall.

Weinberg, G. (1972). *Society and the health homosexual.* New York: Anchor/ Doubleday.

Weinberg, M., & Williams, C. (1975). *Male homosexuals: Their problems and adaptations.* New York: Penguin Books.

West, D.J. (1977). *Homosexuality re-examined.* Minneapolis: University of Minnesota Press.

Wilensky, M., & Myers, M.F. (1987). Retarded ejaculation in homosexual patients: A report of nine cases. *Journal of Sex Research, 23* (1), 85-91.

Wilson-Glover, R. (1987, March 2). *Married men, double lives.* Rochester Times-Union.

5

SINGLE
PARENTS

SUSAN B. DeVANEY, M.Ed.

Teaching Assistant and Student Supervisor
Department of Counseling and
Specialized Educational Development
University of North Carolina at Greensboro

SINGLE PARENTS

AWARENESS INDEX

Directions: Mark each answer true, false, or don't know. Compare your answers with the scoring guide at the end of the test.

1. Fifty percent of all babies born out of wedlock are put up for adoption.

2. Many school personnel assume single-parent children will have difficulties in the classroom.

3. Both widowed and divorced persons suffer a period of mourning for the loss of a spouse.

4. Public policy has traditionally supported the dual-parent family.

5. Whites are more likely to separate and to divorce than Blacks.

6. Twenty-five percent of all children from divorced families now live under joint custody arrangements.

7. Most single parents enjoy reentering the dating scene at the same time as their teenagers.

8. For a child to become overly responsible and nurturant, taking on the role of a substitute spouse, is not unusual.

9. Girls from divorced families are more likely to act out than boys.

10. Equitable property distribution by the courts has virtually eliminated financial difficulties experienced by single parent females.

1. F	4. T	7. F	10. F
2. T	5. F	8. T	
3. T	6. F	9. F	

SINGLE PARENTS, THE POPULATION

In 1985 over 25% of all school aged children lived in single-parent households (Rich, 1987). Eighty percent of those children lived with women, ten percent with men, and ten percent under joint custody arrangements. Between 1970 and 1980 the number of single-parent households increased 79% to 8.5 million families (Morawetz & Walker, 1984).

Reasons for the precipitous rise in single parent families are no secret. America has the highest marriage and divorce rates in the world. Many women have husbands who are incarcerated or working in another state. Other persons are widowed. Ninety percent of unmarried teenaged mothers keep their babies (Morawetz & Walker, 1984; Kitson & Raschke, 1981).

While most single parents are mothers, some custodial women are relatives or even friends. Courts are increasingly awarding custody of children to their fathers, although the percentage is still small. Children living with the male parent tend to be teenagers, a fact that reflects the societal presumption that women are better suited to rear young children.

Among the Black population approximately one-half of all families with children are headed by a single parent, primarily a female (Goldenberg & Goldenberg, 1985). Blacks are more likely to separate without divorcing, to divorce and to remain divorced than are whites (Kitson & Raschke, 1981).

Family incomes in single parent situations are less than one-half that of other families. Government figures in 1985 revealed that 34.6% of households headed by a single woman (some admittedly, without children) fall below the poverty level (Rich,

1987). This figure is a function of the fact that women in general earn only 59 cents for every $1 earned by men in comparable jobs. In addition, only 65% of women entitled to children support actually receive it. The average child support payment was $2,215 in 1985, down from $2,528 in 1983—a drop of 12.4%. For Black families the average payment rose from $1,582 to $1,754 and for Hispanics it increased slightly from 1986 to $2,011. White women, however, are much more likely to have been awarded child support at all. Recent figures show that 71% of white women are awarded payments as opposed to 36% of Black women and 42% of Hispanic women ("Child Support," 1987). With child day care averaging $50 per week ($2,600 per year), it is small wonder that working single mothers are generally in tight financial straits.

Indeed, the average woman's standard of living decreases 73% post-divorce while the man's increases 42 percent (Morawetz & Walker, 1984). More divorces occur among those persons having less education, less income, and lower status occupations than average (Kitson & Raschke, 1981). Moreover, 52% of divorced persons reported hostile post-divorce interactions, thereby creating additional stress on the family (Magrab, 1978).

CURRENT PROBLEMS

In discussing problems associated with single parent families, one must remember that each family member is an individual complete with an array of strengths, failures, beliefs, and characteristic behaviors. Not all difficulties discussed here will be problems for every family or every individual. However, in considering a family system the presumption is that what affects one person affects the others. Whatever particular manifestations of these general problems are present within a family will to some extent affect total family functioning.

The Stigma of Singlehood

In today's America to be a single parent is to contend with a variety of negative stereotypes and prejudices. Television idealizes the two-parent family in Waltonesque dramas. Single women are portrayed as Sirens with expensive wardrobes, impeccable make-up, and perfect bodies. Single men are presented as devilish rakes, rarely encumbered with children. Widows are somehow always pathetic little old women. Even our language reflects the prejudice against singleness. Unmarried women are "old maids" or "spinsters." Children of divorced parents are said to come from "broken homes." Single mothers who have not married are "unwed," a term virtually synonymous in many minds with "welfare mother."

Clearly, marriage is considered not only the norm but also the ideal. Being single, whether by choice or circumstance, carries with it connotations of deviance. Single are encouraged to "find a nice man (woman) and settle down"—even if they do not wish to. Married persons often shun their newly single friends with whom they miraculously no longer have anything in common. Divorced persons are often considered, both by themselves and others, as failures at their life's work while widows and divorcees are thought to be threats to the sanctity of their former friends' marriages. Whether the reaction is pity, fear, or disapproval, single parent families are, in our social milieu, aberations of the "normal" nuclear family.

Overcoming Loss

Persons recently separated, divorced, or widowed suffer acute difficulties in coming to terms with the loss of a spouse. A period of mourning typically occurs wherein the person experiences a mixture of conflicting emotions: regret, guilt, depression, sadness, relief, excitement, loneliness, optimism, and confusion. The severity and duration of this emotional upheaval depend in part on the factors surrounding the loss. The length of a deceased spouse's illness and the quality of the marriage relationship among widows, the presence of infidelity, the amount of social disapproval experienced, the children's current reaction to the situation, the degree of mutuality in deciding to divorce, and the presence or absence of a satisfactory social life all influence an individual's ability to overcome loss (Pett, 1982; Kitson & Raschke, 1981; Wallerstein, 1982).

Lingering attachment to former spouses often inhibits adjustment to singlehood. In general, the longer an individual has been married, the greater the distress experienced. Loss of appetite, concentration, and energy; excessive smoking and drinking; promiscuity; and general self neglect are common during the first year of loss. Headaches, chest and stomach pains, and other somatic complaints are typically present (Kitson & Raschke, 1981).

Restructuring the Household

With the establishment of a new single-parent family, parents, children, relatives, and friends take on new roles, some welcome, others difficult. Newly single fathers may be ill-prepared for child rearing tasks and household chores formerly left to their spouses. Women may be inexperienced at managing auto maintenance, family finances, and other traditionally male occupations. Both males and females, accustomed to sharing duties and obligations with an adult partner, may chafe under the burden of attending to family needs alone. In addition, reduced income often forces strict cutbacks in leisure activities, meals out, housing, and other amenities formerly taken for granted. Moreover, with many single mothers entering the workplace, child care may become a problem for the first time.

Children, too, may be counted on to assume a larger place in household functioning. In addition to cleaning and cooking, older children may babysit for their younger siblings. Many children, even those under the age of 10, are responsible for their own care, staying unattended for long periods of time. With the family in upheaval following divorce or death of a parent, it is not uncommon for a child to take on a parental role, becoming a substitute spouse. Lonely and confused, the parent may come to rely on the child as a helper and confidant. In extreme cases of prolonged role reversal the child may miss out on important aspects of childhood and teenaged years. Seeing that the child has missed a "normal" life by taking care of a needy parent, the parent is often faced with feelings of guilt and depression. In other situations where the child does not assume extra duties, the harried parent feels anger toward the child and guilt at feeling the anger (Morawetz & Walker, 1984).

In the case of divorce, custody arrangements often mitigate hostility among parents and children. With the advent of equitable distribution and communal property laws, child custody has replaced property distribution as the primary source of divorce hostilities. More fathers now have sole custody, joint custody, or extensive visitation privileges than at any other time during this century. After two years, two-thirds of non-custodial fathers see their children at least every other week (Hodges, Buchsbaum, & Tierney, 1983). These circumstances set up opportunities for missed or late appointments, scheduling conflicts, and differing parental expectations. "But Mom lets me do it at her house" becomes a battlecry arousing a wealth of conflicting emotions in a parent who may feel his or her authority threatened. In anger parents may subtly encourage children to ally with them and misbehave with the other parent (Hetherington, Cox, & Cox, 1978; Tooley, 1976).

Thus, despite the fact that the original family is now separated, the absent parent has an abiding effect on family decisions and behavior. Many divorced persons consult each other on matters of finance, child-rearing, and social life. For ex-spouses to date, provide assistance in home maintenance, or otherwise maintain close contact for a number of years is not unusual. These adaptations of former living patterns, even if amicably implemented, may serve as sources of confusion, anger, bitterness, and hostility. Adjustment may be further complicated by the presence of relatives or new opposite-sex companions who presume to take a role in decision-making.

The emotional tenor of this "extended" family is what most affects the psychosocial adjustment of children. Hostility among parties perpetuates emotional distress and confusion while close cooperation is more likely to convince children that their emotional bonds are not severed. In the long run, discord is more damaging to the child than divorce (Hess & Camara, 1979; Hetherington, Cox, & Cox, 1976).

Parenting

While parental conflict is a greater stress for children than divorce, children from divorced families are more prone to a wide range of "deviant" behaviors than are children from happy intact homes. Aggression is by far the most common problem, but many children experience fear of deprivation, psychosomatic complaints, school phobia, enuresis, loss of appetite, and irregular sleep patterns (Magrab, 1978; Leupnits, 1978; Hetherington, Cox, & Cox, 1978; Tooley, 1976; Lamb, 1977). Boys are more likely than girls to exhibit disturbing behavior. Even as early as two years of age, boys with divorced parents have been found to be more aggressive, less helpful, and more impulsive, oppositional, and dependent than girls. However, abberant behaviors (including violative and assaultive actions) frequently do not manifest themselves until adolescence (Beal, 1979; Kelly & Wallerstein, 1976; Tooley, 1976).

Although divorce or widowhood is considered to be primarily a rupture between husband and wife, children inevitably feel a strong sense of separation, loneliness, and loss surrounding the departed parent. For many reasons, few children verbalize their concerns; however, a child will frequently lay blame on the parent who precipitated the divorce or, ironically, the one who tries hardest to explain it to the child. In other cases the child "protects" the needier parent by expressing anger at the one who is better adjusted, developing excessively nurturant behaviors, or becoming a surrogate spouse (Beal, 1979; Kelly & Wallerstein, 1976).

The task of parenting alone, particularly at a time when the person is financially, emotionally, and socially needy, demands more energy than many individuals have at their disposal. Under the strain of the initial adjustment period, relations between child and parent may weaken. Meanwhile, the non-custodial parent, in an effort to protect against the emotional wear and tear of separation, may become increasingly detached (Santrock & Warschak, 1979; Hodges, Buchsbaum, & Tierney, 1983).

With the family in turmoil consistent parenting frequently falls by the wayside. Parents who use laissez faire or authoritarian parenting styles are less likely to have well adjusted children than are those who are authoritative. Inconsistent parenting among separated spouses seems to peak at one year, after which time parents exhibit and demand more appropriate behavior. Children whose parents engage in open communication with them, behave lovingly, and set clear rules and behavioral guidelines by and large exhibit good psychosocial adjustment. With proper parental nurturance a single-parent situation can benefit the child, especially if the marital climate was hostile. Studies have shown adolescents from divorced homes to be better adjusted with respect to delinquency, parent-child relationship, and psychosomatic complaints than children from unhappy intact homes (Santrock & Warshak, 1979; Hodges, Buchsbaum, & Tierney, 1983; Lamb, 1977; Magrab, 1978).

School

Many children of single parents experience difficulties in the classroom. They tend to be late and absent more often, have more health problems, attain lower achievement levels, and have more disciplinary problems than children from dual-parent families. Their intellectual development, however, parallels that of other children. Apparently the child's relationship with the parent is the most important predictor of social and school success. Children whose parents perceive their current situations negatively have less positive school achievement and adjustment than do those whose parents are well-adjusted themselves (Cashion, 1982; Hess & Camara, 1979).

Another difficulty may be that school personnel perceive single parents to be uninvolved in their child's education. On the other hand, parents may view school personnel as arbitrary, uncaring, judgmental, and inconsiderate of work schedules. Many single parents whose children behave well at home are surprised to find that cause for concern at school is present. However, notification of falling grades or disciplinary problems is often late in arriving. Teachers are difficult to reach and parents' work schedules often preclude scheduling after school conferences (Morawetz & Walker, 1984).

In the case of tumultuous home situations teachers may represent the most stable adult force in a child's life. But in other circumstances school personnel may assume children from "broken homes" will have problems and pass judgment on them. In any event, close communication between parent and school is essential for maximizing student success and well being (Morawetz & Walker, 1984; Cashion, 1982; Sheen, Paguio, & McKenny, 1983).

Intimacy

Loss or absence of a spouse opens the questions of whether, when, and how to resume dating or other adult social interaction. Children may pressure a parent to find another mate or, on the contrary, express anger, petulance, or disapproval of social contacts. Some single parents also may find themselves "out of place in time" when they enter the dating scene at the same time as their children. While parents who do engage in adult social interaction appear to experience less distress than those who do not, many are simply unequipped to enter the "dating scene" (Kitson & Raschke, 1981). After years of physical intimacy with a spouse, meeting desirable companions, fulfilling sexual needs, dealing with moral prohibitions, and avoiding sexually transmitted diseases seem unjust burdens to a person already deluged with conflicts. One can readily understand why newly single persons often throw themselves in a headlong dash toward the first man or woman who will agree to see them steadily.

Finances

Hostility, bitterness, and anger often arise from the loss of financial status experienced by many single parents. When desired support is not forthcoming, the mother may retaliate, denying child access to the father and leaving him angry and resentful. Expensive legal costs, which have traditionally been born by the individual, have prevented many women from seeking greater financial support. "Extras" such as braces, camps, and college tuition may become subjects for argument between ex-spouses.

Career Needs

Becoming a single parent necessitates reevaluating one's current employment situation. Women who have been homemakers may be in need of job training or schooling in order to be employable at a reasonable wage. Young mothers in particular may not hold high school diplomas nor have work experience. For others, supporting a family on what was once a second income may not be possible. However, inability to take time away from work or to find money for school can trap single parents in low-paying, dead-end occupations.

Every employed single parent must of necessity learn to negotiate time off for care of sick children, teacher's conferences, and errands that can only be accomplished during working hours. Persons attempting to move up the corporate ladder may encounter difficulty finding child care for irregular work schedules and extended travel. In addition, opportunities for relocation with the company may meet with angry resistance from the non-custodial parent.

Public Policy and Special Services

Public policy has historically endorsed the two-parent family primarily through tax laws and social legislation. For years property was divided between divorced spouses on the basis of income (so much for the value of the homemaker). Enforcement of child support decrees is still notably lax. Alimony has been virtually abandoned by the courts in favor of equitable distribution of property.

Poor single women have felt the brunt of legislation affecting Aid for Dependent Children (AFDC) and the availability of job training and day care. Legal aid for divorce and separation proceedings was denied in the Reagan Family Protection Act. The Job Training Partnership Act eliminated funds for child care and transportation, effectively excluding poor single parents from those programs. Cuts in public housing and supplemental feeding programs and the elimination of CETA and WIN further restricted opportunities for single parents to break the poverty-unemployment-welfare cycle (Morawetz & Walker, 1984).

Until the 1970s services for single parents were virtually nonexistent. The sole exception was Parents Without Partners, a private organization providing workshops, discussion groups, and social activities for both parents and children. Recognizing the need, women's organizations, themselves newly established, sponsored support groups for women reentering the workforce and lobbied for child care legislation. Community organizations and churches followed suit creating day care facilities and classes for single adults. Under pressure from these groups, local governments funded crisis intervention centers, hot lines, referral services, and spouse abuse programs through mental health agencies.

Interest in changes in American family structure has resulted in the adoption and growth of the American Association of Marriage and Family Therapy (AAMFT) as a specialty area among counselors. Requiring special training for certification, AAMFT tracks are being developed by counselor education departments throughout the country.

THE HELPING PROFESSIONAL'S ROLE

In today's society a helping professional may not encounter members of some special populations discussed in this book (Asian refugees, Amish, or even Hispanics), but each and every one will have many dealings with single parents. Single parenthood is a fact of life; no counselor, social worker, friend, or parent can escape the impact of the changing structure of the American family. Of particular importance, then, is that the helper have a thorough understanding of issues, problems, and circumstances common to single parents as well as adequate preparation for working with this group. In the interest of space the following recommendations for helping professions will be listed rather than discussed in detail. For a fuller discussion, consult the references at the end of the chapter.

1. The counselor should examine personal prejudices and stereotypes concerning marriage, divorce, and single life styles that may stand in the way of personal growth and adjustment for the client. While most counselors are careful not to condemn, other attitudes such as pity or acceptance of an untenable situation can create barriers to client problem solving.

2. Even if single parenthood is not the presenting problem, the myriad of conflicting feelings, life changes, and responsibilities faced by an unmarried person will influence the goals and mode of treatment. The counselor must be attune to these concerns and integrate them into the total therapeutic picture.

3. Referrals to vocational rehabilitation, Social Services, child care centers, community organizations, and support groups are part and parcel of work with single parents. Encouraging stable community and social ties, the counselor serves as a liaison between clients and organizations providing help with parenting, social life, finances, education, and job training. Maintaining a book list on topics appropriate for the single parent is a helpful adjunct to agency and organizational referral.

4. Being a single parent does not necessarily mean that parents have no significant partners in the parenting process. The counselor considers who is involved in the family—ex-spouses,

friends, relatives, or lovers whose attitudes influence child rearing practices and lifestyles.

5. Many single parents believe something is wrong with them because they are not married. The counselor can help liberate the parent from excessive self criticism and develop client self confidence.

6. The single parent may be ambivalent about accepting advice from yet another helping professional. Having sensed disapproval in past interactions with pastors, teachers, agency personnel, or employers, the parent may need the counselor's help in overcoming the fear of being blamed for past "mistakes."

7. Counselors should remember that behavior which may appear pathological (depression, promiscuity, fits of temper) may be normal reactions to the stage of separation the client is enduring. One role of the counselor is to work through maladaptive behavior patterns in favor of more successful ones.

8. Many clients will attempt to use the counselor as an ally against the absent partner. The thoughtful counselor will avoid this trap by remaining emphatic but objective, refusing to take sides.

9. The counselor may serve as a mediator between ex-spouses or client and family members. The myth that divorced persons cannot cooperate is detrimental to the adjustment of both parents and children and can be expunged with appropriate help.

10. Initial crises such as a separation, out-of-wedlock birth, or family death may temporarily create a very different family organization—from unstable to stable or visa versa. Thorough assessment of the family system both currently and prior to trauma is essential to anticipating the reemergence of old conflicts.

11. Family members may actively or subtly oppose therapy. Happy for their newfound influence, relatives and companions may

enjoy the client's dependence on them and resist the client's attempts to become self sufficient.

12. Many single parents blame others for their difficulties. A primary task of the counselor is to help the client develop responsibility, self confidence, and an identity apart from a spouse.

13. The experienced counselor recognizes that in crisis situations a parent may be incapable of attending to parenting responsibilities. The counselor encourages examination of client attitudes toward children and parenthood, reduced access to the children, and parental expectations.

14. A single parent needs to be helped to recognize disfunctional strategies used to maintain emotional balance in the family. Excessive focus on the child's needs, adoption of a child as a substitute parent, or refusal to set appropriate limits may inhibit healthy family functions.

15. The counselor can teach a parent to establish a long-term relationship with the child allowing the child some control over his or her life. The parent learns to afford the child privacy, respect, a listening ear, and opportunities to work through feelings.

16. Many single parents deal with a child's misbehavior by either punishing or ignoring it. The counselor can train the parent to use a more appropriate response such as that suggested by Leavitt and Davis (1980):
   a. Begin calmly and using affectionate language
   b. Describe appropriate behavior
   c. Describe inappropriate behavior
   d. Demonstrate new behavior
   e. Give rationale
   f. Ask for acknowledgement
   g. Actively involve the child in practice
   h. Give feedback on the practice
   i. Encourage the child through praise and reward

Other parenting skills, such as use of time-out, behavior charting, behavior contracting, and developing motivational systems also may be taught.

17. Many single parents can be helped to reenter the workplace or modify their career paths through appropriate self assessment, career guidance, and teaching job hunting skills. Again, bibliotherapy and referrals may be important adjuncts for the counselor in these cases.

18. The wise counselor will anticipate scheduling and payment problems and maintain flexibility in order to avoid premature termination.

In short, nothing is inherently undesirable in being a single parent. However, the role brings with it vicissitudes above and beyond those of two-parent families. Counselor sensitivity to the myriad of conflicting pressures and attitudes facing a single parent provides a base on which to build client independence, confidence, and positive self-image. The role of the counselor, then, is to liberate the single parent from any negative beliefs or stereotypes which hinder full adjustment and to open the door to new and happier possibilities for living.

REFERENCES

Beal, E.W. (1979). Children of divorce: A family systems perspective. *Journal of Social Issues. 35*, 140-153.

Cashion, B.G. (1982). Female-headed families: Effects on children and clinical implications. *Journal of Marriage and the Family Therapy.* April. 77-85.

Child support payments drop, census reports (1987, August 23). *Greensboro News and Record*, p. A7.

Goldenberg, I., & Goldenberg, H. (1985). *Family therapy: An overview.* (2nd ed.). Monterey, CA: Brooks/Cole.

Hess, R.D. & Camara, K.A. (1979). Post-divorce family relationships as mediating factors in the consequences of discipline in children. *Journal of Social Issues. 35*, 79-96.

Hetherington, E.M., Cox, M., & Cox, R. (Oct., 1976). Divorced fathers. *The Family Coordinator*, 417.

Hetherington, E.M., Cox, M., & Cox, R. (May, 1978). Family interaction and the social, emotional, and cognitive development of children following divorce. Paper presented at the Symposium on the Family: Setting Priorities. Institute for Pediatric Service of the Johnson & Johnson Baby Company, Washington, DC

Hodges, W.F., Buchsbaum, H.K., & Tierney, C.W. (1983). Parent-child relationships and adjustment in preschool children in divorced and intact families. *Journal of Divorce, 7,* 43-58.

Kelly, J.B., & Wallerstein, J.S. (1976). The effects of parental divorce: Experiences of the child in early latency. *American Journal of Orthopsychiatry, 47,* 20-33.

Kitson, G.C., & Raschke, H.J. (1981). Divorce research: What we know; what we need to know. *Journal of Divorce, 4,* 1-37.

Lamb, M.E. (1977). The effects of divorce on children's personality development. *Journal of Divorce. 1,* 163-174.

Leavitt, S.E., & Davis, M. (1980). Evaluating the effects of a training program for single parents. Paper presented at the Symposium Advances in Behavioral Treatment of One-parent Families, 88th Annual Convention of the American Psychological Association, Montreal.

Leupnitz, D.A. (1978). Children of divorce: A review of the psychological literature. *Law and Human Behavior, 2,* 167-179.

Magrab, P.R. (1978). For the sake of the children: A review of the psychological effects of divorce. *Journal of Divorce, 1,* 233-245.

Morawetz, A., & Walker, G. (1984). *Brief therapy with single-parent families.* New York: Brunner/Mazel.

Pett, M.G. (1982). Correlates of children's social adjustment following divorce. *Journal of Divorce, 5,* 25-39.

Rich, S. (1987, July 31). Proportion of poverty-level families drops. *Greensboro News and Record,* p. 2A.

Rich, S. (1987, August 2). American households just a victim of myths. *Greensboro News and Record,* p. 1E.

Santrock, J.W., & Warshak, R.A. (1979). Father custody and social development in boys and girls. *Journal of Social Issues, 35,* 112-125.

Sheen, P., Paguio, L.P., & McKenry, P.C. (March, 1983). Children and divorce: The teacher's role. Paper presented at the Annual Meeting of the Southern Association for Children under Six, Charleston, SC.

Tooley, K. (1976). Antisocial behavior and social alienation post divorce: The "man of the house" and his mother. *American Journal of Orthopsychiatry, 46,* 33-42.

Wallerstein, J.S. (July, 1982). Children of divorce: Preliminary report of a ten-year follow-up. Paper presented at the Tenth International Congress of the International Association for Children and Adolescent Psychiatry and Allied Professionals, Dublin, Ireland.

6

ON THE RESERVATION

MARILYN JEMISON ANDERSON, B.A.
Human Services Administrator
Seneca Nation Health Department

and

ROBERT ELLIS, Ph.D.
Psychologist
Private Practice
Fredonia, New York

MARILYN JEMISON ANDERSON, B.A.

Marilyn Anderson is currently the Human Services Administrator of the Seneca Nation Health Department, which includes Social Services, Mental Health and Substance Abuse, Community Outreach, and Medical Transportation. She has been actively involved in the delivery of health services on the Cattaraugus Reservation, where she lives with her husband and two children, since 1973. Mrs. Anderson received her Bachelor's Degree in Sociology from D'Youville College, Buffalo, in 1969. At present, Mrs. Anderson is Editor of Si Wong Geh, the Reservation Newsletter. She is on the Advisory Board for a number of local mental health institutions and she is on the Advisory Board to the National Indian Food and Nutrition Resource Center. In 1974, Mrs. Anderson was named an outstanding young woman of America from New York State.

ROBERT ELLIS, Ph.D.

Bob Ellis is a Psychologist in Private Practice in Fredonia, New York, where he lives with his wife and two daughters. He completed a Bachelor's and Master's Degree in Psychology at San Diego State University in California and earned his Ph.D. in Educational Psychology at the University of California at Santa Barbara in 1974. Prior to establishing his Private Practice in 1981, he taught at Idaho State University in Pocatello and State University of New York, College at Fredonia. In addition to his writings on tribal culture, Dr. Ellis works with emotionally disabled individuals including abusive parents and adolescents with anger control problems. He is on the Board of Directors of The National Parent Aide Association and was involved in the development of the New York State Federation on Child Abuse and Neglect.

ON THE RESERVATION

AWARENESS INDEX

Directions: These questions are to help you to evaluate your understanding of the Indian and Indian culture.

Mark each answer true, false, or don't know. Compare your answers with the scoring guide at the end of the test.

T F 1. The Indian behaves differently from non-Indians because of the poverty in which the great majority of Indians must live.

T F 2. The non-Indian counselor is at such a severe disadvantage when working with Indian clients that the attempt should not be made.

T F 3. Indians are at a disadvantage because their social consciousness has not yet developed to the point where they can enjoy the "advantages" of the non-Indian life.

T F 4. Because of their different culture, Indians do not have the western concepts of right and wrong, truth and falsehood.

T F 5. Relatively more alcoholics are on the reservation than are in the dominant non-Indian society.

T F 6. The notion of change to an Indian is negative because of its implication that the present order of things is inadequate.

T F 7. An Indian can live off the reservation without compromising any basic cultural values.

T F 8. Because of their sense of tribal integration, an Indian student may cheat on a test when asked to do so by another member of the tribe.

T F 9. Indians are not punctual because they do not respect non-Indian peoples.

T F 10. The Indian culture could be classified as primitive.

T F 11. In terms of perceived confidentiality, a non-Indian counselor has an advantage over Indian counselor when working with Indian clients.

Scoring Guide for Awareness Index

1. F	5. F	9. F
2. F	6. T	10. F
3. F	7. F	11. T
4. F	8. T	

> The use of ardent spirits amongst the Indians, and the attempts which have been made to civilize and Christianize them by the white people, has [sic] constantly made them worse and worse; increased their vices, and robbed them of many of their virtues; and will ultimately produce their extermination. (Seaver, 1925, p. 48)

Mary Jemison, a white woman, had been living with the Seneca Indians in upstate New York for over 60 years when she wrote the preceding statement. Although the description was written more than 150 years ago, it appears as valid now for this group of Native American as it was then. Her remarks eloquently and succinctly illustrate the Native American's two major problems in American society today: the attempt to interpret Native American behavior in terms of norms and expectations not shared by the tribal culture and, secondly, the continuing attempt to convert the Native American to a "better" culture.

This chapter offers several suggestions for helpers who might provide counseling services to the Native American client, suggestions that will assist counselors in not committing common errors that may lose a client in trouble and damage the counselor's credibility as a helping professional.

Too often, non-Native Americans are admonished to be sensitive to cultural differences when dealing with Native Americans, but one can look far and wide before finding a list or specific statement of those differences. The usual suggestion is for the individual to go and live among Native Americans for a while. But, as many workers in the Bureau of Indian Affairs will attest, mere association is not enough. What is needed is a point of view, a new perspective from which to observe problems. To help you, the reader, develop this perspective, two areas will be discussed:

1. The general relationship of the Native American and the tribe, noting some of the implications of that relationship that have proved confusing and foreign to the great majority of non-Native American observers.

2. The specific problem of alcohol abuse, which is identified quite closely with the Native American, differentiating the problem from alcoholism in the dominant, non-Native American culture.

A point which will be emphasized several times in this chapter is that counselors who interpret a Native American's problem in terms of how that problem functions among non-Native Americans are making a serious error which will be reflected in decreased counseling effectiveness.

The authors recognize the danger of treading in these extremely sensitive territories, especially because a great diversity exists among tribes and individuals both on and off the reservation. The interests, needs, and culture of the reservation Native American may vary greatly from those of the urban Native American. A similar difference may be found between Native Americans living in the eastern, midwestern, and western parts of the United States. However, the difficulties caused by well-meaning helpers justifies the risk. We ask, therefore, that the following be read with the recognition that our comments, based on the experiences of Seneca reservation Native Americans, are offered as suggestions to heighten awareness and not as the final word on the subject.

Several basic assumptions must be understood and accepted before one can begin working with a Native American clientele. The Native American has a culture, a cultural heritage, and a right to that culture as inalienable as any other basic human right. Accordingly, any discussion or suggestion with regard to assimilation—i.e., the suggestion, implicit or otherwise, that an "inferior" culture be abandoned for a "superior" culture—will be viewed, rightly so, as a direct insult and slur.

Most Native Americans, especially those who remain on or return to the reservation, do not prefer assimilation and may not want all of the "advantages" of the non-Native American life. For this reason, a critical position that the counselor must not take is the attitude that a Native Americans' problems are merely cultural. The themes of **cultural disadvantage** and **cultural poverty** have been popular in the social services literature and suggest, as noted previously, that one culture is richer or better than another. Although a Native American may be having difficulty in resolving expectations based on apparently incompatible cultural values, to suggest that the conflict can be consistently resolved in favor of one of those systems, especially if it is the Native American culture, is blatant cultural arrogance.

Native Americans do have problems and do require help and, like everyone else, they are best served by a helper who considers them and their problems individually and with sensitivity to their context. No one is helped when a problem is dismissed by saying, "Oh, it's just cultural"; nor can the individual be helped when his or her basic value system is dismissed casually.

The point that we would like to make is that the dynamics of the problems faced by the Native American are no different from those faced by any other human being; that is, a temporary inability to resolve conflicting pressures in a successful and satisfying way. The difference between Native Americans and others, however, is found in the kinds of pressure with which they have to contend given their particular culture and the dominant society in which they live.

The following preparatory steps are very important for human services counselors working with Native Americans:

1. Recognize that Native Americans approach life with a different set of expectations, values, and interpretations of events and that their approach can be as satisfying and as rich to them as any other culture is to any other person.

2. Become familiar with those specific cultural values so that one can begin to understand and appreciate the pressures being faced by Native American clients.

3. Resist the temptation to interpret a particular behavior or problem as if it emerged in a manner typical of that problem in a non-Native American, middle-class society.

4. Appreciate that Native Americans, like everyone else, want minimal stress and aggravation in their lives.

5. Converse with Native Americans with an attitude of respect rather than paternalism.

THE TRIBE

The first step in understanding the Native American's cultural differences is appreciating that the relationship between the Native American and the tribe is different from the relationship between the non-Native American middle-class person and society. The Native American sees self as an extension of the tribe in the sense that he or she is a part of a whole, and that wholeness of the tribe is what gives meaning to the part. For example, a flower petal has little beauty by itself, but when it is put together with the other parts of the flower, the whole is a thing of great beauty. This relationship stands in contrast to the non-Native American middle-class position where society operates primarily as a set of rules to promote individual accomplishment. Stated somewhat differently, the tribe provides the meaning and justification of existence for the individual from the Native American's point of view, while the individual provides the justification for society from the non-Native American western perspective. As a consequence, Native Americans judge their worth primarily in terms of whether their behavior contributes to the harmonious functioning of the tribe. In contrast, the non-Native American (white, middle-class) judges worth primarily in terms of individual accomplishment, individual prestige, individual power, and/or individual values. While these generalizations are clearly too simple, they do serve to illustrate that the Native American uses a value system that is fundamentally different from that of the dominant culture; basic worth is judged in terms of tribal enhancement and not individual enhancement. On the other hand, the Native American is not against individual accomplishment, for example in craft work or sport, when it reflects positively on the tribe. In short, one would make a mistake to assume, as so many have, that the concept of tribe to the Native American is synonymous with the concept of society to the non-Native American.

Many pressures exist for the Native American to leave the reservation. The main culprits are the public school system with its main-street value system and the television set with its fantasy-consumption value system. At this time, approximately 650,000 of the one million Native Americans still live on or close to a reservation. Pressures to leave the reservation may be more direct as with the explicit termination policy of the Eisenhower Administration whose goal was to "assimilate" the Native American by providing social services support only if the Native American left the reservation. (Some have said that the actual goal was to acquire the now valuable reservation property). The reservation, however, is the physical embodiment of the tribe and for an individual to leave the reservation that individual must, in a sense, reject the tribe and the values it represents. Such a separation, for a Native American, if it is not complete (i.e., accompanied by the adoption of an "individual" point of view), will be traumatic and leave the potential for psychological insecurities and conflicts unfamiliar to the great majority of human-service counselors.

A non-Native American has difficulty in appreciating the trauma of Native Americans leaving the reservation. It means that they must leave behind a value system that has provided nurturance all of their lives and adopt a system of being independent and alone for which they have neither preparation nor relevant role-models. Also an important point to appreciate is that one's family tribe does not extend beyond the reservation. While support and social groups "on the outside" are made up of individuals from different tribes, these provide little satisfaction for they are no substitute for the tribe. In order to leave the reservation, a Native American has to adopt one or more of the values of the non-reservation world and, in so doing, lays the groundwork for potential future problems. Conflicts arise when values from basically incompatible cultures are mixed, and, unless resolved, the resulting anxiety and stress interferes with the performance of day-to-day tasks, just as it would for any other human being. As can be seen, the non-reservation Native American presents a complex and difficult therapy situation. Accordingly, we have chosen to restrict our comments, at this time, to the Native American who has chosen to remain. Because of the ubiquity of the dominant culture, however, even those who choose to stay are not immune to the pressures of the "individual ethic" and as a consequence the reservation counselor can expect to face many situations requiring a surgeon's skill to disentangle the themes of Harmony (tribal culture) and Individuality (western culture) in conflict.

The counselor who wishes to work successfully with the Native American client, then, must dismiss the notion that Native Americans have problems primarily because they lack certain cultural values; that is, because they are "culturally deficient" or "culturally disadvantaged." Rather, the opposite is more often the case; they experience the burden of trying to live consistently within a system of many incompatible values.

Harmony

Differences among tribes and among individuals are enormous, a fact that must be recognized by counselors. On the other hand, the authors believe that common sets of values are shared to various degrees by the great majority of Native Americans and can be identified and discussed as a family of characteristics without suggesting a stereotyped Native American image. Furthermore, the fact that these values are discussed within the context of problems that may bring a Native American into contact with a counselor or human services provider is not meant to suggest that these values are negative or in anyway inferior to other values. As a matter of fact, these values many times contribute to the Native American's problems only because helpers fail to recognize that the Native American has a different, yet legitimate, way of approaching the world. The following, then, is an attempt to clarify some of the ramifications of a tribal society without suggesting either that they are shared in the same degree by all Native Americans or that they reflect negatively on the tribal culture.

As can be imagined, the tribal culture places a high value on the harmonious relationship between an individual and his or her peers, that is, all the other members of the tribe. A high value is placed on behavior that advances harmony and cooperation in the tribe; to not cooperate would be to assert one's individuality and suggest that one is better than the tribe. To be a member of the tribe, then, means that the individual is honor bound to defer to the wishes of others, to be polite, to be unassertive and to work hard to prevent discord. Because of this value of promoting harmony above all, many counselors falsely conclude that because Native American clients fail to disagree, they must agree with the counselor. Then, when the client behaves in a way out of keeping with the "agreement," the counselor jumps to the conclusion that the Native American lied.

The tribal culture, however, does not support lying, and regardless of myth or stereotype the Native American is not a liar. He or she will, however, go to great lengths to develop misdirection and ambiguities to avoid disagreement or contradiction. In the western point of view, such behavior is synonymous with telling untruths (lying) because it does not clarify the truth. Of more value to the Native American is the fact that contradition and dis- agreement are disharmonious and are to be avoided whenever possible. Furthermore, to disagree with someone is in one sense an assertion of ego and individuality and, for that reason also, the Native American works hard to appear to be in agreement.

As a variation of the same phenomenon, consider the dilemma of the Native American student who is called upon to answer a question in front of a group in a class with other Native American students and a non-Native American teacher. To answer it correctly would be an act of individuality and apparent superiority while to answer it incorrectly or to stand mute in indecision would bring humiliation to the individual and to the tribe—a classic no-win situation brought on by the cultural insensitivity of a non-Native American.

By the same token, a Native American student cannot refuse to show a test paper to another Native American student when requested to do so. To refuse would be to violate the mutual dependence, cooperation, and politeness held valuable by the tribal culture. To anticipate somewhat, the Native American is put in rather the same dilemma when asked to have a couple of beers; to refuse would be again an assertion of individuality and a social faux pas.

Other deeply misunderstood consequences of the tribal culture are the Native American's apparent disregard for the punctuality, planning for the future, and the concept of time in general. The Native American's disregard for time has given rise to the stereotype of the Native American being shiftless, lazy, and undependable. Time is a fairly recent invention on the part of the western civilization and is necessary only in a culture that values change. If no change occurs, time to measure that change is unnecessary. Change exists only within the context of time and for a culture that values stability and actively discourages change as the tribal culture does, time becomes an unimportant consideration. Therefore, no support exists for future plans because such plans imply that the individual is trying to better himself or herself at the expense of the tribe.

Accordingly, most Native Americans live in the here and now with little concern for long-term projects that require delayed gratification and sacrifice, such as education or vocational training. In a sense, Einstein's conceptualization of time as a relative phenomenon that is affected by other events is much closer to the Native American idea of time than the western notion of an absolute, quantifiable, and linear quantity. The same holds for the western concept of punctuality: Why would one do something solely for the sake of finishing at a certain point in time? Is not something that is worth doing, worth doing well regardless of how long it takes? In short, when a conflict exists between quality and punctuality, punctuality is sacrificed.

The counselor also must recognize that a tribal culture is inherently conservative and resistant to change. From a western perspective, then, the tribe generates a tremendous amount of social and peer pressure for conforming to tribal custom and tradition. A way to appreciate this pressure is to remember that all behavior is evaluated in the here and now and in terms of how it contributes to the present welfare of the tribe. This concept is changing slowly, but long-term plans such as going to college, which also involves leaving the reservation, are seen as acts of egoism and individuality and suggest that the tribe is inadequate and that things should be done differently. In very general terms, to suggest doing something different is to suggest that you as an individual may know more and may be better than the tribe as a whole. This is not to say that tribes do not change, rather that they do not value and promote change as inherently valuable. As noted previously, behavior that does not contribute to harmony and to the tribe is frowned upon and censured. As a consequence, the Native American client is very sensitive to the expectations of the tribal peer group, and the counselor must recognize and accommodate those sensitivities in work with a Native American if cooperation and a trusting relationship are to develop.

Another consideration is the relationship of the Native American to personal wealth. The Native American tends not to cultivate a life style directed toward either conspicuous consumption or the accumulation of personal property. By now the reader may anticipate why the Native American does not subscribe to those behaviors which are fundamental to the economy of the dominant culture: Conspicuous consumption clearly smacks of individual egoism and a means of communicating superior individual worth. The accumulation of personal wealth requires, as well, both delayed gratification—saving for tomorrow what you could consume today—and active future planning, behaviors that are as foreign to the tribal culture as the cut-throat competition that is required in the struggle to accumulate wealth and power. To the Native American, rugged competition between individuals is an alien and destructive process because of its disruption to harmonious relations and because of the explicit advocacy of individual superiority where one person gains at the expense of another.

The cultural characteristics of harmony and tribal tradition have been interpreted negatively by the dominant culture and, as a consequence, have resulted in many subtle prejudices against the Native American. The primary reason for this interpretation, as far as the authors can determine, is that non-Native Americans tend to assume that the tribal behaviors developed out of an individual-oriented culture. That is, native American behavior has been and continues to be evaluated in terms of standards held by the evaluator and not by the tribe. The consequence is that the tribal behaviors are viewed as manifestation of individual pathology or cultural inferiority. For example, counselors are taught that breakdowns in ego functions are key symptoms of impending mental illness, e.g., schizophrenia. This interpretation is often true for individuals reared within a western culture, but a so-called "weak-ego" is normal within the dynamics of a strong tribal system and therefore is not necessarily a symptom of mental illness for its members. If a counselor confused common tribal phenomena, nonassertiveness and disregard for punctuality, with symptoms of western individual pathology such as time disorientation and loss of the concept of "I," a Native American client would likely receive inappropriate therapy.

Alcohol Abuse

One way to illustrate the problem of evaluating behavior in one culture by standards derived from another culture is to look at the problem of the Native American and alcohol. The misuse of alcohol may occur in one cultural setting for reasons completely different from those of another culture. Likewise, techniques developed to deal with alcohol abuse for one situation may, more than likely, be inappropriate for dealing with it within a different cultural context.

Such is the case with the Native American and alcoholism. Alcohol abuse in the dominant culture quite often operates to insulate the "individual" drinker from both personal responsibility and a stressful environment. As the counselor examines alcohol use and abuse among Native American, what becomes apparent is that such an abuse syndrome is considerably less common among reservation Native Americans, although its incidence increases dramatically as the Native American becomes isolated from the tribe. Rather, the Native American who drinks to the extent that health is endangered drinks in binges and in groups. The Native American does not drink to get through the day but rather to have a good time with his tribal brothers and sisters.

In developing a treatment program, the counselor should not expect a program designed for non-Native American alcoholics to be useful with the Native American problem drinker; rather, the counselor should begin to look at the personal social mechanisms that maintain the behavior. For example, drinking among men, even to the point of stupefication and unconsciousness, is usually not frowned on by the tribe. In fact, for some Native Americans, a certain degree of social approval is associated with an ability to tolerate large quantities of beer. The notion that Native Americans have a lower tolerance for alcohol has never been demonstrated physiologically or psychologically.

For the Native American, drinking is often a social event performed in groups where it acts as a social facilitator. Many individual Native Americans are shy and withdrawn as one would expect in a culture where prescribed social behavior is a key component of an individual's determination of self-worth. As a consequence, the Native American may use alcohol to overcome that reticence. Furthermore, the sociability caused by the first few drinks also heightens the sense of tribe and brotherhood, both of which then operate as powerful reinforcers to maintain group drinking behavior. Also, because many Native Americans believe that to disagree with or contradict another person is bad form, to turn down an offered beer would be socially difficult to do.

One also must remember that without a concern for the future and with an orientation more to the here and now, an individual Native American may be unconcerned about some future, longterm consequence that may result from too much drinking. In addition, excessive drinking may not interfere with the Native American's life style if he or she generally does not work at a job where punctuality is paramount. When the binge is over, the person can return to work with no problems whatsoever. Within that context one can easily understand how alcohol abuse and, increasingly, drug abuse can become a widespread health hazard. To deal with it though, the counselor must first recognize that it more likely develops within and is maintained by the tribal culture. Whatever program is developed, it must be sensitive to the social context dictated by that culture.

PERSONAL AND CAREER GUIDANCE NEEDS OF THIS SPECIAL POPULATION

Clearly, the Native American has special personal and career-guidance needs. For one thing, Native Americans are rarely career oriented because of the necessary long-term planning implied, past oppression by non-Native Americans, and the fact that, in many areas, few career options are open on or near the reservation. In addition, most careers require some college training which again requires long-term planning and an early off-reservation move. Career planning and/or active planning for a college education also carry overtones of personal betterment and egoism. These perceptions or biases against personal development are changing, but the counselor can help by providing guidance in terms of the tribe and explaining how the tribe will be better able to protect its special values and environment if its members are trained to deal directly with the non-Native American world rather than relying on missionaries and the Bureau of Indian-Affairs (BIA).

The career guidance counselor also should be aware that many college-bound reservation Native American students may not stay a full month on campus. Their first trip away from their home is shock enough, but the apparent individual coldness can be too much for the adolescent Native American. What is necessary is that the career guidance counselor make an effort to identify those colleges with a significant Native American population so that the environment will not be too alien and hostile.

If one primary career and/or personal guidance need of the reservation Native American exists in either the schools or society, it is to feel a part of the tribe. Given that the individual Native American may evaluate personal worth in terms of how contributions can be made to the tribe, decisions, suggestions, and recommendations must be qualified in like terms.

The following is a list of what might be described as cultural barriers that must be recognized and accommodated by the helper in order to be effective. Again, these items and characteristics are not universal; they do not characterize all Native Americans nor do they characterize even Native Americans from the same tribe. They do, however, provide a list of cultural differences that should be kept in mind and used to evaluate behavior.

1. The Native American client will most likely be shy, unassertive, passive, and very sensitive to the opinion and attitude of peers.

2. The Native American client may actively avoid disagreement or contradiction and, if allowed, will appear to

agree or conform even though the person has no intention of behaving in that way. Note that the best response in this situation is not to try to outwit the client but to ask questions directly so that no opportunity is available to be evasive.

3. Many Native Americans do not like being singled out and made to perform as in school, especially when peers or Native Americans from other tribes are present. The exception is an athletic competition where the tribe as a whole will benefit.

4. Respect must be earned by the helper. Degrees, experience, and reputation carry no weight on the reservation; counselors must demonstrate their respect and sensitivity to the needs of their Native American clients before respect will be returned. Given the passivity and nonassertiveness of many Native Americans, one has difficulty knowing when that respect has been earned. One indication may be the care the client takes in preparing for the meeting; the more he or she prepares, wearing neat and clean clothes (regardless of the "dressiness" of those clothes), or making the effort to brush hair, the more likely that the client respects the counselor.

5. Most Native American clients have little tolerance for long-range planning and delayed gratification. The counselor, therefore, must not become impatient nor expect a major commitment to complex treatment plan. Taking things one step at a time, demonstrating personal commitment to planning and emphasizing direction at every opportunity are key factors.

6. The Native American client may not view time as a linear ordered process that exists as an objective entity to be chopped up and organized. Patience and recognition that punctuality is not a highly valued behavior are absolutely essential.

7. Property and possessions are most often valued only to the extent that they can be used in the present. Possessions are not used in the sense of reflecting personal worth, nor as a protection against some future calamity.

8. Alcohol plays a positive role in the social functioning of the tribal society but is easily abused because of its social acceptability.

HISTORY OF COUNSELING
AND OTHER SERVICES AVAILABLE

Historically, counseling services have not been available to the Native American client on the reservation; however, since the early 1980s tribes have begun to provide a wide variety of human service programs. The primary experience of the Native American with help services has been in the form of either missionaries or bureaucrats (euphemism for BIA workers) whose philosophy of counseling has been to tell the Native Americans that they are uncivilized savages and that they must change. The attitude that Native Americans are and must be treated as children (paternalism) is not yet history, and potential counselors must always avoid behaving paternalistically if they hope to be accepted and to become effective on the reservation.

THE HELPING PROFESSIONAL'S ROLE

The authors would like to suggest that despite all of the previous warnings and traps to avoid, the non-Native American counselor has certain advantages over Native American counselors in working with Native American clients and, given sensitivity to that potential, can provide effective help.

Because of the close social relationship inherent in the tribal culture, Native American clients may not, in fact, be as open with Native American counselors as with nontribal counselors. They often fear that whatever they say will be broadcast over the whole reservation (via the very effective "tribal telegraph") by sundown. Although a professional counselor, regardless of background, would not break confidentiality in so blatant a way, the Native American client knows only that on the reservation everyone seems to know everything about everyone else and therefore would be extremely reluctant to discuss personal problems with another Native American. Accordingly, a non-Native American counselor has the advantage of not being considered part of the reservation social communication system and should take advantage of that perception at the beginning of a session by emphasizing that all communications will be held in confidence. The Native American counselor, by the same token, is put at a decided disadvantage and must demonstrate over quite an extended time period that confidences are respected.

A new Native American counselor will find the job very trying because tribal members will be suspicious of the counselor who has just returned to the reservation. The best advice to both the new Native American and non-Native American counselor is to keep a low profile and demonstrate trustworthiness through action. With trust, respect will grow.

Given the advantage on confidentiality, non-Native American counselors must nevertheless recognize that they will be approached with suspicion and distrust by Native American clients. Of course, suspicion and distrust are not unique to Native American clientele. All counselors are familiar with it, but the non-Native American counselor must be prepared to undergo testing by clients who resist counseling assistance and who will use the fact of the counselor's non-tribal status as an excuse to avoid or prevent change. The testing may be used to intimidate to a certain extent, but testing primarily will be used to probe the counselor's understanding of the Native American culture with the purpose of finding and exploiting ignorance as a defense against effective counseling. How does the non-Native American respond to the direct challenge: "You're not one of us; you don't understand us; you can't help us; leave me alone!"? Inform the client that you are not there to help "Native Americans" but to help an individual help himself or herself and, furthermore, that the burden of responsibility for change lies with the client and not the counselor.

As a general model of counseling, a good procedure is to make sure that clients assume as much responsibility for change as they are capable. In working with Native American clients, that goal becomes much more difficult to achieve because of the Native American's general non-assertiveness, uncommunicativeness, and tendency to promote harmony through apparent agreement. A strategy that we have found effective in overcoming this agreeable passivity is to ask questions that allow the client to assume some authority in the situation. For example, a noncommital or ambiguous statement can be challenged in such a way that the client is given the opportunity to assume the role of teacher and implicitly take on the responsibility of providing a clear communication. Specifically, one may indicate a lack of understanding and ask for further explanation and detail.

In summary, emphasize any perceived advantage of confidentiality; explain that although you are not a Native American (if you are not) your goal is not to help all Native Americans but to help a single individual; and ask questions in such a way that clients are allowed to assume both authority and responsibility in dealing with their problems. With time you will find your clientele will begin to respect and trust you and will begin to come to you on their own. When that begins to happen it will no longer matter that you are not a member of the tribe. You will have demonstrated that you are both a sensitive and competent helping professional.

With regard to goals counselors may help Native Americans establish, we repeat: Consideration of cultural values must be taken into account. On that note, we conclude with an observation made by a Chief of the Six Nations (of New York) as written in Benjamin Franklin's **Remarks Concerning Savages of North America** (Smyth, 1970):

You who are wise, must know that different nations have different conceptions of things; and you will not therefore take it amiss, if our ideas of this kind of education happen not to be the same with yours. We have had some experience of it; several of our young people were formerly brought up at the Colleges of the northern provinces; they were instructed in all your sciences; but when they came back to us, they were bad runners, ignorant of every means of living in the woods, unable to bear either cold or hunger, knew neither how to build a cabin, take a deer, nor kill an enemy, spoke our language imperfectly, were therefore neither fit for hunters, warriors, nor counselors; they were totally good for nothing. (p. 99, Vol. X)

REFERENCES

Seaver, J.E. (1925). *A narrative of the life of Mary Jemison: The white woman of the Genesee* (22nd edition). New York: The American Science and Historic Preservation Society.

Smyth, A.H. (1970). *The writings of Benjamin Franklin: Volume X, 1789-1790.* New York: Haskell House Publishers.

7

COUNSELING
BLACK PEOPLE

RODERICK J. McDAVIS, Ph.D.
Associate Dean
Graduate School & Minority Programs
Professor of Education
Department of Counselor Education
University of Florida

and

WOODROW M. PARKER, Ph.D.
Professor of Education
Department of Counselor Education
University of Florida

RODERICK J. McDAVIS, Ph.D.

A native of Dayton, Ohio, Roderick J. McDavis received his B.S. degree from Ohio University in 1970, his M.S. degree in student personnel administration from the University of Dayton in 1971, and his Ph.D. degree in counselor education from the University of Toledo in 1974. He is currently Associate Dean of the Graduate School & Minority Programs and a Professor of Education in the Department of Counselor Education at the University of Florida. He also is a co-host of the television program, "The Black Family," aired on public television in Jacksonville, Florida.

Dr. McDavis served as the first President of the Florida Association for Multicultural Counseling and Development and as President of the Board of Directors of Big Brothers/Big Sisters of Greater Gainesville. He currently serves as a member of the Board of Directors of the Gainesville/Alachua County Center of Excellence. His articles have appeared in the *Journal of Counseling and Development, Journal of College Student Personnel, Journal of Multicultural Counseling and Development, School Counselor,* and *Counselor Education and Supervision.* He has served as a member of the Editorial Board of the *Journal of Counseling and Development.*

WOODROW M. PARKER, Ph.D.

A native of Atmore, Alabama, Woodrow M. Parker received his B.S. degree from Stillman College in 1963, his M.S. degree from the University of South Florida in 1971, and his Ph.D. degree in counselor education from the University of Florida in 1975. He served as University Counseling Psychologist in the University Counseling Centers at both the University of South Florida and the University of Florida from 1971 through 1977. Currently he is Professor of Education in the Department of Counselor Education at the University of Florida and is an affiliate member of the staff in the Psychological and Vocational Counseling Center.

Dr. Parker has served as the President of the Florida Association for Multicultural Counseling and Development; has served on a task force for developing competencies for preparing culturally skilled counselors; teaches a course in multicultural counseling; and has recently been cited as one of the most prolific contributors to the *Journal of Multicultural Counseling and Development.* He is currently writing a book on the role of consciousness-raising in multicultural counseling.

COUNSELING BLACK PEOPLE

AWARENESS INDEX

Directions: These questions are to help you evaluate your understanding of Black clients. Mark each item as true or false. Compare your score with the scoring guide below.

T F   1. Being stereotyped is one of the most negative effects of discrimination for Black people.

T F   2. The Supreme Court ruled that racial segregation in public and private schools was unconstitutional in the 1954 *Brown versus Board of Education* case.

T F   3. The least of the problems confronting Black people today is being able to use public facilities.

T F   4. Black people are not included enough in mainstream society.

T F   5. Today, many Black people are working in nontraditional careers.

T F   6. Most Black people are aware of the counseling services that are provided by counselors and counseling agencies.

T F   7. Affective counseling approaches are the most effective approaches to use with Black clients.

Scoring Guide for Awareness Index

1. T	3. T	5. F	7. F
2. F	4. T	6. F	

CASE EXAMPLE

When Derick was very young, his parents told him that he was a good person, intelligent, and capable of achieving anything if he was willing to work hard. Derick believed his parents and, when he started school, was eager to learn as much as he could about science since he wanted to become a medical doctor. During his elementary school days Derick did very well in his studies, but his scores were low on standardized aptitude tests. His White classmates made jokes about how "dumb" Derick was and started telling him that their parents said that Black people could never do as well on these tests as Whites. Derick did not believe his classmates but he was disturbed by their comments. When he discussed his concern with his teachers and counselors, they avoided telling him some of the negative effects that standardized tests have for many Black students.

One day when Derick was walking home from elementary school, a car passed him and he heard someone yell, "Hey nigger, you and your kind should go back to Africa!" When he got home, Derick asked his parents what the person in the car meant. They told Derick that some White people are prejudiced and say unkind things to show their dislike for people of other races. Derick's parents also said that he should not worry too much about being called bad names by White people. Since this was Derick's first encounter with being called a "nigger" he did not know whether he should ignore it, get mad about it, or worry about it at all.

Derick completed elementary school with a "B" average in his studies, but he continued to score poorly on standardized aptitude and achievement tests in high school. He began to think about what his classmates in elementary school had said to him and thought that perhaps they were right—Black people could not score as well as White people on standardized tests. His counselor suggested to him that he might consider a career in some area other than medicine because his standardized test scores were so low, but Derrick continued to make "Bs" in most of his courses, especially in science classes.

During his junior year, Derick decided to try out for the school baseball team. He had played little league baseball, been on the little league All-Star team, and played summer league baseball for three years. On the first day of tryouts, Derick noticed he was the only Black person competing for a position on the team. The manager asked the candidates to catch fly balls and grounders and to practice throwing. Derick was the only one who caught every ball hit to him, and he made accurate throws to the proper people. The next day, however, Derick was cut from the team. That summer, Derick played baseball on the same summer league team as a White student who had played and started on the high school team. Derick started in every game for this team while his fellow classmate sat on the bench. His experience in the summer league confirmed that probably he was cut from his high school team because he was Black.

Derick graduated from high school with a "B" average in his courses and went on to college. His parents told him that if he continued to work hard his dream of becoming a doctor would come true. His major was premed and he maintained a "B+" average in his courses. In most of his classes after his sophomore year, Derick was the only Black student. This situation did not concern Derick until he enrolled in an advanced zoology course during his junior year. He noticed that although his hand was raised the White professor never called on him to answer questions in class. Several times he attempted to make an appointment to talk about this avoidance, but the professor was always too busy. At the end of the term, he received a "C" grade in the course despite having received "B" grades on his tests and projects. Again, Derick tried to arrange a meeting with the professor, but he was never available. He thought about appealing the grade but was afraid he would create more problems for himself. Derick became even more aware that some people will harm, ignore, and/or avoid helping when a person's skin is Black. He began to realize that he would probably be discriminated against at various times the rest of his life.

Derick received a low score on the standardized test required for entrance to medical school but was admitted anyway because of his good grades. He worked hard, finishing in the top third of his class. Ironically, some of his White classmates had initially told him that the only reason he was admitted to medical school was because he was Black. Derick had been through many trials and tribulations to become a physician and yet he knew to some people he was and would always be "just a nigger." As Derick began to plan the rest of his life, he wondered if he would ever live long enough to see the day when he and other Black people would be fully accepted by White Americans.

THE BLACK POPULATION

In 1985, the 28 million Black people living in the United States comprised the largest ethnic minority group in America and 12% of the total population (U.S. Department of Commerce, 1987). The 1985 census also determined the following for the Black population: 54.2% lived in the South, 28.1% were less than 15 years old, 64% were between 15 to 64 years old, and 51% of the families were husband-wife families while 43.7% were headed by a single female.

With regard to education, 33.9% of the Black adults 25 years of age and over were high school graduates, and 11.1% had completed four or more years of college. However, when only those between 25 and 29 years old were considered, the percentage of high school graduates rose to 80.6%. Of the 12.4 million Black people eligible to work, 15.1% were unemployed. The median income of Black families in 1984 was $15,432 with 14.7% of Black families earning under $5,000, 19.2% between $5,000 and $9,000, 15% between $10,000 and $14,999, and 51.1% earning over $15,000.

HISTORICAL BACKGROUND

Black people were first brought to the United States in 1619 when a Dutch ship landed at Jamestown, Virginia, with 20 slaves of African descent (Sloan, 1971). During the first 244 years of their presence in America, Black people were used exclusively as slaves in most part of the country, especially the South. Most Blacks lived on plantations and worked in the fields or houses of Whites without receiving wages. On January 1, 1863, President Lincoln signed the Emancipation Proclamation which freed all Black people from the bondage of slavery. The thirteenth amendment abolished slavery, the fourteenth amendment gave Black people citizenship, and the fifteenth amendment gave Blacks the vote.

Since the 1860s the history of Black people in the United States has been affected significantly by court decisions and congressional legislation. In *Plessy versus Ferguson* in 1896, the Supreme Court upheld the doctrine of "separate but equal" educational facilities for Black people, a decision which resulted in over 50 years of segregated education in the South and contributed to the migration of many Black people to the North in the early 1900s.

Another outcome of **Plessy vs. Ferguson** was the development of predominantly Black colleges and universities. During this period Black people were influenced by two significant figures in Black history, Booker T. Washington and W.E.B. DuBois. Washington's contention was that Black people could be more progressive if they learned skills or trades in agricultural and mechanical fields while continuing to live and work in rural areas of the South. DuBois, on the other hand, believed that Blacks should pursue education in professional fields and become leaders of the race. Both men inspired Black people to acquire more education in a wide variety of occupations during the period between 1900-1950.

Segregated school systems lasted until 1954 when the Supreme Court declared racial segregation in public schools to be unconstitutional in **Brown versus Board of Education.** For the first time in 335 years, Black students were permitted to attend the same schools as Whites. This integration led to a larger number of Black people being educated in such professional fields as law, medicine, business, and engineering. The Civil Rights Act of 1964 provided Blacks with basic human rights that had been previously denied. Black people were able to eat in any public restaurant and stay in any public motel. In 1965, through the Voting Rights Act, Congress gave Black people in the South the right to vote, a right which had been denied in past years. In the Bakke decision of 1978, the Supreme Court ruled that race could be used as a factor in admitting students to colleges and universities; these institutions were permitted to use affirmative action measures to increase the numbers of Black students admitted to undergraduate and graduate programs.

Court decisions and congressional acts have had both positive and negative effects on Black people. Although Blacks are beginning to perceive themselves as equal under the law, some majority group members have not accepted Supreme Court decisions and congressional acts and still view Black people as inferior.

The history of the Black population in the United States has been dismal. It has been filled with oppression, discrimination, and unfair treatment. While true the plight of Black people in 1987 is better than it was in 1619, many still find themselves in a society that does not fully accept them. This fact continues to be in their minds and results in mistrust and dislike for some majority group members.

CHARACTERISTICS OF BLACK PEOPLE

In order to provide effective counseling for Black clients, counselors need to know what distinguishes Black people as a group. Counselors need to have at least a general knowledge or an awareness of certain characteristics, behavior patterns, and values that differ from those of the White majority culture. Acquiring this knowledge is essential if counselors hope to facilitate Black clients toward the development of their full potential.

Characterizing Black people as a distinguishably different group from White people is a monumental task for at least two reasons. First, such characterization reinforces and perpetuates stereotypes, a limiting and destructive force against the development of human potential. Second, Black people are almost impossible to describe owing to the broad spectrum of racial and cultural variations within the group culture as well as within the Black race. Even among slaves, diverse subgroups existed. Blassingame (1972) reported that there were three kinds of slaves during the years of slavery in the United States: Nats—the militant fighters (Harriet Tubman, Nat Turner, and Frederick Douglas); Jacks—slaves who accepted life as it was, did not shun work, but ran away if the opportunity existed; and Sambos—shuffling, grinning, happy slaves who used their image as a mask to help other slaves escape. Even within the slave community to classify the slaves was difficult.

Distinguishing certain characteristics that are uniquely Black may be even harder today. Atkinson, Morten, and Sue (1979) outlined differences within Black and minority groups based on their reaction to racism and oppression through a five stage *Minority Identity Development Model.* Persons in stage one (conformity) identify more strongly with dominant cultural values. Persons in stage two (dissonance) feel confusion and conflict about the values and beliefs of dominant cultural values and beliefs, and they question them. Individuals in the third stage (resistance and emergence) actively reject the dominant culture and demonstrate greater identification with the Black culture. Those in stage four (introspection) question their rigid rejection of dominant cultural values. People in stage five (synergetic articulation and awareness) work toward a sense of fulfillment regarding cultural identity.

Explaining that Black people are different within their own race is one way of emphasizing the importance of looking at Black people as individuals rather than arbitrarily assigning group traits to all Black persons. According to Sue (1981), social scientists have characterized Black people from a deficit perspective indicating that something is wrong with being Black. In this regard, the authors want to be sure that our discussion of distinguishing characteristics of Black people as a group does not perpetuate such stereotyping.

While the case has been made that differences exist within Black people as a group, certain characteristics still distinguish Black people from White people. What distinguishes the group? An exhaustive discussion on characteristics, values, and behaviors of Black people is beyond the scope of this chapter. The authors would, however, like to provide enough information to help counselors gain a better understanding of Black people by detailing two primary distinguishing features of the Black population: the family and the church.

The Black Family

The Black family has been generally described in social science literature from a deficit perspective. While negative aspects of the Black family are indeed present, the authors choose to focus on the positive qualities and values that have facilitated the survival of the 28 million Black people living in America today. Some of the qualities or values include the extended family, filial piety, respect for elders, and socialization of children.

The extended Black family often consists of many members including the mother and father, children, grandparents, aunts and uncles, nieces, nephews, and cousins. There appears to be a willingness on the part of Black family members to accept all relatives regardless of their circumstances. For example, a common practice is for a mother and her children to live with relatives when life circumstance, death, divorce or pregnancy warrant. Generally, they would be permitted to live in a given home until their life circumstances changed.

Filial piety refers to Black children's devotion to their parents. In many families children are taught early to take care of their parents and to be genuinely devoted to them. Black children know that making a negative comment about another's parents, particularly their mothers, is an invitation to a serious confrontation. Such activity in many Black communities has been commonly known as "playing the dozens." Black children, especially Black males, may become angry to the point of fighting anyone who questions the honor of their mothers.

Another aspect of filial piety is the devotion of Black children to one another. Many well known Black people have reported that they owe their success to an older brother or sister who helped them along the way. Usually, older siblings are responsible for the younger siblings. A Black female graduate student told the authors that her sister came from another state to keep her children while she did her internship in another part of the state. The willingness of Black family members to help one another has been a major contributing factor to the survival of the Black community in America.

Elderly persons are a prized commodity in the Black family. Elderly Black people play key roles in the family, church, and community. Younger Black family members who experience difficulty in their development are often referred to their grandparents for counsel. Many Black grandparents accept the responsibility for rearing their grandchildren while the parents of those children acquire more education or continue working.

In addition, elderly Black family members play a significant role in passing on cultural values, customs, and traditions to Black children. One of the authors, whose grandparents live in his home, remembers the stories they used to tell about the family history. The author's recollection of these stories helped him understand his family and himself as a Black man growing up in America.

Partly because of the large measure of respect accorded them, the elderly in the Black community enter nursing homes only as a last resort.

While socialization of children is one of the most important functions in Black families, parents encounter challenges and difficulties in the process. A recent study (Coleman, 1987) showed that feelings of racial inferiority among young Black children are as strong in 1987 as they were 40 years ago when the original Clark study was conducted. Coleman recommended that Black children can be helped to develop self-esteem through teachers and parents and by changing the ways that Black people are portrayed in the media. The Black family in general, and Black parents in particular, have the responsibility to teach their children that it is as honorable for a Black child to be Black as it is for a White child to be White. Black parents must first be secure in and accepting of their own Blackness as a model for their children.

A second socialization process for Black parents to teach their children how to survive in the White society. Black children must be taught how to respond when they are the only Black person in the presence of Whites, how to respond to name-calling, or what to do when they are stereotyped or labeled. Education is another value that Black parents must instill deeply in their children. Unfortunately, many Black children do not take advantage of the educational opportunities available to them. They are not taking the courses needed in math and science to prepare them for the technological world in which they will live and work. Acquiring an education is critical for Black people because it is often the only vehicle through which they can achieve upward mobility.

The Black Church

Douthis (1985) described the Black church as, "A rock in a weary land" and "a shelter in a time of storm." According to Douthis, the early Black church was not only concerned with the spiritual needs of Black people; it also played a major role in their education, politics, economics, and social welfare. He reported that early Black church groups formed and supported schools and colleges, mutual aid societies, and banks. It served as a meeting place for spiritual leaders and community workers in the fight against slavery and again during the civil rights movement. Well known leaders such as Dr. Martin Luther King Jr., Dr. Ralph David Abernathy, and Reverend Jesse Jackson used the church as a launching pad for victories.

Today, the church remains the cornerstone of the Black community. The Black church is the last extant institution in the Black community since the elimination of Black neighborhood schools. The church continues to be a place for spiritual renewal, educational development, political awareness, and social and psychological support. One church's slogan typifies the character of most Black churches: "Our church is the church where everybody is somebody." The membership of most Black churches represents people from various occupations and economic levels; therefore, a janitor might as easily serve as a church officer as a judge or medical doctor. Roles that many Black people serve in Black churches are significant to their self-concepts because church may be the only place in society where some Black people feel accepted and worthwhile. The church allows each member to participate in the worship service in some meaningful way which might explain why some Black church services last nearly three hours.

Finally, an important point for counselors to note is that the church is viewed by many Black clients as their major support system. Simply going to church makes them feel rejuvenated, less depressed, and less anxious. Because many Black people seek ministers for psychological help, the authors suggest that counselors build rapport and working relations with Black clients through ministers from selected churches in their communities.

PROBLEMS CONFRONTING BLACK PEOPLE

Labeling

Physiological differences exist within the Black race. That is, skin color, texture of hair, and so forth vary within the Black group and influence their lives politically, economically, socially, and psychologically. While some may argue that differences in Black people's skin color have not mattered since the 1960s, results from recent studies have shown that Black people with lighter complexions are preferred over those with darker skin (Gaines-Carter, 1985). If this is true, or perceived to be true, then skin color is a variable by which Blacks are labeled in society.

Simply being labeled a minority group member is a problem that all Black people face. While the word **minority** is not necessarily negative, the term causes many Black people to wonder if they are perceived as equals by majority group members. As Black children grow older, they soon realize that they are labeled as minorities by majority group members. This label imprinted on their minds by society becomes another stigma that Black people must learn to cope with throughout their lives.

One effect of this label is that many Black people develop negative self concepts and do not strive to fulfill their potentials. For example, some Black students begin to believe that being a member of a minority group means being unable to achieve as do majority group students. A second effect is a growing mistrust of majority group members. As Black children learn the history of their people, they may doubt that White people will ever understand, accept, and respect them. Hence, Black children wonder if they can or should trust any majority group members. Third, the minority level causes many Black people to dislike members of the majority group. When a person is perceived to be untrustworthy, then to establish healthy interpersonal relations with her or him is difficult.

Discrimination

Another problem that faces all Black people is discrimination. In spite of all the legislation and court decisions that have provided legal rights to Black people, they are still discriminated against in society and schools because of the color of their skins. In the area of housing, the vast majority of communities in the urban centers of society are still segregated or minimally integrated. In other words, most Black people live in one part of the city and most White people in another. Many Whites do not want Black people living in their neighborhoods and when they do move into these communities, White flight occurs. Further, some real estate companies will not sell homes in some White neighborhoods to Black people.

Discrimination in our society also affects the employment rate among Black people. While many factors contribute to the high unemployment rate among Black people, one of those factors is racial discrimination. Many Black people have had the experience of applying for a job, being told they were not qualified, and discovering that the only difference between them and the person who received the job was the color of their skins.

Discrimination in schools is reflected in the attitudes of many administrators, teachers, and counselors toward Black students. In order to perform well in school, students must believe that those responsible for their education are genuinely interested and concerned about them. Unfortunately, many educators have negative attitudes toward Black people and are unable or unwilling to work with Black students effectively.

Standardized and competency tests are other examples of discrimination in schools. Research indicates that Black students score lower on these tests than their White counterparts. When Black students learn this fact, they begin to doubt their intelligence and potentials. Many of these students lose interest in their school work and begin to look for other ways to become successful. While many educators are aware that these tests are biased against Black students, they continue to use them to judge their knowledge and potentials. Students have difficulty in being motivated or believing in themselves when they know they are being tested unfairly in school.

Lack of Role Models

A third problem that faces all Black people is the lack of role models in traditional and nontraditional careers. There are no Black senators or governors, no significant number of Black people in chief executive positions of major corporations or television networks, few Black administrators in predominantly White colleges and universities, and a relatively small percentage of Black people in medicine, dentistry, law, college teaching, engineering, pharmacy, architecture, and aeronautics. Without appropriate role models, these and other technical professions are perceived as career areas that Black people do not enter. Likewise many Black parents, educators, and counselors tend not to encourage children to seek careers in nontraditional areas. Labeling, discrimination, and lack of career role models will continue as pressing problems and sources of disillusionment until a concerted societal effort is mustered to dispel them.

PERSONAL AND CAREER GUIDANCE NEEDS OF BLACK PEOPLE

Personal Needs

Black persons, like all human beings, need to be understood, accepted, and respected. Many White people have had limited contact with Black people as individuals and minimal involvement in activities sponsored by Black organizations. Hence, White people have not been exposed to some of the differences in the culture, lifestyle, and communication patterns of Black people. For example, some White people criticize and penalize Black people for using Black dialect when they do not understand that this style of communication is accepted in the home and community. Denigration of their very speech leaves many Blacks feeling ignored and rejected by White people to the end that mistrust and hatred is fostered, leading to further separation of the groups.

Negative stereotypes about Black people have existed since Africans were brought to America as slaves. Many White people learn these stereotypes at an early age, believe them, and never challenge them. Sensitive to negative stereotypes, some Black people may consent to the attitudinal and behavioral expectations of White people and assume certain roles for survival. Others may learn to rationalize or deny the existence of negative stereotypes, while still others may absorb them as part of a negative self-concept. Thus a second personal need of Black people is to be perceived as individuals who are judged by character rather than color. In other words, Black people do not want White people to have expectations of them that are based on stereotypes; they want to be seen as individuals who have different as well as similar needs to those of White people.

A third personal need of Black people is to be treated as equals rather that unequals. As Black people become aware of history in America, they learn that their ancestors have been treated as second class citizens. The effect has been an expectation of unfair treatment in their associations with majority group members. Black children learn from their parents at an early age that they should be very cautious about trusting Whites. Most of these parents can share personal experiences of their unfair treatment by White people. Many Black parents have stories to tell about having to drink from separate water fountains, sitting in the balconies of movie theaters, not being able to stay in certain hotels or motels, and not being able to obtain loans to start businesses.

A fourth personal need of Black people, one that perhaps encompasses the others, is to be included in the mainstream of society. Black people rarely have been able to feel an integral part of society. The effect of this is that Black people have learned to live in two worlds, one Black, the other White. Black parents teach their children that they must learn to function in White society as well as they function in Black society. Developing a "dual personality" is necessary for Black children in order to survive in both worlds. For Black people, they have no other choice; they must learn to function within the White system so as to avoid being isolated and segregated in society. Black people want to be included in society's mainstream without having to sacrifice those qualities that make them different. In other words, Black people want to be themselves and to be perceived by majority group members having something to offer society.

Career Needs

Black students need to be provided with information about nontraditional careers, including examples of Black males and females who currently are working in nontraditional fields. These nontraditional careers would include engineering, architecture, mathematics, basic sciences, computer science, and medicine, career areas that for a variety of reasons Black people historically have not entered. Through the provision of culturally relevant career guidance materials, including slide/tape presentations, career scrapbooks, Black speakers, and the like, students can be made aware that Black people have entered these career areas and experienced success.

Since Black students may perceive nontraditional career areas as unrealistic for them, counselors should explode this myth through encouragement of active career planning that can help Black students to identify career alternatives, develop strategies, complete appropriate course work, and seek information about appropriate areas. Thus, a person can better understand the education necessary to acquire the skills needed to do the job, the amount of time involved in preparing for this career, and the career options available within an area of interest. Furthermore, because many Black students respond well to challenges, counselors should not be afraid to encourage them to explore and enter nontraditional as well as traditional career areas. Challenging these students to enter nontraditional careers communicates in a positive way that counselors believe that Black people can achieve in these areas.

COUNSELING SERVICES FOR BLACK PEOPLE

Being generally unaware of the services that counselors provide, many Black adults do not utilize the available community counseling services nor do they encourage their children to seek the help of school counselors. Most Black students, however, have become familiar with counseling and counselors through their attendance at public schools. Black people who have not had positive experiences with counselors in schools are most likely not to seek the help of counselors in the community when they really need help. Based on these observations, one can understand why counseling services in the community are under-utilized by many Black people. Moreover, many Black people assume that significant others (ministers, relative, friends) in the community are more interested and qualified to help them than are professional counselors.

Another reason why Black people have not utilized counseling services is that many of the counseling agencies expect clients to come and ask for help, the traditional way that counseling has been made available to all people. In Black communities, however, this system does not work well because Black people are not accustomed to sharing their personal problems with strangers. Thus, a substantial increase in the utilization of counseling agencies and services by Black people has not occurred.

During the 1980s a significant decrease has occurred in the availability of counseling services in the Black community. Federal budget cutbacks coupled with the lack of new legislative domestic programs have discouraged many Black people from seeking mental health services in their communities. At a time when the need is growing for more counseling services in Black communities to address very serious problems, apparently only a few politicians want to champion programs that provide such services.

The recent trend of establishing some community mental health agencies directly within the Black community has improved the availability of counseling services to Black people. The fact that these agencies are highly visible means that Black people will begin to perceive them as a part of their community and thus begin to make better use of them. An important point to recognize is that a long period of time may be necessary before these agencies become totally accepted by Black communities because of the negative stigma that has been attached to them in the past. It is, however, a step in the right direction in terms of increasing awareness of such services, of making use of counseling agencies, and of establishing the overall need and purpose of counseling services in Black communities.

ROLE OF HELPING PROFESSIONALS

One problem that faces many helping professionals in their attempt to provide better counseling services for Black clients is their lack of experience in working with Black people. Not having lived among or developed friendships with Black people, many helping professionals leave preparation programs unsure of how to approach and counsel Black clients. A frequent practice is for these professionals to refer Black clients to Black counselors if the inexperienced professionals find themselves unable to work effectively with Black clients. While this practice may seem plausible, it is nonetheless limiting and unprogressive. Counselors must learn to work with different clients and not provide less than adequate or appropriate counseling services for Black clients.

A question that might be posed is "Are helping professionals responsible for being able to counsel Black clients effectively?" Without hesitation, the answer to this question is "Yes." A necessary first step is being aware of how one thinks and feels about Black people. Awareness of attitudes can help individuals determine if they as counselors have a need to increase experiences with Black people in general to learn more about their culture, lifestyles, and communication patterns. Experiences with Black people also can serve as a vehicle for individuals to dispel myths or stereotypes that counselors may hold. Clients have a way of knowing whether a counselor is being genuine. We do not fool any of our clients, any of the time. They know whether we are being genuine when we talk to them, or whether we are just talking to them because it is our job. If a client is racially, ethnically, or culturally different, helping professionals must find ways to appreciate those differences, as opposed to saying something is wrong with clients who are different. Neither can it be assumed that because helping professionals have received graduate training, they are well equipped to work with all clients who come into their offices, regardless of the clients' race, culture, or language.

Helping professionals who are not Black have some homework to complete before they begin to counsel Black clients. Essentially, this homework includes two basic tasks. The first task is exploring and perhaps changing some attitudes toward Black people. The second is acquiring knowledge of the differences and similarities among Black people. Neither of these tasks is easy. Changing attitudes requires commitment. Acquiring knowledge of Black people places us in strange environments. We may feel uneasy, uncomfortable, and even insecure. These are the same feelings Black people experience when they visit helping professionals. In other words, helping professionals have to be willing to take the same risks they ask of their clients. Helping professionals may stumble and fall in their attempts to learn more about Black people, but they have to be willing to stand up and try again.

How can helping professionals acquire more knowledge about Black people? The most effective way is for these professionals to place themselves in situations which enable them to feel what it is like to be different. Attending social affairs sponsored by Black organizations, such as dances, parties, and picnics, is one way to better understand how it feels to be a member of a minority group Also, by eating meals with Black people at restaurants in the Black community and having informal conversations with Black people, helping professionals can begin to learn the culture, lifestyle, and language of Black people. The aim is to become helping professionals who believe that all people have an inherent right to retain their identities, make their own choices, and be self-directed individuals.

An Eclectic Counseling Approach

All of life centers around our constant struggle to strive to become better persons, to develop better self-concepts, and to become all that we can become. When Black clients have problems, and they bring those problems to us in counseling relationships, what they are really saying is that—"I'm stuck, I cannot move, and I need you to help me learn how to move from this point to a better point in life." We have to say—"Yes, I can help you, and this is how I can help you." Therein lies the essence of counseling: the ability to help somebody. Counseling is not for counselors; counseling is for clients. The client's needs are what are the most important ingredients in the entire counseling relationship.

During the past 20 years much has been written about counseling Black clients. Most authors suggest that counselors use a counseling approach based on one of the directive—cognitive theories, such as reality therapy. Others recommend that counselors use a counseling approach based on one of the nondirective-affective theories, such as client-centered therapy. Our view is that an eclectic approach with an existential philosophical base can be used effectively with Black clients. Existentialism is a school of thought that is concerned with individuals and their attempt to develop their identities, make their own choices, and provide self-direction. Existentialism means viewing racially, ethnically, or culturally different clients as individuals. It also means understanding that we all have different physical and mental characteristics and that we all have an inherent right to be who we are. Thus the role of the counselor is to understand clients as they exist in their worlds. Counselors should try to imagine what Black clients are experiencing so that they may better understand their meaning, values, lifestyles, concerns and choices. We advocate an existential philosophy for counseling Black clients because it places emphasis on existence, humanity, and individual differences.

The seven steps in the eclectic approach include building rapport, identifying the problem, setting goals, working, planning action, following-up, and terminating. The first step is building rapport. At the beginning of our counseling relationships with Black clients, we should take some time to establish a personal relationship. Building rapport communicates to Black clients that we care about them as persons, and that we want to know more about them. A simple hand shake is a way of saying "I'm okay—you're okay." An important part of introducing oneself to Black clients, to promote trust, is shaking hands. It is one quick way of saying, "I do not mind touching you." Counselors may also share some personal information about themselves, thus inviting Black clients to share similar information. In addition, providing an orientation to counseling, (i.e., telling Black clients what happens in counseling relationships) lets Black clients know what to expect, prevents confusion and misunderstanding, and helps build the client-counselor relationship.

The second step in the eclectic approach is identifying the problem. Black clients must be allowed opportunities to indicate in their own words why they are seeking help. Counselors identify the problem by asking probing questions, clarifying and sharing hunches. They search with Black clients within their worlds to identify problems. An important procedure is to help Black clients to understand causes of their problems or concerns. If counselors only work with Black clients' symptoms, they have not helped them; they have put band-aides on open wounds that need stitches.

Having identified the problem or problems, the third step in the eclectic approach is setting realistic goals. Setting goals that are outcome oriented is important with Black clients, because it helps them to understand the purpose of counseling. They should designate the outcomes of the counseling relationships in clear, simple language, indicating that help is available to solve the problem.

The fourth step in the eclectic approach is working. Working involves both Black clients and counselors in a mutual enterprise. By investing in the partnership, the counselor challenges the client's irrational beliefs and negative self-concepts. The counselor must remember that Black clients have their own experiences, and it is within those experiences that they are sharing their problems and concerns. While accepting what clients say is very important, doing so does not mean that the counselor should not debate what they say, or discourage irrational thinking patterns. Counselors have to be able to respond to Black clients in a way that says, "I understand what you are saying; I'm trying to understand what you are feeling; and I want to struggle with you."

The fifth step in the eclectic approach is planning action. The action that counselors plan must involve both themselves and their clients. The focus in planning action is on what can Black clients do to help themselves and what can counselors do to help them help themselves. A practice instrument in action planning is the use of homework assignments. Making homework assignments is effective not only for Black clients but also for the counselor as well. These homework assignments need to be specific actions that counselors and Black clients are going to do between the counseling sessions. Counselors and clients both need to make a commitment to the plan of action. Facilitate the counseling process through the client and counselor becoming we and us. Thus both Black clients and counselors are involved in the planning and the implementing of the plan.

The sixth step in the eclectic approach is following-up. Counselors must find out whether the action plan worked and for what reasons. Have clients to be involved in deciding effectiveness. Were action plans effective or ineffective? Is there a need to create another action plan or modify the existing one? What blockers exist to effective implementation?

The seventh and last step in the eclectic approach is terminating the counseling relationship. Here counselors become teachers with Black clients by explaining what was done, why it was done, and how clients use similar techniques to help themselves. Moreover, this is the time for counselors to offer encouragement to Black clients, to communicate that whether or not we walk with them when they leave us, we will be with them in spirit and we believe in them. So often the difference between effective and ineffective counseling relationships lies in whether clients leave believing they can solve their problems. In other words, we can make a difference in the lives of Black clients by simply believing that they can become better persons.

The eclectic approach is a viable one for counseling Black clients. The authors no longer believe that counselors can afford to debate which counseling theory or approach is more effective with Black clients than another. All counseling approaches can be effective with Black clients if used properly. The only thing that matters in counseling relationships is that counselors meet the needs of their clients. If that means needing to be directive, then we should be directive. If it means needing to be nondirective, we should be nondirective. If it means needing to listen, we should listen. If it means needing to talk, we should talk. The eclectic approach provides a process through which counselors enter Black clients' worlds, enter their struggles, and together create alternatives and plans for action.

During the last 20 years much has occurred in the area of counseling Black clients. Many articles and books have been published on the subject. Conferences and workshops on counseling Black clients have been sponsored by many helping professional organizations. Counselor education and psychology departments now offer courses and other academic experiences in an effort to better prepare future helping professionals to work with Black clients. Indeed, counseling Black clients has become a legitimate area of scholarly thought and research in helping professions. As we move closer to the twenty-first century, counseling Black clients will become an integral part of all helping professions. Our challenge is to equip ourselves and future helping professionals with the necessary skills to respond effectively to the needs of Black clients. The authors believe that counselors can meet this challenge.

REFERENCES

Atkinson, D., Morten, G., & Sue, D. (Eds.) (1983). *Counseling American Minorities (2nd ed.)*. Dubuque, IA: Brown Company Publishers.

Blassingame, J. (1972). *The slave community: Plantation life in the ante-bellum south*. New York: Oxford University Press.

Coleman, D. (1987, September 1). Study finds feelings of inferiority among Black children. *Gainesville Sun*, p. 1D.

Douthis, J. (1985). *Black churches provide more than spiritual needs* (Report No. 44). Washington, DC: Smithsonian Institution Research Reports.

Sloan, I. (1971). *Blacks in America 1492-1970*. Dobbs Ferry, NY: Oceana Publications.

Gaines-Carter, P. (1985, September). Is my "post-integration" daughter Black enough? *Ebony*, pp. 54-56.

Sue, D. (1981). *Counseling the culturally different.* New York: John Wiley & Sons.

U.S. Department of Commerce, Bureau of the Census. (1987). *Statistical abstract of the United States.* Washington, DC: U.S. Government Printing Office.

8

WOMEN ENTERING
OR RE-ENTERING
THE WORK FORCE

HELEN B. WOLFE, Ed.D.
Associate Dean
Academic Affairs
Western Maryland College
Westminster, Maryland

HELEN B. WOLFE, Ed.D.

Helen B. Wolfe is Associate Dean of Academic Affairs at Western Maryland College, Westminster, Maryland. She combines her administrative role with teaching in the counselor education program at the college. Prior to her present employment Dr. Wolfe was Executive Director of the American Association of University Women. Her career has actively involved her in counseling, politics, research, evaluation, and teaching. She holds degrees from the State University of New York at Albany, Cornell University, and the State University College at Buffalo. Her involvement in counseling women stems from the mid-sixties when she began studying the work values of women.

WOMEN ENTERING OR RE-ENTERING THE WORK FORCE

Whether consciously or unconsciously, we have all absorbed an attitude toward the phenomenon of large numbers of women entering or re-entering the labor market. This attitude has been shaped by our past experiences, by the feelings of others around us, by the mythology of a previous generation concerning women, and by any reading or serious reflection we may have done. The following awareness index has been designed to assist the reader in separating fact from fiction in the specific attitude which one brings to the consideration of the problems that confront this segment of American women.

AWARENESS INDEX

Directions: Mark each answer true, false, or don't know. Compare your answers with the scoring guide at the end of the test.

T F 1. Employed women now receive equal protection under the law.

T F 2. The changed socio/economic climate has produced a significant diversity in the proportion of women employed in jobs traditionally dominated by men.

T F 3. Most women work because of economic necessity.

T F 4. While the wage gap for women has remained the same in jobs in the clerical and service area, it is barely discernible in the professions.

T F 5. Women born after 1940 are the group most responsible for the great increase in women workers.

T F 6. Employed women experience more psychological problems than other women.

T F 7. The Federal government has consistently enforced the laws aimed at ending discrimination against women.

T F 8. American women have greater security in the work force that European women.

Scoring Guide for Awareness Index

1. F	5. T
2. F	6. F
3. T	7. F
4. F	8. F

CASE-EXAMPLES

Beth is a young woman in her early thirties who is pursuing a career as a lawyer in a high-powered metropolitan law firm. Her equally ambitious husband is a lawyer with a competing firm in the same city. They postponed having children until they could be well launched in their professions, but when the point of no return came, they determined not to be childless. Now after a three month maternity leave Beth must decide whether to remain home with her baby, to return to her seventy hour a week law practice, or to scale back her occupational goals. What is to be done with the baby? Grandparents are too actively engaged in their own careers to offer a solution. The cost of a live-in nanny would consume most of one of their salaries. Does our society want such a young woman to be able to have it all, to achieve professional and personal fulfillment? Or must she be compelled to choose between vocation and motherhood?

Sarah is a young nurse, who worked in hospitals before her marriage and for several years afterwards. When the children came, however, she decided to stay home with them. With two young children still at home, her husband decided to fulfill his dream of opening a sporting goods store. Nursing lends itself better than most professions to an interrupted career pattern, and so Sarah returned to work in order to help cushion the financial changes caused by her husband's self-employment. Since she works nights and weekends, one of them is always able to be home with the children.

Carole was a happily married full-time homemaker with four children. She enjoyed her role and viewed marriage as her economic bedrock. When she was in her early forties, her husband died unexpectedly. Economic necessity forced her to enter the work force. She cleaned houses, for this was her only marketable skill. Now she has been able to find a part-time job as a short order cook.

Joan has a job as a secretary which she took in order to supplement her husband's salary and provide the family with some luxuries. She enjoys getting out and meeting people now that her school age children require less of her time. However, her husband has recently lost his job and now she is the sole supporter for the household. The supplemental income has become the sole income; it is not sufficient.

Marjorie is a college professor with a son in elementary school. Until their divorce, she and her husband shared child care responsibilities. Now, however, Marjorie is on her own, and providing child care coverage is a major problem. She worries about the necessity of the "latch key" between the time her son gets home from school and the time she is able to leave work. Leaving town for a professional conference requires careful planning and also a bit of luck. The day she counts on being able to leave immediately after he boards the school bus, he may wake up with a fever and not go to school at all. She earns enough to afford baby sitting fees, but not enough for a housekeeper.

DEFINITION

The focus in this chapter is upon problems and needs of those women who become part of the work force, either willingly or under some compulsion. Fifty million women cannot be ignored, and so during the past decade they have increasingly attracted the attention of those who provide counseling services. Economist

Carolyn Shaw Bell (1975) has noted: "With irreversible changes in the culture in response to all facets of the women's movement, the revolution in the status of women can most simply be summarized in the fact that these women can't go home again." Many can't go home again because of the economic demands which are made upon them, and many others won't go home again because now their aspirations have become linked with the rewards associated with employment. The bottom line is that fifty million women are seeking equality in the world of work.

Significant improvement has occurred in the status of women over the course of the past century, but during this time women's expectations have risen enormously. This means that, in spite of the gains, no greater congruence has occurred between expectation and achievement than was the case a century ago. The ratio between expectation and achievement is not always understood, especially by those who think that women should be grateful for the gains that have been made and not press so hard for their next stage of freedom.

The sex role stereotypes under which both men and women chafed in the 60s and 70s were outmoded relics of the American frontier. Rigid sex roles made sense under those difficult conditions; the division of labor into carefully prescribed male and female roles was necessary for the family's survival. When the American physical environment changed, however, these roles no longer made sense. The incongruence made women increasingly impatient about the retention of stereotypical roles that were inappropriate in the new environment. The American family shifted from a producing unit to a consuming unit as the economy shifted from a manufacturing to a service emphasis. These changes have inevitably increased the ambiguity inherent in traditional male/female roles. Elizabeth Janeway (1974) wrote, "The social changes that we are trying to cope with do not arise from some fiendish plot of bra-burning females, but from our old, old friend the Industrial Revolution. It has remade work, remade society, and now it is remaking the family" (p. 141). A new picture of men, women, children, and families has taken shape. Rigid sex roles have become obsolete. Our society is characterized by smaller families, reconstituted families, dual career families, increased employment of women, and many female heads of household from the middle and working classes.

CURRENT PROBLEMS CONFRONTING EMPLOYED WOMEN

One of the most significant and pervasive problems with which women must cope is the persistent myth that the majority of American women freely choose to enter the labor market for reasons other than economic necessity. Gerson (1985) described the social conditions which must be in place in order to permit a woman's decision to remain at home. These are

1. a family system characterized by permanent, stable marriage;

2. a household economy founded on a one-paycheck, male family wage;

3. limited work opportunities for women; and

4. sufficient behavioral similarity among women to provide mutually reinforcing support for female domesticity (p. 204).

Although these conditions may have existed in previous generations, they do not now exist for American women nor do they seem likely to reappear in the foreseeable future.

Statistics from the United States Department of Labor show that by 1960 the trend away from female domesticity toward economic independence had begun. In that year 37.7% of all women between the ages of 16 and 70 were employed outside the home. By 1987 the figure was 51.9%, fewer than half of American women remaining at home. If projections for 1990 materialize, 70% of all women will either be employed or looking for a job. The full-time homemaker is becoming rare. The average woman who comes of age in the 1980s can expect to spend more than 30 years of her life in the workforce. Of the women currently in the workforce, 70% are there because of economic necessity: they are single, widowed, divorced, or married to men who earn less than $15,000 a year (***Children's Defense Fund Budget,*** 1985). Moreover, the definition of what constitutes an adequate family income is a highly individual matter, and many additional women would no doubt claim economic necessity as a reason for working.

Having entered the work place, women have discovered a two-tiered reality. As relative newcomers to the labor market, women find themselves in the lower tier because of the scope of their jobs and the pay associated with them. Women earn approximately 60% of what men earn, and this differential is constant across the entire spectrum of jobs from the corporate woman to the cleaning woman. The pay differential has remained constant for five decades, and has been seemingly unaffected by equal pay laws or female entrance into non-traditional occupations. The growing acceptance of the concept of equal pay for jobs of comparable worth may eventually help redress this inequity.

The demographics of the woman worker indicate the problem areas. Gerson (1985) depicted the majority of women workers as "married, rearing young children, working throughout the middle adult years, and working full time throughout the year" (p. 7). Therefore, not surprisingly, the center of the problems confronting employed women is child bearing and child rearing issues. Department of Labor Secretary William Brock (1987) stated, "We still act as if workers have no families." Since 90% of all American women will bear a child, child care concerns are inevitable. Between 1960 and 1986 the number of women with children under the age of six tripled. Now 9 million preschoolers require care while their mothers work. We like to say that women are free to choose both motherhood and careers, but social supports to enable such dual decisions are weak. As women have observed this harsh reality, the rise in the number of employed women has been accompanied by a sharp decline in fertility rates. Susan Brownmiller (1984) has summed up the problem: "For many women, perhaps most, motherhood versus personal ambition represents the heart of the feminine dilemma."

Is it unfair for a woman to expect that her desire to be a full-time mother should be accommodated for an unspecified number of years?

Should another woman avoid motherhood entirely in order to secure the full chance that any man might have for economic autonomy and satisfying work?

Does a society that understands the need for successive generations have a moral obligation to ease the way for a woman intent on fulfilling both aspects of her dual purpose ambition? (p. 231)

When a woman decides to combine motherhood with a career, her protection under the Federal Pregnancy Discrimination Amendment (1978) is limited. The law requires all employers who have disability plans to treat pregnancy as any other disability. New York, New Jersey, Hawaii, California, and Rhode Island, however, are the only five states that require private employers to provide disability coverage; therefore, 60% of employed pregnant women are not covered (Kamerman & Kahn, 1984).

In addition, the decision to have a child frequently jeopardizes a woman's employment status because she puts at risk her seniority and employee benefits. Guarantees are not present that she will be able to return to her same job after the birth. This is but another reminder that, in spite of the sentimentality surrounding Mother's Day, motherhood is accorded little status in American society. Noting the negative impact it has had upon others, many women have opted to delay motherhood until today a frequent occurrence is for women to become mothers for the first time in their mid-to-late thirties after their careers have stabilized.

Regardless of the age at which mothers bear children, the problem of finding adequate child care confronts women when they return to work. Whether the child is a month old or in middle school, the logistics involved can seem overwhelming. "What can I afford to pay for child care?" "Do the qualities of the caregiver satisfy me?" "What contingency arrangements can I make when the child or the caregiver is ill?" These questions plague women.

The premise that children are primarily the mother's responsibility is being re-examined by American families. With fathers increasingly sharing the parenting obligation, parental responsibility is becoming a family issue rather than solely a concern of women. Child care has emerged as a major political subject and is debated in Congress and by Presidential candidates. It has moved from being a problem for the less affluent to being a general issue which crosses socio-economic class lines. Serious attention is now given to maternity/paternity leave policies, parental leaves to care for sick children, flextime, job sharing, and part-time options. Some institutions have opened child care centers at the workplace for their employees. Child care is becoming urgent, as Betty Friedan (1981) predicted, "not just for the individual woman, but for the very survival of the family" (p. 228).

To compound the problem, current social policy, as expressed in the Tax Reform Act of 1986, fails to recognize the irreversible changes that families have experienced. The tax benefits in this legislation go to families who own large houses, have many children, and earn one income. In Gerson's (1985) view, "Working mothers cannot and will not return to the home; decreeing that women belong at home and refusing to ease their movement out of it will not stem the tide of women, with and without children, moving into the world of work" (p. 230). The regressive stereotypes which the federal government is now seeking to promote fail to address the new constraints faced by today's families.

When marriage no longer represented a stable means of fulfilling their economic needs, women looked to contemporary divorce laws for financial protection. Weitzman (1981) has shown that a woman's standard of living following a divorce tends to fall about 73%. Hewlett (1986) faulted the courts for interpretations placing an equal burden of child support on both partners. She found that many women were caught between a generation which revered domesticity and a generation which relied on the economic independence of the sexes. Many women are not financially able to bear an equal burden of support.

PERSONAL AND CAREER NEEDS

Although women face similar economic and social conditions, a mistake would be made to assume that their responses are all alike. As much variation among women exists as among men and between men and women. The personal and career needs of women are highly individualistic, and as a group they are no more homogenous than are men. Counselors should operate from the premise that women have many choices in creating their individual life patterns. Role models are diverse and numerous: women can choose domesticity or nondomesticity with or without children; their participation in the labor force may be full-time or part-time; and their work patterns may be stable or interrupted. Whatever their specific choice, however, what is predictable is their need for assistance in life planning, decision making, and goal setting.

Since more and more women are finding that a critical importance issue for them is to become economically self-sufficient, then a sensible procedure is for them to make significant investments in education and vocational training. Such an investment will produce substantial dividends in comparison to drifting without plans which will leave career decisions to chance and in so doing will produce costly mistakes in the long run. Inderlied (1979) has pointed out that "goal setting has been consistently associated with career planning and aspiration and with effectiveness in occupational choice" (p. 34).

Gilligan (1982) encouraged counselors to see women's developmental models as different from male models, but not as deviant. Since women's experiences have been different, to subject them to male models in order to explain psychological, moral, and career development is erroneous. By using male models, doubts that women may still have about their worth and their experiences are reinforced. Gilligan's research has enabled us to understand that women's judgments are based on a "relational bias, i.e., a tendency to see themselves and issues in terms of themselves in relation to other people" (p.164). Women define their identity through relationships of intimacy and care so the problems they encounter are somewhat different from those of men, who frame their identities in other ways. The critical experience becomes choice, "Changes in women's rights change women's moral judgements, seasoning mercy with justice by enabling women to consider it moral to care not only for others but for themselves" (p.149). Brownmiller (1984) used the work of Gilligan to suggest that "ambivalence in making and sticking to some hard decisions (motherhood, career choice), long considered to be a feminine weakness, stems from the ethics and responsibilities of motherhood and the importance of caring relationships for women" (p.230).

The career needs of women, however, have become virtually identical with the career needs of men. All workers need skills for entering the labor market, for retention in the world of work, for upward mobility, and for acquiring strategies to allow men and women to mesh careers and marriage. Married women, however, do need help in coping with such facts as the following:

1. They may find themselves constrained in their aspirations because of the geographical location of the husband's job. This reality causes underemployment or unemployment frequently for married women, as well as psychological

distress posed by seeing the husband's job as more significant than hers.

2. Women's careers are more affected than men's by the other partner's career choice (Nieva & Gutek, 1981, p. 50).

3. Dual career families must be distinguished from two job families. The former implies careers of both spouses require development, persistence, and nurturing. This poses special challenges to negotiate a family life style that will fulfill these requirements.

4. Although married women may feel greater time pressures than their husbands, Pleck (1985) pointed out that this does not appear to have negative consequences for them. Initially, women were overloaded as they tried to fulfill home and family demands on top of their work requirements. This problem seems to be working itself out, because now a woman's over-all work day averages only 12 minutes longer than her husband's work day (Pleck, p. 140). Men and women are moving toward convergence in their family time, and for both the family role is far more psychologically significant than their paid work roles (Pleck, p. 134).

The Wellesley Center for Research on Women (Friedan, 1983) also found that women who combine homemaker and worker roles have better psychological health than do those who maintain only one of these roles. This is credited to the fact that employment allows them to exercise more control over their lives, thus providing outlets for achievement and mastery needs without sacrificing pleasure and intimacy.

Single women, whether heads of households or on their own, because of their total self-sufficiency, feel greater economic pressures and personal demands. Counselors should be aware that these women often do not find adequate psychological support, since they have no one in the family to whom to turn.

All women need information regarding their rights and responsibilities as workers. Empirical knowledge of the legislation protecting them as workers gives them the power to gain their rights. Subtle sex discrimination and sexual harassment are sufficiently widespread that women need special skills allowing them to recognize harassment and take steps to gain redress from violations of their civil rights.

Women need career information which is gender free. Gerson (1985) called for counselors to use a developmental approach because "women are reared with ambiguous expectations and so we must look at how people's motives, goals, and capacities develop as they move through life stages and confront a series of choices in which they must make consequential life commitments" (p.37). She finds earlier theories, i.e., the childhood socialization model and the social-structural coercion model, insufficient for understanding women's behavior.

HISTORY OF COUNSELING AND OTHER SERVICES AVAILABLE FOR WOMEN

Economic and social conditions have always determined whether American women choose domesticity or nondomesticity. Historically, unless a woman was enrolled in an educational institution that offered counseling and guidance services, for the most part she received no counseling from any source. More recently, the availability of counseling services for working women tended to follow the Federal dollars. Money was allocated according to whether or not the country needed "Rosie the Riveter" during a war-time economy. Janeway (1974) pointed out that "one aspect of the war between the sexes not often noted is its manipulative use of women by the State and the Establishment. Wars put women into the labor market and recessions and depressions put them out of it" (p. 79).

As a profession, counselors too often have allowed Federal dollars to establish their priorities; thus they have followed more frequently than they have pioneered. After World War II a great effort was made to integrate veterans into a post-war society, but few were concerned about the working women who were pushed out at the same time. The launching of Sputnik dictated that counselors master the techniques required to produce scientific and technocratic career decisions. In the early 1960s some legislative advances for women, such as the Equal Pay Act of 1963, were achieved, and a few governmental commissions were appointed to focus upon the changing roles of women. In 1965, I attended a pilot conference sponsored by the Women's Bureau of the Labor Department to examine the counseling needs of women and girls. Women counselors and women counselor educators interacted with the Women's Bureau, but the profession as a whole showed little interest.

The civil rights movement helped rekindle the women's movement, but the funding basically emerged for Blacks rather than for women. The specific drive for passage of the Equal Rights Amendment generated enough energy to create some helpful legislation for women. In 1975, Title IX of the Educational Amendments Act of 1972 was passed. It was intended to eliminate sexual discrimination in college admissions, financial aid, physical facilities, curricula, sports, counseling, and employment in educational institutions receiving Federal funds, but lax enforcement and the narrowing of the scope of the legislation by subsequent court decisions resulted in minimal effects for women in educational settings.

The Comprehensive Education Training Act (CETA) provided programs in the late 1970s and early 80s to retrain women who suddenly found themselves in the work force after many years as homemakers. The program was designed to address the particular educational and/or training needs women required in order to become economically self-sufficient. CETA programs were limited in that they tended to perpetuate occupational segregation for women, but even these were lost when the Reagan administration ended them in the early 80s.

The general apathy of the counseling profession for the needs of women during the 1960s and 70s caused feminists to take up the slack in providing services for women. The advent of women's studies in higher education, changes in gender stereotypes depicted in standard elementary school textbooks, the initiation of legislative reforms helping women, and the integration of women into work force unions and professional societies increased the visibility of women and represented a greater commitment by all components of society to meeting their needs.

Women became important consumers to higher education institutions concerned about declining enrollments from the traditional pool of high school graduates. Marketing and recruitment practices by colleges and universities utilized the available counseling services offering life planning and career planning services to recruit nontraditional students. Women embarking on a first career or a change of career comprised a large proportion of this population. Professional counselors are now providing services for women designed to increase their marketability as workers.

THE HELPING PROFESSIONAL'S ROLE

Counselors need to engage in an on-going process of self-evaluation. Even the growing feminization of the counseling profession does not preclude the need for all counselors to ensure that we do not constitute a barrier for women seeking to close the gap between their aspirations and the realities of life. Counselors must examine their own perceptions about women's development and their role in present society. An important procedure is to help women to see real alternatives so that they can continue to move beyond traditional barriers in the workplace.

Women need reassurance that their aspirations are not deviant. Group counseling is an effective technique for providing this assurance because women in similar circumstances offer support and encouragement to one another. Women need to be encouraged to discuss what they can do. They need to understand that communication skills, including self-promotion, are part and parcel of labor force participation. Women have been conditioned by society to minimize their qualifications. Professional counselors and others must help women move toward greater self-awareness and to refine their ability to project this confidence.

In addition to the cohort support that single-sex group counseling can provide, family counseling takes on a greater role for counselors working with married women who are employed or seeking employment. We have seen how the participation of both husband and wife in the labor force is becoming the norm in American society. Challenges are found in the new options and the new roles that this phenomenon brings. Both partners need assistance in exploring strategies which allow them to combine careers, marriage, and parenting more effectively. Values clarification, problem solving, time management procedures, and conflict resolution are topics which counselors can address effectively.

Diversity in occupational choice can be presented to women through meaningful career counseling. The diversity is important for women not only in the professional classes but is of critical importance for women in the working classes. Hewlett (1986) reminded us that the United States labor market is still largely segregated, 75% of women being employed in traditional women's jobs with the accompanying limitations on earnings and job mobility. Occupational variety is especially important because the job outlook in some of the traditional occupations for women tends to be bleak. The counselor must be careful, however, to adequately prepare women entering nontraditional fields for both the challenges and the obstacles they can encounter. Awareness of potential problems and psychological pressures will better equip women for these vocations.

Career planning is just as important for women as it is for men. Because women tend to have a history of short-range planning they may initially have difficulty with sequential, long-range planning. The counselor who understands this heritage which women bring, rather than erroneously assuming this is "just the way women are," will be able to overcome this attitude. Women can be taught to integrate the long range view in their career decisions, but the counselor cannot assume the current existence of this skill. Careful discussion of life stages can be supplemented by suggested readings to provide factual data.

Interest, aptitude, and ability tests continue to have less relevance for mature women than for mature men. Although test publishers have made significant revisions, the dependency upon the relevance of the male role model and the assumption of the female as deviant rather than different continue to be problems. The decision of test use, therefore, must be highly individualistic and done with an awareness of the appropriateness and validity of these measures.

Since educational institutions have more deliberately extended their outreach to women, the decision to seek further education appears to generate less stress in women today than a few years ago. The counselor, however, has a significant role in assisting women to make the transition from school to work. The marketplace imposes its own expectations which the woman can address by acquiring effective job hunting skills. The counselor must be able to help the woman learn to develop an effective resume. Since many women are unpracticed in resume writing they tend to include too much data, such as date of birth, marital status, and number of children. They need help in assessing their skills adequately and then expressing them on paper.

Upon entry into the workforce, the "superwoman syndrome" is a problem which faces many women. Gilligan (1982) found that women perceive and construe social reality differently than men (p. 171). Gerson (1985) observed that "in order to justify their own embattled positions, domestic and nondomestic women denigrated each other's choices and the tradition of men's careers taking precedence over women. Many women may feel a trace of residual guilt when they go to work, and this guilt must be dealt with." This guilt is manifested in the tendency to compensate by becoming Superwoman, the need to do it all—the job plus the myriad of other tasks that the wife and mother who is not employed performs. A few exceptional women are able to do these tasks without damage to themselves, but we should not assume they are the majority. Most women need to share tasks with their husbands and/or children. The employed mother also may seek to assuage this guilt by over-indulging the children and should have an opportunity to examine this issue. Counselors can help women define their priorities and to live comfortably with a series of compromises and fewer absolutes involving meal preparation, housecleaning, and social life.

James Michener wrote a book entitled **The Quality of Life** (1972). In reflecting upon educational and occupational opportunities for minorities he made the telling point that we cannot afford as a society to cut anyone short of his or her full potential for we all have too much at stake. What great novel has not been written because we blocked the full potential of someone through destructive stereotypes? What cure for cancer might have been discovered by a woman or a Black? What improvements in the quality of life have we lost by this suicidal cutting off the brain of a large part of our population? Because of their sensitivity to human personality, and their skill in surmounting problems, counselors as a group are in a position to pioneer in the task of helping women achieve their full potential. Full integration into the workplace is a vital starting point.

REFERENCES

Bell, C. (1975). The next resolution. *Social Policy, 6,* 5.

Brock, W. (1987, June 22). In Wallis, C., The Child-Care Dilemma, *Time,* Vol. 128, No. 25, p.59.

Brownmiller, S. (1984). *Feminity.* New York: Linden Press.

Children's Defense Fund Budget. (1985). Washington, DC.

Friedan, B. (1981). *The second stage.* New York: Summit Books.

Friedan, B. (1983, February 27). Twenty Years After the Feminine Mystique. *The New York Times Magazine.*

Gerson, K. (1985). *Hard choices: How women decide about work, career, and motherhood.* Berkeley: University of California Press.

Gilligan, C. (1982). *In a different voice.* Cambridge: Harvard University Press.

Hewlett, S. (1986). *A lesser life: The myth of women's liberation in America.* New York: William Morrow.

Inderlied, S. (1979). Goal setting a career development in women. In B.A. Gutek, *New directions for education work and careers.* San Francisco: Jossey-Bass.

Janeway, E. (1974). *Between myth and morning: Women awakening.* New York: Morrow.

Kamerman, S. & Kahn, A.J. (1984). *Maternity policies and working women.* New York: Columbia University Press.

Michener, J. (1972). *The quality of life.* New York: Fawcett.

Nieva, V. F. & Gutek, B. A. (1981). *Women and work: A psychological perspective.* New York: Praeger.

Pleck, J.H. (1985). *Working wives/working* husbands. Beverly Hills: Sage Publications.

United States Department of Labor. (1984, 1985, 1987). *Monthly Labor Review.* Washington, DC.

Weitzman, L.J. (1981, August). The economics of divorce: Social and economic consequences of property, alimony and child support awards. *UCLA Law Review 28,* 1254.

9

INDIVIDUALS WITH A PHYSICAL DISABILITY

NICHOLAS A. VACC, Ed.D.
Professor and Chairperson
Department of Counseling and
Specialized Educational Development
University of North Carolina at Greensboro

and

KERRY F. CLIFFORD, Ed.S.
Clinic Coordinator and Counselor for Union County
Bradford—Union Guidance Clinic
Starke, Florida

KERRY F. CLIFFORD, Ed.S.

Kerry F. Clifford is currently Clinic Coordinator and Counselor for Union County of the Bradford-Union Guidance Clinic with offices in Starke and Lake Butler, Florida. As a scholarship athlete at Kansas State University, he received a B.S. in Mechanical Engineering in 1957. In 1967, as the result of an industrial accident, he became paraplegic. His Masters of Rehabilitation Counseling was received at the University of Florida in 1971, where work toward a Ph.D. continues. In the recent past he has served as an instructor at Santa Fe Community College in the Work Exploration Unit and in the CETA program Vocation Preparation Class. He is a member, and past chairman, of the Gainesville, Florida, chapter of The Governor's Committee on the Employment of the Handicapped. He also serves on the Handicapped Advisory Committee for the North Central Florida Regional Planning Council. Mr. Clifford has been involved in the development of, and has participated in wheel chair athletics in the Gainesville area. He has served as a volunteer consultant on architectural barriers and designed his home. A major hobby is CB radio with which he has assisted in the promotion and organization of the local REACT team, which monitors and assists motorists on the national emergency channel nine on CB radio. He and Suzanne, his wife of 35 years, have three children and their first grandchild.

INDIVIDUALS WITH A PHYSICAL DISABILITY

AWARENESS INDEX

Directions: These questions are to help you to evaluate your understanding of individuals with a disability. Mark each item as true or false and then compare your score with the scoring guide at the end of the awareness index.

T F 1. The term "wheelies" refers to a common expression used for individuals who need to use a wheel chair for mobility.

T F 2. Individuals, who have a disability, like to be recognized as an example for "normal" individuals.

T F 3. Fund raisers have been very helpful in assisting individuals with a disability to change the attitudes of others.

T F 4 Generally speaking, society places a high premium on physical perfection.

T F 5. The paraplegic personality can be summarized or characterized by the word angry or hostile.

T F 6. Society is increasingly recognizing the capability of individuals with a disability to assume competitive employment.

T F 7. Counselors as helpers need to focus attention on advocacy for helping individuals with a disability.

T F 8. As helpers, we must recognize those aspects of our behavior and society that provide limits on individuals with a disability.

Scoring Guide for Awareness Index

1. T	3. F	5. F	7. T
2. F	4. T	6. T	8. T

REFLECTIONS

The authors of this chapter care deeply for the welfare and productive existence of all individuals. Their interest, however, evolved from two very different sets of events. The first author very early in his professional career became conscious of inequities in our educational system for children with handicapping conditions and has been involved since then with the education and welfare of individuals with disabilities. The second author experienced an accident on the job that resulted in a severed spinal cord and a disability that immeasurably affected both his professional and personal life. Although a paraplegic and a "wheelie," he does not view himself nor does he wish others to view him as a disabled person. Yet, during the 10 years that have passed since his injury, he has had many experiences which have conveyed to him that the majority of people regard him as disabled. The first person accounts included in quotation in this chapter convey some of his own personal experiences and feelings.

To speak of individuals who have disabilities, who differ from the non-disabled in physical, emotional, and/or mental ability, is to speak of a minority group. As with any minority group, this one is/and will continue to be faced with hostility, lack of understanding, indifference, and prejudice.

Many wheelies believe that they really cannot condemn members of the general public for their attitude toward an individual with a disability because "walkies" (people other than wheelies) have not had the opportunity to learn anything different. Some non-disabled think that the wheelie and other individuals who have a disability should stay at home, while other non-disabled individuals believe that those with disabilities should be protected from the rough and tumble world. Thus, attitudes toward these individuals range from complete ignorance and lack of understanding to the over-sympathetic and protective.

Many individuals cannot camouflage their disability because a wheelchair or prosthetic device is not easily concealed. The wheelie is literally looked down upon. However, while they cannot "stand tall" in a wheelchair, wheelies are not less than a full grown person.

One day when I had on my braces and was just about to stand up, a neighbor woman dropped in. She had never seen me standing, only sitting in the chair. I stood up, moved out into the room and stopped. She sort of stared at me with a "funny" look on her face. I immediately checked the air by nose to see if, as often happens when I get up in braces, I had done a "no-no." There were no signs. I then quickly looked to see if my "plumbing" was in order. Everything was all right, but she was still looking at me the same way. Suddenly she smiled, ran over and put her arms around me and said, "Man! You are a big one aren't you." I didn't ask her, "A 'big one' of what?" but after that event, a subtle change was made in her attitude towards me.

CURRENT PROBLEMS

Even in this enlightened age, a stigma is often attached to a disability. Some paraplegics have expressed their concern that people tend to think they are paralyzed from the neck up as well as the waist down. Some people find it difficult to talk directly to anyone in a wheelchair; they may talk over their heads or discuss them as if they were not present. Martin (1974) characterized the public's response to the handicapped by saying, "They are different, they trouble us in deep, unexplainable, irrational ways, and we would like them somewhere else, not cruelly treated, of course, but out of sight and mind" (p.150). Many non-handicapped individuals appear to be uncomfortable in the presence of anyone with a disability, and some try to hide their feelings by over-attention, over-kindness, or maudlin sympathy.

It is difficult for many paraplegics to accept the attitudes of some people towards them. At first they resent the people who, meeting them for the first time say, "You poor thing, what is wrong with you?" Or, the more common situation of manner and tone of voice when they say, "Boy! You can sure handle that thing! How do you do that?" These same people would never dream of saying to Carlos Alvarez, "Man! You sure can catch that ball! How do you do it?"

Historically, society has not expected people with a disability to function as normal people and therefore, has been somewhat hesitant to accept the achievements of individuals with disabilities. As a result people may cover-up their feelings by being over-lavish in their praise, with some being patronizing as if praising a child or someone from whom such a standard of achievement is not expected. These people may look on an achievement by the disabled in the same way that Dr. Samuel Johnston did a dog walking on two legs. As Dr. Johnston stated, "It is not the fact that he does it well, but the fact that he is able to do it at all that brings praise."

The person with a disability wants to be recognized as an individual, not a statistic or a wonderfully courageous person—an example for the world. And many do not enjoy being objects used to stimulate fund raising. Individuals with a disability do not enjoy seeing a campaign picture of a child on crutches, standing in the shadows, with a woeful look as he or she gazes into the distance where other boys and girls are playing. A more desirable image would be to have the same child mixing with playmates and sharing in the fun, even if he or she is only sitting in the sandpile making roads while the rest run and play.

Mass media sometimes hinders the cause of individuals with disabilities. In many plays and novels, the disabled male person has been portrayed as a miserable tyrant who is often very wealthy and makes life unbearable for all who come in contact with him; or an evil villain who seeks revenge for his disability by committing horrible crimes; or a meek pitiful creature who suffers greatly and tries to smile, but must spend the rest of his life wrapped in a blanket sipping hot milk. Fortunately, current literary works are beginning to portray these people as believable human beings. The television series, "Ironside," was a good attempt to show a paraplegic in realistic terms. Ironside, however, did not propel his chair by himself as much as he might have.

One of the myths about well-adjusted persons whom have a disability is that they are always supposed to be happy, or at least pretend to be. However, these individuals have feelings that parallel those of non-disabled individuals: happiness, fear, loneliness, and anger. The latter often accompanies problems with architectural barriers where none should exist.

If you would like to see and hear a display of anger by a paraplegic, come to the hospital parking lot with me some day. I have, upon several occasions, arrived early enough to have a pick of parking spaces. I always choose one that is the last in line at the west end of the lot. This space is chosen so that the door on the passenger side of the car is free to swing wide open, for easy egress and ingress of the car. However, several times upon returning to the car a small car has been parked next to the passenger side of my car with two wheels up on the grass and the other two almost in my car's fender wells. Of course, I have passed about fifteen empty spaces on the way to the car. The temperature of the air rises about five degrees centigrade and the tar in the road melts under my wheelchair. Of course, events arousing similar reactions include exams or a paper being due which I have not yet finished.

An injury that confines one to a wheelchair does not change a person's personality. However, some feelings may be lessened such as fear, anger, and sex drive (Hofmann, 1966). If these feelings are indeed lowered, their manifestation is not. The shy, returning person will still be shy though confined to a chair; the complainer will still complain; and the aggressive person will still be aggressive. There is no paraplegic personality; each wheelie is an individual. Physically disabled people do not want to be viewed as handicapped or disabled, but as individuals with a disability. They can be well adjusted if they receive love, understanding, and tactful help in meeting problems. They want to be judged competitively in their community, with emphasis upon what they can do, not what they cannot do.

Today, more than ever before, there is growing recognition of the potential capability of individuals with a disability to assume independent living and competitive employment. With this recognition, change is occurring in the direction of a more comprehensive attack on the problem of providing resources, facilities, and services to help integrate these individuals into the community. The following verse by an unknown, presumably paraplegic author aptly conveys the frustration of being separated from society:

> I burn the rubber off my wheels.
>> I can hardly wait;
> My wheelchair's 30 inches wide,
>> the john is 28.
> Some plead for civil justice
>> when they are set upon.
> I ask for just one freedom,
>> the right to use the john.
> I've thought about reforming
>> and changing my evil ways;
> To be a model of deportment
>> for the remainder of my days.
> But when I get to heaven
>> and face the Pearly Gates,
> St. Peter will say, "You're 30 inches wide.
>> Our gates are 28."

Unknown

NORMALIZATION

Normalization is usually defined as enabling people to participate in the normal range of societal activities as much and as independently as possible. With the requirements of normalization principles as stipulated by law, it has become increasingly important that the schools and other agencies of society find ways of working with and helping individuals with disabilities who may differ from the "normal" population in emotional stability, learning capability, and/or physical capability (Ballard & Zettel, 1977).

Helping persons to cope with problems in their natural environment, so that the handicapping aspects of their disabilities are minimized and the level of life functioning is maximized, has produced a need for a change in counseling services to include advocacy. At this time, however, there appears to be an inadequate response to this need for extended and strengthened services. As with any special population, helpers must be conscious of the present inequities for individuals with disabilities and strive to adjust the "system" to allow for maximum personal achievement. Tennyson so capably put it:

How dull it is to pause
to make an end,
to rest unburnished,
not to shine in use.

A disability represents a massive assault on an individual, and how he or she acts will depend on environmental experiences. These experiences are influenced by the nature of the disability, the realistic problem(s) it creates, the person's attitude, material resources, and the attitude of family members and/or people in the immediate environment as well as that of society in general. Helpers should be sensitive to developing an understanding of these factors and their manifestations relative to the individual.

The importance of helpers striving to "adjust the system" can be dramatically illustrated by the case of a Vietnam War veteran whom the second author was requested to assist. This pleasant, good-looking young man, who will be referred to as Joe, had attempted suicide two times within a three-month period.

We talked initially of the things that two "paras" usually discuss, especially in a hospital setting with one person being a relatively novice wheelie and the other a more experienced one. The topic included incidence of injury, medical/surgical course, hospitals and care, bowel/ bladder control, decubitus ulcers, types of chairs, and operations. After a while it became evident that Joe had two major concerns. The most important by far was sexual function; the other was mobility, especially operating an automobile without assistance. That these subjects were important to Joe was not surprising. What was surprising was that he had not been offered coun- seling and information concerning them. According to Joe, his inquiries about the subjects had elicited vague, confusing, and unsatisfying responses.

Counseling after two suicide attempts had never touched upon these two main concerns. The question is whether the non-disabled do not view with importance those activities which they take for granted or whether they view the disabled as having no needs other than those directly related to the disability (McBain, 1976).

Joe's ignorance of whether or not he could obtain a reflex penile erection paralleled my own experience seven years earlier. A few suggestions on procedures plus health and safety precautions were offered on determining whether an erection, plus degree of erection, could be obtained. With this, the two-hour visit with Joe terminated. His smile and demeanor during my visit the next day answered the question of whether he had been successful. During the ensuing months, sexual-function education and possible procedures were presented and discussed with the veteran. At the same time, Joe obtained an automobile with hand controls and instruction and training on how to use them. Subsequently, Joe became very busy in living. Times for the unofficial counseling visits became increasingly short and finally ceased. When Joe was discharged from the hospital, he rented an apartment which had been made architecturally adequate, set up independent living, and started classes at the nearby community college.

Sad but true Joe did not continue to "live happily ever after." He had other handicaps with which to contend in addition to his physical disability. He was young and had experienced a rather protected earlier life. As a result, he was psychologically and emotionally immature, lacking experience in coping with the demands of independent living. He developed behaviors indicative of arrogance and pride, spurning further counseling and even friendship. Alcohol and other drugs became more and more part of his lifestyle. He quit school, wrecked his car several times, and finally, due to improperly caring for himself, developed a chronic urinary tract infection as well as a decubitus ulcer on his buttock. He became rather desperate and his parents took him back to the home area. I have not heard from Joe since that time.

In the case of Joe, the system was eventually adjusted so he could function independently in society—he was helped in learning how to function adequately with his disability. In the past, many individuals like Joe, in addition to not receiving the type of assistance they desired, would have been separated from their natural environment based on the rationale that their removal would eliminate the problems and frustrations they might encounter in their everyday life. School aged children with disabilities have often been removed from the public classroom and/or placed in special care facilities. Fortunately, a change is currently taking place via the significant movement toward improving educational programs for school-age individuals with handicapping conditions, a movement which resulted from the full enactment of Public Law 94-142. Perhaps schools may be the place where bridges can be built between the past and the future, changing old policies of separation and passive service to new ones of involvement and aggressive action that will result in full relationships with society for all individuals.

CHANGES IN EDUCATIONAL PROGRAMS AND RELATED SERVICES

Even people not immediately affiliated with the education profession seem to be aware of the law passed which acknowledges equal educational opportunities for all children. Public Law 94-142 resulted from the work of parents and other individuals who brought public attention to the handicapped through policy victories won in the nation's courts and state legislatures. This legislation was designed to insure that all public education agencies provide an appropriate educational program for a child with a disability or handicap.

The Education for All Handicapped Children Act applies to all persons aged 3 to 21, who require special education and related services. As defined by this Act, handicapped children are those who are mentally retarded, hard of hearing, deaf, orthopedically impaired, other health impaired, speech impaired, visually handicapped, seriously emotionally disturbed, or children with specific learning disabilities who by reason thereof require special education and related services. (Ballard & Zettel, 1977, p. 178)

The major purposes of Public Law 94-142, as summarized by Ballard and Zettel (1977) are to

Guarantee the availability of special education programming to handicapped children and youth who require it.

Assure fairness and appropriateness in decision making with regard to providing special education services for handicapped children and youth. Establish clear management and auditing requirements and procedures regarding special education at all levels of government.

Financially assist the efforts of state and local government through the use of federal funds. (pp.177-178)

Section 504, which was enacted through the Vocational Rehabilitation Act Amendments of 1973, applies to all Americans with a handicap or disability but has special meaning for school age children because it guarantees them, when appropriate, access to regular education programs. As the statute indicates:

No . . . qualified handicapped individual in the United States shall, solely by reason of his (sic) handicap, be excluded from participation in, be denied the benefits of, or be subjected to discrimination under any program or activity receiving Federal financial assistance. (Ballard & Zettel, 1977, p. 178)

The school in particular has the potential for providing intervention for children with a disability because it is a major part of a child's natural environment. Accordingly, this section of the chapter will focus on the school as an agency that is potentially capable of providing important assistance with helping these individuals achieve preparation for "normalization."

Because children and youth with disabilities have greater contact with the school than any other agency, there should be personnel in the schools who are adequately trained to work with these children concerning their career, personal, and social problems. The goal for significant adults working with those children should be to develop a milieu that prescribes normative behavior and ways of problem solving that can be followed when facing dilemmas in their lives.

HISTORY OF COUNSELING SERVICES FOR CHILDREN WITH DISABILITIES

Relatively speaking it has only been in recent years that children with disabilities have been provided for in the public schools. Even then it has been done mainly through special education classes. DeBlassie and Cowan (1976) indicated that counseling for the handicapped was first mentioned after 1950 with the formation of the National Association of Retarded Children (NARC), the organization that brought pressures to provide services for the mentally retarded in areas previously neglected. Gowan, Demos, and Kokaska (1972) reported that

> The guidance of exceptional children is one of the last areas of guidance to be developed. Consequently, guidance theory and practice in this area are, in many instances, in a rather primitive state. Typical of this situation is a view which regards guidance as equivalent to vocational information or involved only in the identification of exceptional children. (p.1)

Counseling assistance in the schools for children with disabilities, if available at all, has often been limited to practical information-providing or advice-giving efforts. Most counselors are aware of students in their schools who have a disability and are concerned about providing appropriate services for them. Yet, it seems fair to conclude that incomplete services are provided. The counselor's inadequate involvement may be attributed to lack of time and/or apprehension caused mainly by his or her limited knowledge of and experience with such children. Consequently, it appears that many counselors are not meeting the career development, social, and personal adjustment needs of children with a disability. There needs to be an operational awareness that the career and personal-social needs are inextricably bound. Children with a disability, no matter how well trained they may be in academic skills, cannot hold a job if, for example, they cannot get along with their fellow workers or have limited knowledge of career opportunities.

In order to meet the needs of children with any disability, an urgent change must be made in the traditional behaviors of school counselors to counter the results reported by Hanna's (1976) investigation of the role of the counselor in working with educable mentally retarded children. His study revealed that in the past, counselors have been perceived by special educators as failing to assume the appropriate responsibilities with handicapped children.

HELPING PROFESSIONAL'S ROLE

Helpers need to examine and realistically appraise their own attitudes when working with an individual with a disability. They need to be cognizant of not over-simplifying the problems as being directly related to the disability alone. Mental, emotional, and career problems of those individuals are likely to originate from as wide a spectrum as do those of non-disabled individuals. The individual with a disability is likely to have not only diverse career goals and leisure interests but also limitations concerning life management. Accordingly, it is important that we as helpers do not categorize individuals and limit our involvement with them to concerns that are only directly related to their disabilities.

McBain (1976) summarized three facts which helpers need to acknowledge in order to assist a person with a disability:

1. There is great variation in functional limitation among those classified as possessing a particular type of disability.

2. Technological change has created vast new possibilities for compensating for physical limitations.

3. The individual's attitude and will to accomplish can bring about achievement that may seem impossible with a given disability. (p.7)

Basic Assumptions

Four basic assumptions need to be underscored.

1. Each individual with a disability is a unique person varying in his or her wish to receive and respond to life's experiences.

2. Elements of a helping relation advocated for the non-disabled are equally applicable to those individuals who have a disability.

3. Individuals with a disability are limited by having to function in a non-disabled world with architectural obstacles, debilitating attitudes, and assumptions which until recently, have separated them from the "normal" world.

4. Because an individual with a disability has more than the usual amount of contact with helping professionals, a helper must necessarily become involved with a number of other helping professionals such as physicians, rehabilitation counselors, and staff members of community agencies.

Important Daily
Functions to Address

Helpers working toward possible solutions for individuals who have a disability must gain an understanding of four areas of daily life functioning in which handicapping aspects of a disability come into play; mobility, time, physical or body requirements, and personal and social disposition. These areas should be considered as a point of departure for helping individuals toward a solution of problems in their environment. Although these daily life functions are interrelated, they are separated here to highlight their importance to an individual with a disability. The salient points relative to each area are presented in the following paragraphs.

Mobility. Mobility is being able to move freely in one's environment. Each of us, from infancy to adulthood, desires being as physically independent as possible. We hold dear the ability to be able to go wherever we want whenever we want. The individual with a disability is no exception.

Time. Generally we are not concerned with time per se, but rather with its utilization. It is this utilization of time concerning daily living that affects some individuals with a disability. Common functions such as getting dressed, preparing a meal, or other tasks that are taken for granted by the non-disabled, may occupy a place of major importance to an individual with a disability. Time is finite and if daily living requirements involve longer time frames, a person's choices of activities become restricted.

Physical or Body Requirements. Physical or body requirements of an individual with a disability may vary from those of non-disabled persons, depending on the nature of the disability. The conditions that are of importance include additional safety requirements, avoiding activities that may run the risk of creating injury to the body, and assistance with physical or body care.

Personal and Social Disposition. The personal and social attitudinal disposition starts at the most basic point of the individual's commitment to growth and a desire to set goals in the search for an improved quality of life. Personal and social attitude is the desire to command the physical environment and to acquire social knowledge of self. The authors' view concerning individuals with a disability is to treat the disability as a challenge, another life problem to be solved. As such, the helper seeks to teach new skills for adapting to one's environment.

SERVICES HELPERS CAN PROVIDE

Services which helpers can provide individuals with a disability can be divided into two areas: (1) direct service and (2) advocacy. Suggested services include the following:

Direct Service

1. Providing career, personal, and social counseling on an individual and group basis.

2. Assisting individuals to
   a. obtain appropriate in-school placement and/or employment,
   b. secure admission for appropriate training, and/or
   c. participate in leisure and/or extra-curricular activities.

3. Consulting regularly with employers and/or appropriate school personnel.

4. Assisting in arranging the transition of an individual with a disability from one setting to another.

5. Identifying needs of family members.

6. Evaluating the efficacy of the counseling program.

Advocacy

1. Sensitizing other staff members to practices and materials which may be prejudicial to individuals with handicaps.

2. Informing family members of mandates and regulations concerning the rights and opportunities of disabled individuals and their families.

3. Assisting individuals in seeking and using school/community resources.

4. Participating in identifying at all developmental levels the needs of individuals with disabilities.

LAST WORDS

Certain issues should be addressed in order to provide for more and better services for individuals with a disability. Research needs to be conducted in the area of guidance services for these persons, our training programs need to be improved to include the development of skills for working with the disabled, and inservice training programs need to be included for helpers in all agencies to improve their skills for direct-service roles.

Assistance can be provided with some immediacy by focusing attention on self-appraisal of existing services. Consideration should be given to whether each of the following services is or should be incorporated into the program. Services which any agency should provide disabled individuals include

1. providing information to the individual concerning his or her legal rights and opportunities,

2. using assessment materials to assist individuals in understanding themselves in relation to educational and career opportunities and requirements,

3. cooperating with significant others to develop or review and revise programs and plans, and

4. conducting workshops on topics such as careers, human relationships, and decision making for the individual and significant others in the agency's environment.

In the earlier sections of this chapter, emphasis was placed on the importance of recognizing those aspects of our behavior and society that impose limits on individuals with a disability. Public Law 94-142 and Section 504 of the Rehabilitation Act of 1973 have increased public awareness of an individual's right to have a productive and meaningful life. It is up to us helpers to create ways to assist the members of this special population and their families to expand control over their own life styles. Passiveness on our part is a compromise of our professionalism. Continual evaluation of both our attitudes and our services is necessary to improve the total milieu for all individuals in society. We should keep in mind the words of Szasz (1961) which were spoken in another context, but are applicable to this situation: "...although there are certain biological invariants in behavior, the precise pattern of human actions is determined largely by roles and rules" (p. 13). Helping people to understand, as much as possible, that their perceptions and anticipations of behavior further handicap individuals with a disability and curtail their freedom to a greater extent than do the individual's physical limitations is a step toward full humanity for all people.

REFERENCES

Ballard, J., & Zettel, J. (1977). Public Law 94-142 and Section 504: What they say about rights and protections. *Exceptional children. 44,* 177-184.

DeBlassie, R. R., & Cowan, M. A. (1976). Counseling with the mentally handicapped child. *Elementary School Guidance and Counseling, 10,* 246-253.

Gowan, J., Demos, G., & Kokaska, C. (Eds.). (1972). *The guidance of exceptional children* (2nd ed.), New York: David McKay Co..

Hanna, R.C. (1976). *The role of the counselor in working with educable mentally retarded students.* Unpublished doctral dissertation, University of Florida.

Hofmann, G.W. (1966). Some effects of spinal cord lesions on experienced emotional feelings. *Psychophysiology, 3*(2), 143-156.

Martin, E.W. (1974). Some thoughts on mainstreaming. *Exceptional Children, 41,* 150-153.

McBain, S.L. (1976). *Enhancing understanding of students with physical disabilities.* Palo Alto, CA.: National Consortium on Competency-Based Staff Development.

Szasz, T.S. (1961). *The myth of mental illness.* New York: Dell Pub.

10

OLDER
PERSONS

HAROLD C. RIKER, Ed.D.

Professor of Education, Emeritus
Counselor Education Department
College of Education
University of Florida
Gainesville, Florida

and

JANE E. MYERS, Ph.D., CRC, NCC

Associate Professor of Education
Counselor Education Department
College of Education
University of Florida
Gainesville, Florida

HAROLD C. RIKER, Ed.D.

Harold C. Riker is professor of education emeritus, Counselor Education Department, University of Florida, Gainesville. He is a faculty associate of the Center for Gerontological Programs and Studies and a member of its steering committee. Dr. Riker received his B.A. and M.A. degrees in English literature and history from the University of Florida and his Ed.D. degree in student personnel administration from Teachers College, Columbia University.

Active in local, regional, and national professional associations, he is currently a member of the State Advisory Council on Aging and the State Committee on Housing for the Elderly. He has served as a member of the Governor's Committee on Aging; delegate to the 1981 White House Conference on Aging; past Chairperson of the Gainesville Housing Authority; past president of the Florida Council on Aging; member, planning committee, 1980 Governor's conference on Aging; member, Association for Adult Development and Aging; member, the Gerontological Society, National Council on Aging; and member NRTA-AARP. His publications include **College Housing as Learning Centers** (1965); "Learning by Doing," a chapter in **Perspective on the Preparation of Student Affairs Professionals,** (1977); "Potential Crisis Situations for Older Persons," a chapter in **Counseling the Aged,** (1978); and "Residential Learning," a chapter in the **Future American College,** (1981).

JANE E. MYERS, Ph.D.

Jane E. Myers, Ph.D., CRC, NCC, received her graduate training in gerontological counseling at the University of Florida. She has worked as a rehabilitation counselor, administrator of aging programs, and rehabilitation and counselor educator. She also has directed two national curriculum development and training projects in gerontological counseling. Dr. Myers has written and lectured extensively in the field of gerontological counseling and was the founding President of the Association for Adult Development and Aging.

OLDER PERSONS

AWARENESS INDEX

Directions: Mark each answer true, false, or don't know. Compare your answers with the scoring guide at the end of the test.

T F 1. An older person is one who has attained 55 years of age.

T F 2. Older persons are very much alike.

T F 3. The number of older persons is increasing rapidly.

T F 4. Over 21% of all older persons have incomes below or near the poverty level.

T F 5. Physical impairment is largely limited to those who are 65 years of age and above.

T F 6. Stereotypes of older persons often become self-fulfilling prophecies.

T F 7. Counselors are likely to have some degree of prejudice against older persons.

T F 8. Self acceptance is an important counseling need of older persons.

Scoring Guide for Awareness Index

1. F	5. F
2. F	6. T
3. T	7. T
4. T	8. T

OLD OR NOT?

Age is a quality of mind.
If you have left your dreams behind,
If hope is cold,
If you no longer look ahead
If your ambition fires are dead,
Then you are old.

But if from life you take the best,
and if in life you keep the just,
If love you hold;
No matter how the years go by
No matter how the birthdays fly,
You are not old.

—Author Unknown

TWO CASES

Mrs. G.

Two delightful women illustrate the range of differences among older persons. The first, Mrs. G., is 72 years of age and lives alone in a college town where her husband was a member of the faculty before his sudden and unexpected death. She is representative of white, professional, middle-class families.

Mrs. G. has lived through her grief and has joined a small group of widows who, after a short training period, are active in assisting older, recently widowed women to work through their sense of loss and fear of the future.

A vivacious, attractive woman, Mrs. G. participates in a variety of community activities. She attends her church regularly and is a member of several of its committees. She has joined the Retired Senior Volunteer Program (RSVP) and spends four hours each week at the City Hall Information Desk.

Mrs. G. is usually busy, primarily with other busy women of about her same age. Together they are involved in helping others through a number of community agencies. Mrs. G. enjoys a warm relationship with a son and his family who live in the same town. She has a number of friends in other communities where she and her husband have lived, and maintains an active correspondence. Mrs. G. is a vigorous person who finds happiness and support in her family, her friends, and her service for others. She finds that age has brought new opportunities.

Mrs. C.

Mrs. C., on the other hand, represents a very different segment of U.S. society. In her mid-nineties, she is Black, poor, and dependent for her existence on food stamps and supplemental security income provided by the Federal Government. When her two sons were very young her husband deserted her, and she assumed the full burden of the sons' support. Now in their 70s, these sons remain strongly attached to their mother, who has helped to rear their children and their children's children. Both sons have returned to live with Mrs. C.; their time seems to be spent primarily in playing cards.

Mrs. C. spends much of her time in bed watching television. When she leaves the house, it is to see the doctor or attend church. Somewhat hard of hearing, she has a slight tremble in her voice and arthritis in her hands. Her physical environment is incredibly impoverished. The three room house in which she lives is in poor condition, has no running water or inside toilet. Near the house is a water pump and old wooden privy. The house and yard are unkept; flies and other insects abound. For her meals, Mrs. C. relies on her neighbors and junk food.

For over 60 years, Mrs. C. worked as a house maid; for most of those years she was with one family and was regarded as a family member. Although life for Mrs. C. has been far from easy, she has been sustained and supported by the affection of her former employer and the bonds of love and loyalty which have held her family together.

WHO ARE OLDER PERSONS?

In the sense that every person is older than someone else, all persons are older. In the sense that attitudes toward life and living influence aging, those persons who habitually look backward to the past rather than forward to the future are older, regardless of their chronological age. By stating that persons sixty years of age and over are eligible for benefits under the Older Americans Act, the U.S. Congress has so defined older persons. Because retirement from jobs has traditionally been set at 65 years of age, those who are 65 and over often are described as older persons. Should retirement age increase upward, the definition of **older** may be expected to change as well.

In order to define older persons as a special population, the chronological age of 65 and above is used in this chapter, principally because much of the demographic information about older persons is based on this age group. At the same time, one should recognize that those who are 40 years of age or more are often classified as older, particularly by employment agencies. Persons in this age group experience longer periods of unemployment than those who are younger.

Several points should be made about older persons. First, they are a diverse group, with wide variations in family background, education, income, abilities, and interests. Second, each person is an unique individual, very much like he or she has always been, only more so. In other words, arrival at a certain age, whether forty, sixty, or sixty-five, in no way marks any fundamental change in in personality, interests, or abilities. And, third, the rapid rise in numbers of older persons has created a special and growing segment of the total population with particular needs, interests, and concerns which demand attention and response on the part of the U.S. society.

THE AGING OF AMERICA

U.S. citizens are living longer. As early as 1800, the median age was 16; by 1970, it was just under 28; by 2000, it will reach 35 (*Graying of America,* 1977). Between 1900 and 1983, the average life expectancy of men and women increased by more than 50%, from 47.3 to 74.7 years. For men, life expectancy in 1983 was 71.0; for women, 78.2. Currently, 75% of the U.S. population can expect to reach 75 years of age; in 1900, 40% could do so (U.S. Senate Special Committee on Aging, 1985-86). Men who arrive at 65 years of age can anticipate living for 16.8 more years; women can expect 18.8 more years (American Association of Retired Persons, 1986).

The number of older persons is increasing dramatically. In 1900, about 3 million persons age 65 and over were counted by the U.S. Bureau of Census. This number expanded over six times to more than 20 million in 1970 (Atchley, 1977). The 1985 total is about 28.5 million, and the estimate for 2000 is almost 35 million, a ten-year growth of nearly 22% (AARP, 1986; Challenges of the 1980s, 1979).

Of particular interest is the increase in the numbers of older persons by age groups. During the period 1900 to 1985, the 65 to 74 age group grew eight times; the 75 to 84 group by 11 times, and the 85 plus group by 22 times (AARP, 1986).

Demographic Characteristics

An appalling fact about this population is the sizeable number who live at or below the poverty level. As of 1985, approximately 3.5 million were below the poverty level, described as an income of $5,156 for a person living alone or $6,503 for a couple. Over 21% of the older population is described as poor or near poor. In an inflationary period, with rising costs and the declining value of fixed incomes, older persons are especially vulnerable to financial difficulties. To assume that a person can maintain a decent standard of living on $5,156 a year, or $99 per week, is, to say the least, unrealistic (AARP, 1985).

Race, Sex and Marital Status

On the basis of race, approximately 90% of persons 65 years of age and over are White; 8% are Black; 2% are of other racial origin. Persons of Hispanic origin represent 3% of the older population. The sex ratio is weighted toward females, who represent 59% of the total, while males represent 41%. The current sex ratio among older persons is 147 women for every 100 men. In 1985, half of all older women were widows (51%) and one-fifth of that number were widowers. Only 40% of older women are married compared to 77% of older men, and 4% of all older persons are divorced (AARP, 1986).

Older persons have substantially less formal education than those under 65 years of age. A decade ago, 63% of the older person group had some high school education or less compared to 26% of those under 65 years of age (Harris & Associates, 1975). Steady growth in the educational level of older persons is reflected in a rise in the median number of years of schooling from 8.7 to 11.7 years in the period from 1970 to 1985. This reflects a median of 11.8 years for females and 11.4 years for males. The number of years completed varies considerably according to ethnic origin. In 1985, the figures were 12.0 years for Caucasians, 8.1 years for Blacks, and 7.1 years for Hispanics (AARP, 1986).

Employment

The percentage of employed older persons has dropped steadily. In 1900, 63.1% of men over 65 were employed; by 1985 this percentage had fallen to 16%, and by 1985 to only 11% (AARP, 1985). Among the factors involved was encouragement by the Federal Government for workers to retire early, in order to create more jobs for others. Organized labor also bargained for pension plans that would permit early retirement, opening up employment and promotion opportunities for others. Inability to find or keep regular work has led some workers to use their retirement options. However, efforts are being made to encourage older persons to continue working if they have the interest and capability to do so. Mandatory retirement has been banned legally, and employers are encouraged to hire older workers.

Trends toward earlier retirement apparently do not reflect the preferences of a substantial proportion of workers and retirees. According to a 1979 Harris study, 51% of the surveyed employees expressed a preference to keep working rather than to retire; 48% in the 50 to 64 age group preferred to keep working after age 65; while 56% of the retired group wished they had not stopped working.

Health

Most older persons, about 86% of them, reported one or more chronic diseases which limit their daily activities, yet only 32% reported their health as fair or poor (AARP, 1986). The most commonly stated conditions were arthritis (53%), high blood pressure (42%), hearing impairments (40%), heart disease (34%), cataracts (23%), orthopedic impairments (19%), visual impairments (14%), arteriosclerosis (12%), and diabetes (10%). In spite of such conditions, these persons remain generally active and independent. At least 85% live in their own communities, with about 5% in institutions such as nursing homes. At the same time, the 65+ age group is responsible for about 25% of our country's health costs and makes use of as much as 25% of all drugs. Worth noting is that 72% of those in the 45 to 64 age group also may have one or more of the chronic diseases listed previously (Butler, 1975). Physical impairment, therefore, is by no means limited to those who are 65 years of age and above. In fact, statistics concerning functionally disabled persons indicate that one-third are below age 16, one-third are aged 16 to 64, and one-third are aged 65+ (Rehab Group, 1979).

In the past, aging and disease were often regarded as part of the same process. More recently, the importance of distinguishing among changes resulting from aging, disease, and social-psychological factors have been recognized. For example, Comfort (1976) has concluded that, in general, physical changes are not as significant to the aging process as are "sociogenic" factors which are imposed on individuals by the negative stereotypes about aging maintained through the culture of which they are a part. If indeed aging is, to some considerable extent, socially imposed, changes in negative stereotypes should receive high priority.

STEREOTYPES OF OLDER PERSONS

A basic problem experienced either directly or indirectly by older Americans is discrimination because of age. By means of discrimination, younger persons place older persons in a category of inferiority and describe older persons as different from themselves. This kind of discrimination enables younger persons to deny the possibility of their own aging. The irony of this situation is that these younger persons eventually find themselves the victims of their own prejudice.

An insidious effect of ageism, as Butler (1975) has described prejudice against older persons, is that many older persons accept and believe in their inferiority and the weaknesses attributed to them. Older persons place their peers in a category of inferiority. What, then, are some of the common stereotypes?

Stereotype of Unproductiveness

Older persons are believed to become unproductive and, hence, useless, a point of view long supported by the concept of mandatory retirement. However, the facts are that, given the opportunity, many older persons continue to be productive and actively involved in work and/or community life.

Contrary to popular belief, older workers can be as effective as younger workers, except perhaps in jobs requiring prolonged physical stamina or rapid response behaviors. Older workers are dependable, maintain excellent attendance and safety records, and require minimum supervision after job requirements are learned.

In terms of creativity, some persons remain active in their 80s and 90s. Examples include Pope John XXIII, working at church reform; Christopher Wrenn, designing St. Paul's Cathedral in London; and Michelangelo, completing St. Peter's Cathedral in Rome.

Stereotype of Disengagement

One theoretical explanation of the behavior of older persons is that they gradually withdraw from customary life activities and become more concerned with self. Such withdrawal can be selective so that relationships with some persons are retained, but the emphasis is on less interaction with others and on living with memories of the past.

While this theory of disengagement explains the behavior of some older persons, it by no means has application to all. The fact is that many older persons are very much involved in the life of their communities, to the extent that an "activity theory" has been stated to account for this type of behavior. A "continuity theory" suggests that individuals tend to continue in retirement the behaviors they have followed throughout their lifespan. The problem is, of course, that the stereotype of disengagement can mislead older persons to believe that they should withdraw from others after active work experience.

Stereotype of Inflexibility

Older persons are commonly believed to be set in their ways, insistent on following specific patterns of behavior, and unwilling to consider change. At least two factors may be involved. The first could be preference for what is familiar and customary. The second could be fear resulting from awareness of a slowdown in personal reaction time coupled with an acceleration in the tempo of life in the world around them.

However, healthy older persons do respond positively to change, shifting points of view and altering life styles as part of their continued personal growth. The ability to change and adapt seems to be related more to lifelong behavior patterns than to age.

Stereotype of Declining
Ability to Learn

The notion that persons can no longer learn when they grow older is expressed by the popular saying, "You can't teach an old dog new tricks." A common belief is that intelligence slides downward from adult years through old age.

Actually, healthy older persons can continue to increase their ability to organize their thinking and can successfully complete training and college degree programs with notable efficiency. Some evidence has been found to show that older persons can be helped to improve their response speed on intelligence tests (Baltes & Schaie, 1974). The possibility is that reduced learning speed may be related to environmental deprivation.

Stereotype of Senility

The term **senile** is loosely and inacurrately applied to older person who are forgetful, confused, or unable to maintain attention to one topic for any period of time. Both older and younger persons experience anxiety, grief, and depression; yet when the former give evidence of these problems they are sometimes assumed to have brain damage! Overuse of drugs, malnutrition, psychosocial stresses, and undiagnosed physical ailments may produce behavior labelled senile. Prompt diagnosis and treatment generally relieve all symptoms. A major complicating factor is the lack of willingness on the part of physicians to treat older persons. Many of their diseases are in fact "iatrongenic," or physician induced (Butler & Lewis, 1983).

Permanent brain damage, correctly described as senility, is irreversible. However, much of what is called senility can be successfully treated but may be ignored for the unstated reason that older persons are sometimes regarded as dispensable.

Alzheimer's Disease is a progressive form of mental deterioration which may last for as many as 20 years before death occurs. Its symptoms include loss of memory, inability of the person to make changes quickly, and destruction of mind and personality. Eventually, total care is required. Certain drugs show promise, but a cure is not yet known.

Stereotype of Declining Interest in Sexual Activity

The stereotype of loss of sexuality has two elements. The first is the belief that sexual relationships for persons over 65 years of age are improper. A typical description of older men involved in sexual activity is "those dirty old men." Lustiness in younger men becomes lechery in older ones. Older women who reveal a sexual interest in men may be labelled as suffering from emotional problems.

The second element is the common impression that older men and women lose with age their physiological capacities for sexual activity. On the contrary, healthy older persons who have maintained some degree of continuity of their sex lives continue to enjoy sexual relationships throughout most of the lifespan. Physiological changes do occur, but they tend to be gradual, and the body usually accommodates to them. At the same time, because of the emotional problems which can develop in this area of sexual relationships, accurate information and warm understanding on the part of both partners are important to the mental and physical health of those involved. Age does not place a time limit on sexuality or sexual capacity.

A common emotional problem experienced by older persons is fear of impotence. However, sexual activity provides feelings of well-being and positive self-regard. Recent studies indicate that about 80% of older persons are sexually active; less than 30% find that sexual responses and feelings diminish with age (Hittner, *Golden Years,* 1987).

Stereotype of Serenity

Popularized by fiction and the news media, untroubled serenity often is pictured as the reward of those who grow old. Grandma bakes cookies in the kitchen while Grandpa rocks contentedly on the front porch. The apparent conclusion to be reached is that the storms of active life are over.

Actually, older persons often face more stressful conditions than any other age group, and exhibit a remarkable ability to endure crises. Their resilience suggests that living longer has prepared them, somehow, to handle new stress.

The youth-oriented society of this country has effectively segregated its older membership, perpetuating a host of false beliefs about aging, and dooming many older persons to lives of little hope and declining enjoyment. The stereotypes about aging seem to undermine important personal qualities of self-confidence and self-worth and to forecast a dismal, decaying future which hardly seems worth the effort. The social prejudice confronting older Americans implicitly denies the possibilities for continued personal growth and explicitly imposes barriers to those striving to develop their own capabilities.

COUNSELING NEEDS OF OLDER PERSONS

Counseling needs vary widely among older persons. For sizeable numbers, these needs are minimal. For some, perhaps as many as 30% of the 65 plus population, needs for counseling range from moderate to great. The array of possible needs for counseling interventions also is considerable. Some method for categorizing these needs may be helpful to counselors working with older persons.

Myers (1978) developed a classification system for the counseling needs of older persons which includes four components:

personal concerns, interpersonal concerns, activity concerns, and environmental needs. She later added special categories of older persons as important areas of concern for counselors. Certain demographic categories, including age, gender, and race, seem to be related to the needs of older persons for counseling (Ganikos, 1977; Myers, 1984).

Personal Concerns

Personal matters of concern to those over 65 include psychological concerns related to death and dying, mental health, and independence; physical concerns related to health; and psychological and/or physical concerns related to acceptance of the aging process and acceptance of oneself as one who is aging. These concerns combined with the changes and losses of aging contribute to decreased self-esteem and increased difficulty in decision making for many older persons. Other areas of personal needs, as identified by Ganikos (1977) in a study of older adult persons, include personal adjustment and adjustment to life situations.

A major area of counseling need is for assistance in resolving personal problems and/or continuing or renewing progress toward self-fulfillment. Personal problems often grow out of personal losses such as loss of a spouse, friends, job, health, and youth, and generalize to feelings of loneliness, worthlessness, and depression. The passage of time awakens the older person to the realization that youthful dreams remain unfulfilled and that death is inevitable. Two frequently asked questions are "Who am I?" and "Why am I here?"

As older persons find and are helped to find answers to these questions, additional needs arise. Such needs revolve around the development or renewal of realistic, short-term goals for living. Of particular value is training in decision making skills to enable older persons to consider alternative courses of action and resolve problems with a greater sense of purpose. An important element of purpose is focusing on the present in terms of lifestyle.

Interpersonal Concerns

A second area of counseling needs identified by Myers (1978) includes psychosocial concerns such as relationships with significant others. Significant others can include family (spouse, children, parents, other relatives), neighbors, and friends. Ganikos (1977) also identified family relationships and social-interpersonal adjustment as key areas of need for older persons.

Studies of life satisfaction among older persons have demonstrated that support networks are essential to the maintenance of self-esteem and morale. Factors that correlate with high life satisfaction include marital status (married) and frequent personal and telephone visits with family and friends. The presence of at least one close relationship, usually a spouse, has repeatedly been found to be the single dominant factor determining life satisfaction over the lifespan, with children a close second.

Family relationships are not always positive, however, and counselors can intervene when difficulties arise. Older persons with physical or emotional disabilities are most at risk for developing family stress situations. When caretaking is required for an older relative, the potential for abuse increases significantly. The frail elderly tend to be most at risk for physical, psychological, and financial abuse (Myers & Shelton, 1987).

Group memberships are an important psychosocial concern. Such memberships serve to mitigate against isolation as well as provide identification with age-peers. Groups serve an important function in the support network of older persons, and can relieve family members of the stress involved in caring for aging relatives.

Activity Concerns

Within the third category of needs are concerns related to work, leisure time, and utilization of skills. Work involves the concerns arising from gainful employment and retirement. Leisure time encompasses hobbies, service, and recreational activities. Skill utilization includes vocational evaluation and learning new skills. Ganikos (1977) identified needs in this area as among the most important for older individuals. In particular, vocational and educational needs were important for her sample of adult learners, which would be expected based on their attendance in college coursework.

For many Americans, retirement from a full-time job has been viewed as the beginning of the end of life. For some, this view has been correct; they have declined rapidly in associations with others, in activities, in interests, and in health. Why? High among the possible factors is loss of the sense of personal worth derived from the job. In U.S. society, employment has long been the focal point for self-definition, association with others with similar interests, social contacts, and development of a personal value system. To deny employment to those who want to keep working and have the capabilities for doing so is, in fact, to destroy a significant support for life itself.

Fortunately for older persons, the reasons for enforced retirement are changing and conditions are favorable for continued employment, at least on a part-time basis. Individuals are living longer and are in better health than in years past. Research supports the fact of continued intellectual capabilities of older persons and their qualities of dependability, loyalty, and effectiveness on the job are confirmed by employers' experience.

Decline in the availability of labor is leading business and industry to encourage employees to remain on the job rather than retire. Dramatic increases in the costs of pension plans and special services for older persons are leading planners to suggest that the age for retirement be raised beyond the traditional 60 to 70 years. In addition, inflation has added so much to the costs of living that income to supplement pension payments is becoming essential.

Environmental Needs

Environmental concerns are basic because they relate to independence in meeting environmental demands and obtaining needed services. In fact, another important type of information needed by older persons includes the various forms of assistance which are available to them from federal, state, and local governments as well as privately operated agencies.

This category of needs includes the many services which help some older persons to live independently, such as transportation, shopping assistance, help with meal preparation, and housekeeping or chore services. Also included are financial and budgeting needs and legal assistance.

Needs Related to
Demographic Categories

Ganikos (1977) was one of the early researchers to identify demographic variables which seemed related to needs for counseling. Age was one of the variables. The younger subjects in her study, with an age range of 59 to 65, reported greater educational and vocational needs than the older subjects, age 65 and above. Younger widowed persons seemed to have greater educational needs than older widowed persons.

Other variables which appeared to affect expressed counseling needs were sex, marital status, and educational level. Subjects who were not married and in the lowest education groups (0 to 11 years of schooling) indicated more counseling needs related to personal adjustment than married subjects in the highest education groups (college and graduate school). In terms of adjustment to life situations, females reported greater needs than males, with both groups being at the middle educational level (high school and college). These results were supported in an extensive literature review by Myers (1984), who also noted that low income correlated highly with needs for counseling among older persons.

Needs of Older Women

Older women have some special problems. They live longer than men so that 51% of the women 65 years of age and over are widowed (AARP, 1986). Because society frowns on their dating and marrying younger men, widows generally continue to live alone. Many have never worked except as housewives; those who have worked usually have received low wages. As a result, older women often are living on limited incomes with few, if any, opportunities for social activities.

Social roles of older women may become indeterminate, particularly with the loss of the husband. Self-identity may develop as a central issue. Loneliness is a common problem. Relationships with sons or daughters may change, with conflicts arising from differences of opinion regarding degrees of responsibility for each other. Women at lower socioeconomic levels are likely to experience greater feelings of isolation and loneliness than those of the middle-class because the latter often have more friends and more community interests. Widowhood seems to be less of a problem for working class Black women than for White women primarily because open hostility between the sexes is more common among Blacks (Atchley, 1985).

Older women are overrepresented in the 30% of noninstitutionalized older persons who live alone—some 41% of older women compared to only 15% of older men (AARP, 1986). When disabled, they are far more likely to receive institutional care. They also have a greater tendency to live in poverty.

Needs of Older Minority Persons

Older minority persons exist in a situation best described as "multiple jeopardy." They are at risk because of their minority status, because of their age, sometimes because of their gender, and often because of their health status and income. They are a minority within the minority of older persons. Their quality of life usually is low, and their needs for counseling are correspondingly high.

Needs Related to Families

Some 67% of older persons lived in family setting in 1985, including 14% who lived with children, siblings, or other relatives. Family members who become caretakers for older persons may experience numerous stresses, which are intensified when the older person has a physical or emotional impairment. These stresses can lead to abuse, an increasingly common problem. Estimates are that 10 million older persons each year are victims of abuse (Myers & Shelton, 1987).

DEVELOPMENT OF SERVICES FOR OLDER PERSONS

The principal vehicle for federal, state, and local government assistance to older persons is the Older Americans Act passed by the Congress in 1965 and subsequently amended several times. This Act defined a national policy for older persons and included these specific objectives:

an adequate income; the best possible physical and mental health; suitable housing; full restorative services; opportunity for employment without age discrimination; retirement in health, honor, dignity; pursuit of meaningful activity; efficient community services when needed; immediate benefit from proven research knowledge; and freedom, independence, and the free exercise of individual initiative...(Butler, 1975, p. 329).

The Older Americans Act provided for the Administration on Aging, one of the major agencies now functioning under the auspices of the Department of Health and Human Services. For at least the first seven years of its existence this agency suffered from insufficient funds and limited authority.

During fiscal year 1966, Congress appropriated $6.5 million to carry out the provisions of the Act. By the end of the first year of operation most of the States had qualified for grants based on approved state plans. In a number of years following 1966, this Act was amended and funding increased. For fiscal year 1969, appropriations amounted to $31.9 million; for 1973, $213 million; for 1978, $720.4 million; and for 1985, $1.027 billion. Thus, during a sixteen-year period, appropriations have grown tremendously (National Association of State Units on Aging, July, 1985).

The 1978 Amendments represented a strong Federal effort to encourage the comprehensive coordination of services in order to better serve older persons. Title III, Part B, was re-written to include social services, senior centers, and nutrition services. Congregate meals and home-delivered meals were funded and preretirement and second career counseling for older persons were made available. Legal services, such as assistance with taxes and finances, were continued under the definitions of social services. The Administration on Aging's proposed regulations implementing the 1978 Amendments amplified the term **counseling** to include welfare and the use of facilities and services (Administration on Aging, 1979a, p. 45042).

Aging Network

As part of the recently designated Federal Department of Health and Human Services, the U.S. Administration on Aging is the first element of the Aging Network and is responsible for implementation of the Older Americans Act, which authorizes many of the services provided for older persons.

The second element of the Aging Network, is the State Unit or Agency on Aging. Specifically designated by action of state legislatures, this agency advocates for the state's older population and coordinates all activities in the state relating to the Older Americans Act. Organized during the years immediately following passage of the Older Americans Act of 1965, state units are organized administratively in the federal regions.

Area Agencies on Aging, the third element of the Aging Network, were authorized by the U.S. Congress through 1973 amendments to the Act. State Agencies on Aging were required to divide the state into planning and service areas, to decide which areas would have an area plan, and to designate for each of these areas an Area Agency on Aging. Currently more than 625 area agencies are operating in the United States.

Two general purposes of these agencies are to serve as both advocate and focal point for older persons within the area and to develop and administer the area plan for a coordinated and comprehensive system of social and nutrition services.

The number of organizations actively involved in the field of aging probably exceeds the 284 listed in the National Council on the Aging Directory of 1971. Each of these organizations has an impact on a particular group of older persons. Some organizations compete for grants funded by public and private agencies; many exert political pressure on elected representatives to support legislation favorable to their programs and concerns. A smaller number are engaged in multiple programs and activities.

The American Association of Retired Persons and the National Retired Teachers Association (AARP-NRTA), with an approximate membership of 25 million, is the largest organization of its kind in the world. Dedicated to the well-being and activities of retired persons, AARP-NRTA is built on a well-developed network of local, state, regional, and national units which maximize membership participation. In each state a joint legislative committee considers political issues affecting older persons and initiates specific recommendations for legislative action. This organization also makes recommendations concerning federal legislation.

The Gerontological Society is another sizeable national organization which is actively involved in the development and dissemination of information regarding aging and older persons. Its three branches focus on biological sciences, clinical medicine, and behavioral sciences. Its two journals, the *Gerontologist* and the *Journal of Gerontology,* are useful resources in the field of aging. The American Society on Aging and National Council on the Aging are two additional professional associations having similar purposes. A variety of regional and state professional associations affiliate with these groups.

Variety of Services

Many services provided older persons by federal, state, and community agencies have in common two objectives: the first is to improve and expand quality of life; the second, is to extend personal independence, delaying or avoiding dependence on long-term institutional care. Holmes and Holmes' (1979) study of human services for older persons described in detail most of the following services: information and referral services, multi-purpose senior centers, homemaker and home health services, legal services, residential repair and renovation services, services for employment and volunteer work, daycare for older persons, nursing home services, and counseling services.

THE HELPING PROFESSIONAL'S ROLES

For many years counseling has been associated primarily with helping younger persons. Considering older persons as possible counselees opens up a new area of opportunity for helping professionals. At the same time, problems quickly emerge.

Problems Affecting
Role Performance

The first problem is for counselors to recognize that older persons differ from younger persons in several important ways. They have an extended background of experience. Their problems tend to be the result of losses. Their life tasks may involve a shifting and redirecting of fairly well-established attitudes, goals, and behaviors. They probably recognize that life is indeed finite; their needs are likely to be short-term or immediate.

A second problem is recognizing and appraising the degree to which older persons may have been overpowered by some of the stereotypes with which they have been surrounded by society. In some instances, stereotypes about the aging process have so influenced the behaviors of older persons that change is difficult, if not impossible. For example, one stereotype is that older persons are inflexible, unpleasant, difficult, and hard to get along with. At a time when an older person is losing family members and friends who move away or die, that person may believe that the circle of family and friends is shrinking because of his or her behaviors. This conviction, reinforced by the stereotype, becomes a self-fulfilling prophecy.

Associated with the second problem is a third, which is the prejudice against older persons likely to be held, often unknowingly, by counselors and others who work with older persons. This prejudice can have a profound influence on the attitudes of helping professionals toward older persons. For example, when older persons are confused, forgetful, or depressed, the helping professional's first reaction may be that these behaviors are typical and expected. Yet such conditions can often be corrected. Likewise, the helper's reaction to the older person who is ill and unlikely to recover may be, "Nothing I can do will make any difference." This attitude ignores the importance of the older person's emotional state in the immediate present.

Approaches to this problem of ageism include expanding the helper's knowledge about aging and older persons, increasing frequency of association, stimulating sensitivity to older persons as unique human beings, and maintaining personal awareness of the subtle existence of ageism. Despite the best intentions of counselors and other helpers, some degree of prejudice against older persons is inevitable because of the common fear of death and entrenched societal attitudes.

An additional problem for helping professionals is defining counseling, particularly counseling for older persons, and clearly and perhaps frequently interpreting this definition for both older persons and those who work with them. One useful definition is that counseling is "the process through which a trained counselor assists an individual or group to make satisfying and responsible decisions concerning personal, educational, social, and vocational development" (U.S. House of Representatives, 1977). This definition makes the important points that counseling is a process which involves a relationship, one or more decisions on the part of the counselee, and positive action which can result in the counselee's further development.

Counseling older persons, known as gerontological counseling, is perhaps best identified as helping individuals to overcome losses, to establish new goals in the process of discovering that living is limited in quantity but not quality, and to reach decisions based on the importance of the present as well as the opportunities of the future.

Gerontological counseling occurs most effectively within the context of activities which meet the immediate needs of older persons. For example, counseling may occur while the counselor is transporting the counselee to the food stamp office. Likewise, counseling may take place when meals are delivered to older persons at home by paraprofessionals trained by professional counselors.

PERCEPTIONS OF COUNSELING

For many reasons older persons tend to be reluctant clients for counselors. One point to remember is that most of today's older persons are unlikely to have had experience with counselors during earlier years. In addition, discussing issues of a personal nature with someone outside the family was, in the past, frequently discouraged. Today's older persons were reared prior to the emergence of counseling as a profession. To many of them, mental health care is equated with significant psychiatric illness. Thus, to seek counseling is seen as an admission of serious problems. Further, today's older persons were reared to value independence in solving one's own problems. Seeking help from a professional is equivalent to an admission of inadequacy.

In addition to barriers among older clients to seeking counseling, the mental health system itself prevents older persons from receiving the services they may require. Therapists tend to hold negative views of older persons and their potential for growth and change. Thus, they are reluctant to use their time and resources in counseling with this population. Current estimates are that more than 25% of older persons could benefit from mental health care for significant problems. Yet, only 2 to 4% of persons seen in community mental health clinics are over age 65. If this condition continues, more than 80% of older persons needing mental health care will never receive that care (Butler & Lewis, 1983).

Murphey (1979) studied perceptions of counseling services in Florida by administrators, direct service supervisors, and service providers associated with aging programs. He noted apparent differences of opinion about the definition of counseling and concluded that counseling should be more clearly defined. Interestingly, while only 10% of the 220 responding aging projects in Florida offered counseling services, most of the direct service staff tended to see most of their work as counseling.

Most of the service providers who claim to do counseling have not been trained in counseling. In Murphey's study, service providers thought that counseling should be integrated with other services and not be provided separately. Moreover, they did not consider any special training to be necessary for the provision of counseling. While administrators thought that adequate funds were available for the provision of counseling, service providers thought that more money should be available but should be used to hire paraprofessional staff. The loose usages of the words "counseling" and "counselors" can leave little doubt that they are perceived in a wide variety of ways by the general public and, in fact, by counselors themselves.

COUNSELOR ROLES

Perhaps the many roles taken by counselors account for the differing perceptions of their functions. In the case of gerontological counselors, they function like all counselors, as trained helpers equipped with specialized knowledge and skills. These skills are applied to a diversity of situations and conditions which involve older persons. Gerontological counselors assume a variety of roles: information and referral counselor, counselors for independent living, counselors for personal growth in aging, preretirement counselors, employment counselors, financial counselors, leisure activities counselors, marital and family counselors, counselors for nursing home patients, counselors for the terminally ill, bereavement counselors, trainers for peer counselors, consultants, and advocates.

SUPPORT SYSTEMS

To consider roles of gerontological counselors separately is to risk overlooking the fact that these roles are closely interrelated. More importantly, the needs of older persons are intermeshed, with the significant consequence that older persons must be understood and helped in their totality as human beings.

Regrettably, this point of view seldom prevails at the present time. Current federal legislation places heavy emphasis on the physical needs of older persons, with considerably less attention to mental and emotional needs. Thus the efforts of the Aging Network have been largely directed toward meeting physical needs. The Mental Health System Act, while targeting services for older persons, in most states is not effective for these persons. Possibly a more balanced approach to meeting the needs of older persons might have more effective results over a period of time. From the viewpoint of gerontological counselors, an assessment of total needs is indispensable to corrective action aimed at a total effect on the life of the older individual. Also indispensable is the development of interrelated support systems.

Educational Support System

One continuing goal for this system is to explain the aging process to young people in order to combat the fear of growing old and the discrimination caused by the negative stereotypes of older persons. A second continuing goal is to develop lifelong educational programs which will enable older persons to keep abreast of social, economic, and political changes in the world and maintain a competence level that will make it possible for them to participate in meaningful ways in the life of their communities.

Social Support System

Because a social support system tends to become smaller as people grow older, efforts must be made to replenish and revitalize it as necessary. One possibility is to encourage older persons to remain active in part-time employment, leisure activities, civic affairs, and educational programs. Another is to suggest that older persons move into housing projects or form small living groups which have membership responsibilities.

Health Support System

Health insurance and hospital care are basic elements of a support system. Lifetime health care training and lifetime programs for physical exercise need further development. In addition, medical training should include greater attention to geriatric medicine and close working relationships with professional counselors so that physical and mental health care can be coordinated effectively.

Services Support System

The services support system includes access services such as transportation, information, and referral; in-home services such as homemaker and home health aid, visiting, and telephone reassurance; legal services; nutrition services; multipurpose senior centers; and housing. Additional efforts are needed to coordinate these various services in order to maximize their results for older persons. Congregate housing and community care programs represent positive steps in this direction.

For helping professionals who work with older persons one basic requirement is knowledge about the available support systems and access to them. An equally important requirement is recognizing the complexity and diversity of the needs of older persons. Success in helping older persons may well rest on the recognition that emotional needs and physical needs are inevitably interrelated. When older persons are the clients, the helping professional's scope of information and activities must indeed be broad.

COUNSELORS OF OLDER PERSONS: SPECIAL OR SPECIFIC CHARACTERISTICS?

Counselors of older persons are, first and foremost, counselors. Thus, the generic skills required of all counselors are necessary for their repertoire. All counselors must have basic counseling and communication skills, knowledge of theories and techniques of counseling, familiarity with vocational development theories, methods of assessment, and group counseling strategies. Counselors of older persons must have all of these general skills, as well as others involving special training geared to the specific needs of older persons.

Knowledge of the needs, concerns, and life situations of older persons is essential for gerontological counselors. Such information will allow counselors to use their generic skills in their work. This knowledge can be gained through integration of concepts about aging and the needs of older persons into each of the core counselor preparation areas. For example, theories of aging can become part of the curriculum in the core course on counseling theories. Assessment methods for older persons can be addressed in psychological testing courses (Myers & Blake, 1986).

In the absence of integration of information about older persons into core courses, or perhaps in addition to such integration, specialty courses in preparation of gerontological counseling are needed. The authors believe that a sequence of courses will best meet the training needs of gerontological counselors, and the senior author has developed such a sequence at the University of Florida. The five courses in this program for training counselors to meet the needs of adults across the lifespan are: Counseling Needs of Older Persons, Theories and Techniques of Counseling Older Persons, Mid-Life Counseling, Pre-Retirement and Retirement Counseling, and Practicum in Counseling Older Persons. The practicum is a supervised work experience in a setting where older persons are the primary clientele.

Continuing education coursework is recommended for gerontological counselors to help them keep abreast of new developments in the field and apply these to their work. Although standards for preparation, certification, and continuing education for gerontological counselors are not yet a reality, such standards are currently being prepared and may be implemented within the next decade.

As today's counselors-in-training plan for work with older clients, they may find few opportunities available to meet their needs. Creativity, coursework in departments other than counseling, and attendance at professional conferences will help to overcome gaps in training. Counselor educators, even in the absence of available coursework, can assist trainees through individual coursework and practicum experiences to examine their attitudes toward older persons and motivation for wanting to work with this population.

A helpful procedure is for both students and educators to remember that, just as gerontological counselors are first of all counselors, older persons are first of all persons. They have the same kinds of needs and emotions as persons of all ages. The circumstances of aging may lead to a difference in the degree to which these needs and emotions are experienced. Counselors of older clients must be aware of their attitudes toward the needs and potential of older clients. If those attitudes are negative, they will be communicated to the older person and inhibit rapport. If one firmly believes that persons possess the potential for growth and change regardless of age, then he or she can be a successful counselor to older individuals.

REFERENCES

Administration on Aging. (1979, July 31). Grants for state and community programs on aging, *referral register, part II.* Washington, DC: U.S. Government Printing Office.

American Association of Retired Persons. (1985). *A profile of older Americans, 1985.* Washington, DC.

American Association of Retired Persons. (1986). *A profile of older Americans, 1986.* Washington, DC.

Atchley, R. C. (1985). *Social forces in aging.* Belmont, CA: Wadsworth Publishing.

Atchley, R. C. (1977). *The social forces in later life.* Belmont, CA: Wadsworth Publishing.

Baltes, P., & Schaie, K. (March, 1974). The myth of the twilight years, *Psychology Today, 40,* pp.35-38.

Butler, R., (1975). *Why survive? Being old in America.* New York: Harper & Row.

Butler, R., & Lewis, M.I. (1983). *Aging and mental health: Positive psychosocial approaches.* St. Louis: Mosby.

Challenges of the '80s. (October 15, 1979). *U.S. News and World Report,* pp. 45-80.

Comfort, A. (1976, Spring). Age prejudices in America. *State Government.* no pagination.

Ganikos, M. (1977). *The expressed counseling needs and perceptions of counseling of older adult students in selected Florida community colleges.* Unpublished doctoral dissertation, University of Florida.

Graying of America. (1977, February 28). *Newsweek, 55* pp. 50-52.

Harris, L., & Associates. (1975). *The myth and reality of aging in America.* Washington, DC: The National Council on the Aging.

Hittner, C. B. (1987). The truth about senior sexuality. *Golden years. 9*(2).

Holmes, M., & Holmes, D. (1979). *Handbook of human services for older persons.* New York: Human Sciences Press.

Murphey, M. (1979). *Counseling services for older persons as perceived and provided by selected Florida aging program administrators and direct service personnel.* Unpublished doctoral dissertation, University of Florida.

Myers, J. (1978). *The development of a scale to assess counseling needs of older persons.* Unpublished doctoral dissertation, University of Florida.

Myers, J. E. (1984). *Counseling older persons: An information analysis paper based on a computer search of the ERIC data base November 1966 through May 1984.* Ann Arbor: University of Michigan.

Myers, J. E., & Blake, R. (1986). Professional preparation of gerontological counselors: Issues and guidelines. *Association for Counselor Education and Supervision, 26*(2), 137-145.

Myers, J. E., & Shelton, B. (1987). Abuse and older persons: Issues and implications for counselors. *Journal of Counseling and Development. 65*(7), 376-380.

National Association of State Units on Aging. (1985, July). *An orientation in the older Americans Act.* Revised Edition, S.C. Ficke (Editor). Washington, DC.

Rehab Group. (1979). *A digest of data on persons with disabilities.* Washington, DC: Author.

U.S. House of Representatives. (1977). *HR Bill 1118, Counseling Assistance Act of 1977.* Washington, DC: U.S. Government Printing Office.

U.S. Senate Special Committee on Aging. (1986). *Aging America, 1985-86 Edition.* Washington, DC: U.S. Department of Health and Human Services.

11

SOUTHEAST
ASIAN
PERSONS

RHONDA L. ROSSER-HOGAN, M.Ed.
University of North Carolina-Greensboro

and

JOSEPH NGUYEN
Chairperson
Board of Directors
North Carolina State Legal Defense Corporation

RHONDA L. ROSSER-HOGAN, M.ED

Rhonda L. Rosser-Hogan, M.Ed., is past Montagnard Project Director for Lutheran Family Services in North Carolina. She received her degrees from Guilford College and the University of North Carolina at Greensboro where she is studying for her doctorate in counseling with a special interest in counseling Southeast Asian refugees in America. She has traveled extensively to refugee camps in Southeast Asia and is actively involved in refugees advocacy.

JOSEPH NGUYEN

Joseph Nguyen is a student at North Carolina State University where he is a Caldwell Scholar and a North Carolina Fellow. He learned English in a Malaysian refugee camp called Pulautanga where he arrived as a Vietnamese boat person. In 1980 at the age of 15 Nguyen and his family settled in the U.S. He is currently the Chairperson, Board of Directors, North Carolina State Legal Defense Corporation.

SOUTHEAST ASIAN REFUGEES

AWARENESS INDEX

Directions: Mark each answer true, false, or don't know. Compare your answers with the scoring guide at the end of the test.

T F   1. The biggest barrier to Indochinese refugees in seeking professional counseling is their lack of fluency in English.

T F   2. The socioeconomic and psychological characteristics of Indochinese students are virtually indistinguishable from those of Asian students in general.

T F   3. For the Indochinese refugee with family members left behind in transit, life is often full of guilt.

T F   4. The Indochinese are relative newcomers, with most of them arriving in the U.S. after 1975.

T F   5. There are tremendous diversities within the small Indochinese community.

T F   6. Because of the Indochinese's strong attachment to their families, the basic family unit and power structure has remained unchanged over time.

T F   7. The Indochinese community is almost always the greatest source of support for the Indochinese refugee in time of mental distress.

T F   8. The overwhelming need to gain command of the English language compels most Indochinese refugees to encourage their youngsters to practice English at home.

T F   9. Among the newcomers from Asia in the past two decades, the Indochinese are the only true refugees.

T F 10. As a group, the Indochinese tend to be at least as affluent and educated as other Asian-American groups.

T F 11. Vietnamese and Cambodians, because of their emphasis on hard work and family orientation, have a lower than average rate of depression and marital discord.

T F 12. Most Indochinese share Confucian or Buddhist values with other Asian-Americans.

Scoring Guide for Awareness Index

1. F	4. T	7. F	10. F
2. F	5. T	8. F	11. F
3. T	6. F	9. T	12. T

THE SADNESS IN GREENSBORO

Written in Rhade by Y Sung Ding Plai
Translated into English by Rmah Dock

This deserted evening I am very sad to be alone.

This deserted evening I lonely contemplate the East, all of the mountains, I look towards the West. I only see the brook and stare at the trees. I only see the red leaves are falling down to make me sadder, this is my dream.

How miserable is my lonesome life now.

My mother is already quite old. My people are already too far from me. My life is as sad as the running river that does not return.

I am already very far from you, my beautiful highland. I am already very far from you, my beautiful highland, days and nights I never forget you.

Oh, Sadness! Who may give me a consolation?

Contemplating the sky, I only see the flying cloud. How sad my life is, when will I be able to get the happy chance?

Y Sung Plai was born in 1959 in Darlac Province of Vietnam. He fled his country during the war and came to the United States in November of 1986. Y Sung is a Montagnard refugee from the central highlands of Vietnam.

A CASE EXAMPLE

Y Nie Eban came to this country with his young wife, H'Bel, and his two preschool-aged children, Dethai and Uno. He and his family escaped the communists by hiding in the jungle for many years before fleeing to a refugee camp on the border of Thailand and Kampuchea. He witnessed the death of his two older children, one from starvation and the other from the brutal hands of the Khmer Rouge. He prefers not to talk about his two deceased children or the atrocities and persecution he and his family have suffered.

Life in the United States is perplexing to Y Nie Eban. The smells; the language; the sounds; the customs; the big, rich American people; and the many automobiles are strange to him. He has come to accept and understand that Americans are always in "the big rush," as he puts it, but he wonders why it is necessary for Americans to move so very fast in all of their pursuits.

Y Nie Eban is struggling to keep his family self-sufficient. Although he was a chief administrator in his own country, his past experience and degrees are of no use in America. He is only beginning to really understand or speak English as a second language. He finds it hard to concentrate on learning English after working as many as ten or eleven hours a day.

After working long hours and trying hard to understand his American co-workers, some of whom resent him and harbor deep prejudice, Y Nie Eban arrives home to his family. He knows his wife is lonely and longs for her family and friends, whom they both know she will never see again. Y Nie Eban tries to be cheerful upon his arrival, but it is very hard for him. He thinks to himself that the suffering in this life is sometimes too hard to bear, but he knows he must be strong for his family. Late in the evening, when the children are asleep, he and H'Bel soothe the aches of their homesickness by softly talking about the days before the Communists, the days when their lives were not so full of pain and sorrow, the days when they had a country to call their own.

Each and every day here in this strange land of America, Y Nie Eban prays for strength and patience to deal with the many frustrations that he and his family experience. Other refugees who have lived in this new land remind him that with time his life will become easier. He can only hope this is true. For now, the disturbing dreams of the brutality and hardships his family endured are haunting, and this new culture of America is overwhelming.

THE SOUTHEAST ASIAN REFUGEE POPULATION

The Southeast Asian or Indochinese refugee population is comprised of three nationalities: the Vietnamese, Laotians, and Cambodians. It also includes Vietnamese of Chinese ethnicity, tribal groups from the central highlands of South Vietnam, and various tribal groups from the mountains of Laos. Since the fall of Saigon in 1975 over 818,000 of these refugees have arrived in the United States.

These refugees all share one main characteristic. They have fled their country to escape persecution. They have among them tremendous diversity in background and education. The Vietnamese are by far the most educated, averaging nearly ten years of formal education, while the Hmong and Khmer of rural Laos and Cambodia have an extremely low educational level, averaging only 1.5 to 5 years of schooling (McLeod, 1986).

Within each nationality are vast differences in background. Among the Vietnamese, particularly those arriving immediately after the evacuation of Saigon, were academicians, bureaucratic workers, and governmental officials as well as merchants, laborers, and maids. The Vietnamese arriving after the "first wave" (termed "boat people" because of their method of escape) tend to be less educated and, consequently, less affluent than the first group. The Cambodians or Khmer come primarily from rural backgrounds influenced by the past purging of academics under Pol Pot. Khmer children were virtually unexposed to formal schooling after 1975. The Hmong people of Loas perhaps have had the most difficult time adjusting to their new culture as they come from an agrarian culture where no written language existed until 30 years ago (Doerner, 1985).

The most recent refugee group to come to the United States are the Montagnards, or "mountain people," which represent tribal groups from the central highlands of Vietnam. This ethnically distinct group of Indochinese refugees are diverse in formal education within their own group. They are Christian, both Catholic and Protestant, unlike other Indochinese refugee populations that are predominantly Buddhist or Confucian. Most of the last eleven years they spent hiding in remote jungle areas of Southeast Asia.

The Indochinese refugees have all lived through extensive and brutal civil wars and have endured incredible suffering both in their country and during their escape. They have lived under oppressive governments. Almost all Indochinese refugees have experienced the death of one or more family members, and many have witnessed these deaths. The mass killings and forced relocations of the Pol Pot regime have caused 80% of Khmer refugees to be completely cut off from family members left behind, while this percentage is 30% for the Hmong, 21% for the Chinese, and 5% for the Vietnamese (McLeod, 1986).

Indochinese refugees have lost their country, their occupational status, and their family and friends. Many have lived through the horror of forced labor camps. Upon arrival in the United States, the refugee must learn a new language and culture, find employment, and learn to attend to totally new daily tasks of living in America: paying rent, buying groceries, opening a checking account. A great tribute is due these refugees because despite the many stresses and frustrations, they are coping and succeeding in America.

PROBLEMS CONFRONTING INDOCHINESE REFUGEES

Stereotypes

MYTH #1: The "Super Achiever" Myth. The media have recently given a great deal of publicity to the super achievements of Asian-American immigrants. This has given rise to false perceptions and expectations of Southeast Asian refugees. As aforementioned, the Indochinese refugees represent three nationalities: Vietnamese, Cambodian, and Laotian. Within these three nationalities is great ethnic diversity. The Indochinese are similar in racial and physical characteristics to other Asian immigrant groups, and the majority of Americans are unaware of differences between the two groups. In reality, Indochinese are less affluent and educated than similar Asian groups with whom they are often confused.

Contrary to common perceptions that Asian students are over-achievers in school, professional high school counselors have noted that the majority of Indochinese are not college material. Hmong and Khmer students are particularly ill-prepared for academic success because of extensive warfare and unfortunate economic situations in their homeland. One high school counselor commented that to keep these students for a few semesters and teach them the rudiments of language and cultural skills before they dropped out in frustration is a major accomplishment.

An undeniable fact is that some Indochinese do excel academ-ically. These students generally tend to be from educated families in their native country. Because of their success they are the focus of media attention. Consequently, they innocently perpetuate the myth of super achievement. The fact remains, however, that most Indochinese refugee students arrive at their American schools with no language skills and must go through language training such as "English as a Second Language" (ESL) courses. The brighter few who move out of ESL classes into remedial courses tend to possess better study skills than the American children in these remedial classes. Because of their language deficiency, they do not move to regular classes but do make high marks where they are, thus perpetuating the super achiever myth.

Those students unexposed to academics in their native country and those unable to live up to the super achiever myth often experience guilt and intense family pressure. Indochinese refugee students often report that they are "shaming" their ethnic group. They try to live up to their teachers' and peers' expectations (both ethnic and American) to do well.

The Buddhist/Confucian cultural values of hard work and education are extremely important in Indochinese families. Often, well-meaning refugee parents equate poor grades with laziness, and refugee students are compared to superior Indochinese peers. At a time when refugee children are in great need of support because of "loss of face," these students remove themselves from their two most valuable assets, their ethnic peer group and family. The result is withdrawal for these Indochinese refugee students who are already conditioned by their culture to be obedient and quiet.

MYTH #2: The Indochinese as a whole are less likely to seek professional psychiatric counseling and are therefore adjusting well. While true Indochinese refugees are less likely to seek professional counseling than their American counterparts, they are far from being problem-free. The first obstacle in obtaining professional help is often financial. Although mental health centers have available free services, few refugees are aware of these services or can afford a private professional counselor.

The reluctance to enlist professional help is also rooted in their culture. All refugees suffered material and family losses during the war and in transit. However, being unfamiliar with the treatment of psychiatric problems, refugees choose not to receive help. Furthermore, the Asian culture attributes sorrow and grief to the "natural" course of one's life and does not label such mental states as "sickness" or mental distress.

The family is the basic social unit in Asian culture and individual family members rely on one another for support in times of distress. However, they are faced with a dilemma. In a culture that discourages outward expressions of emotion, family members are found needing support but being unable or unwilling to ask for it. In these cases the ethnic community is helpful if someone is present in whom they can confide. However, the ethnic community in general discourages individuals from seek professional treatment for fear that once they are "discovered," those individuals may cause the family to lose face. Many refugees with whom the authors have worked reported that they either tried to internalize their stresses or rationalize their grief rather than risk losing face for themselves and their families.

Prejudice

One major problem Indochinese refugees face in this country is pure and simple discrimination. Many Americans ignorant of the plight of these refugees believe they should not be in our country, they are lazy, and they are living on welfare. They are also often perceived as stupid because of their inability to speak English. Most Indochinese refugees in America have proven themselves to be fiercely independent, self-reliant, and hard-working individuals of normal intelligence. Negative stereotypes concerning Indochinese refugees stem from ignorance and xenophobia, conditions which may be remedied in part through education.

PERSONAL AND CAREER GUIDANCE COUNSELING NEEDS OF INDOCHINESE REFUGEES

Indochinese refugees in this country have experienced the horrors of war, near starvation, displacement, and untold other miseries. They, among other ethnic minorities, have special problems that schools and society need to recognize. First, sex roles are vastly different in America and Southeast Asia. This is a cause of family discord during adjustment to American life; Indochinese men are often disturbed that they are no longer the ultimate decision maker in the family. In his book, *From Vietnam to America*, Kelly (1977, p.119) reported that some Vietnamese men thought that "women in the United States have too much power." One counselor has noted that the greater the discrepancy between social standings in the old and new countries, the greater the stress for men. For many Indochinese men the new culture is a great test of their resourcefulness, tolerance, and courage. Prestigious employment that took years to attain in their own country has vanished from their lives. Many refugee men weather the difficulties of supporting their families here in America by performing jobs for which they are vastly over-qualified.

For many families often an economic necessity is for the wife to work. In one family, after the wife began to work she became more outgoing and questioned her husband's household supremacy. Her husband resorted to sabotaging the family's second car to prevent his wife from continuing to work. An Indochinese man is caught in a delicate dilemma. He must consider the economic necessity of having a two-income family while subsequently losing rigid control over his wife. He is also judged by his ethnic peers on his ability to exert control over his family, a large componant in his "face" in the community. He must court voluntary agencies or sponsors by showing his cooperation while at the same time often resenting them for introducing "destructive" values in his family. Many men resolve this conflict by condemning the new culture, pointing especially to the high divorce rate. They then tighten the rein over their own family, justifying their increased control as merely trying to preserve the traditional values.

During the early adjustment period, Indochinese refugee children rapidly absorb their new culture through school, television, and American peers. The teenage sub-culture the children model challenges the dominance of Indochinese parents and contributes to stress within the family unit. Indochinese parents are especially distressed by their youngsters' rapid absorption of their new culture and their own inability to make meaningful and authoritative suggestions to guide them. A senior high school counselor of Indochinese adolescents spoke of a "power shift" within the family unit with the youngster gaining control due to a quicker command of the new language and culture. Parents have difficulty retaining control when they must interact with the world through the language skills of their children. The counselor suggested that such a situation be remedied by supplying the parents with skill and information to promote greater sharing of influence within the family unit.

The older generations, wanting to retain their familiar values, are especially frustrated by their children's adoption of new American values. Children with a quicker command of English and the culture begin to see the "imperfections" of their parents and elders and actively question the traditional supremacy of the latter in the family. The parents react by tightening the grips. For example, in many Vietnamese and Laotian families, an unspoken rule is that speaking English is forbidden in the home. Parents struggling for day-to-day survival become more and more detached from the younger generations who are desperately trying to fit in with their American peers in fashion, behaviors, and values.

The result of this intergenerational cultural dilemma is an unspoken duality. Adolescents realize that in order to acculturate they must learn assertiveness and behaviors that are discouraged by their parents. They also know that they must learn and practice these values and behaviors outside of the family. Within their families, these adolescents go along with the status quo by not allowing their new values and behavior to show at home. Many Indochinese families that have adjusted successfully report a reconciliation over time between the two generations with the younger generation retaining important aspects of their cultural heritage and the elders gradually accepting some aspects of the youths' assimilation into American society.

Another problem of Indochinese refugees is that of tremendous grief for families that were left behind. Many Indochinese feel guilt for "abandoning" family members and frustrations for not being able to help them. Refugees here in America often feel the need to help family members left behind by sending home money and gifts they can ill afford. One Vietnamese high school student recently dropped out of school because he felt he needed to work more to send money home to his family.

The double burden of supporting a family in America while sending money home causes extreme frustration for the refugee and a feeling of failure in comparison to those peers whose families are intact. This causes some refugees to feel bitter, withdrawn, and removed from their peers.

The intense feeling of guilt for abandoning family members often has profound deleterious effects on adjustment to American life. One Khmer girl became extremely withdrawn from her adjusting Indochinese peers. She refused to speak English while conversing with them and looked upon her slowly Americanizing friends with disgust. She reported that she felt her adjusting friends were betraying their heritages and had no right to enjoy themselves in this country while people such as her own family were suffering at home. For many of these refugees the intense sadness over their losses, compounded by feelings of guilt, leaves them embittered, unhappy, and less able to adapt to life in their new country.

Another case example is a Laotian family that arrived in the United States without their father. The eldest son, S., was an honor student in high school and excelled at a local community college. Financial support for the family was provided by a younger sister who worked to support S, his invalid mother, and younger sister. The stress and guilt S. felt finally became overwhelming and he dropped out of school. He now works at a toy factory to support the family. S. expressed bitterness and blamed himself for "failing" when he had less than three semesters left to complete his engineering degree.

Career Needs

Indochinese students are often at a distinct disadvantage because of the stereotypes held by school personnel. Counselors and teachers often assume these students will enjoy and excel in the physical sciences and mathematics. Because of their stereotypical perceptions, they often fail to expose these students to areas and career possibilities the Indochinese are reluctant to explore.

Indochinese students often try harder at math and physical sciences because these fields allow the student to operate at a high level with little command of the English language. Additionally, many Indochinese students believe to "follow the footsteps" of their elders, who often succeeded in math and physical science-related careers, is a necessity. Furthermore, Indochinese students were victims of unjust political and social systems during the war. Consequently, they are often cynical towards the social sciences and feel a certain degree of safety in the pursuit of pure scientific truth.

In assessing and assisting Indochinese students with their career needs, the single most important task is to encourage, guide, and teach Indochinese students to become more assertive. Assertiveness is not encouraged or admired in the Asian and Indochinese cultures. While one may be successful in a technical career without having to assert oneself, the humanities require greater language fluency, confidence and, therefore, a greater degree of assertiveness. Assimilation, acculturation, and time remove some of the cultural barriers and give the student more confidence. However, as seen by the continued tendencies of second and third generation Asian students, "Americanization" is not sufficient in itself. Counseling and a concerted effort to expose Indochinese students to a wider variety of career choices are needed.

COUNSELING SERVICES FOR
INDOCHINESE REFUGEES

Indochinese refugees in this country have a need for counseling services that are germane to the experiences they have suffered. Research has pointed to the fact that for a variety of reasons only a small percentage of Indochinese refugees use mental health services. Higgibotham (1980) suggested refugees do not have access to information about types of mental health services that are available or an understanding of the types of problems mental health services are meant to address. Cultural minorities in large part do not know mental health services exist nor are they referred to mental health facilities (Padilla, Ruiz, & Alvarex, 1975). In addition, Indochinese do not perceive mental health to be separate from physical health and therefore seek mental health assistance from medical practitioners.

One primary reason for non-utilization of mental health services is the notion in Indochinese culture that mental illness is a cause for ridicule for both the refugee and the family. The strong Asian concept of "face" within the ethnic community discourages many refugees from seeking help for their emotional problems. Additionally, talking to a stranger about private problems is not within the realm of experience of the refugee. Indeed, talking about feelings is simply not a Southeast Asian behavior. Tung, (1985) related that although depression, regret, guilt, and shame weigh heavily on the Southeast Asian's mind and life, they are perceived as essentially private concerns.

Wong (1985, p. 348) found that "mental health services and support to Southeast Asian refugees have consisted of a hodge-podge of intervention attempts." The federal government funded projects in the early 1980s for mental health for Southeast Asian refugees, and in some areas of the country major projects such as the Bay Area Indochinese Mental Health Project that began where mental health providers were specifically trained to work with the special needs of Southeast Asian refugees.

Overall, however, only a paucity of trained professionals is available to help these refugees with their unique problems. Robinson (1980) aptly stated that community mental health centers are inadequate in serving Indochinese refugees. Their staffs do not possess enough expertise in their particular concerns and culture and are not bilingual. Local volunteer agencies that provide translation services to refugees are generally overworked and understaffed and do not have the necessary time to translate for refugees' mental health problems. The volunteer agencies involved in refugee resettlement have precious little time to devote to finding housing, securing employment, obtaining clothing, attending to medical appointments, and the many related concerns of helping non-English speaking families begin life in a new country with no money and no resources.

Mutual Assistance Associations, or "MAAs," that have begun in many Indochinese ethnic communities are the most helpful to the newly arriving refugee. These ethnic community groups help the refugee obtain necessary information concerning all aspects of life in America. Most importantly, these MAAs give a feeling of strength and support in absorbing the shock of being in a new country. Many leaders in these ethnic communities are the primary mental health providers for the refugee. Wong (1985) emphasized that these leaders are refugees themselves and are often dealing with concerns they have recently experienced in the trauma of relocation and resettlement. These helpers are still struggling themselves and may have unresolved grief and conflict, an important fact to remember if, indeed, ethnic leaders are to be trained mental health providers.

For the resettled Southeast Asian refugee, appropriate and culture-sensitive counseling services are sadly lacking in America. Although some areas of the country have excellent programs and experts in refugee mental health, this is not true in most areas where the largest numbers of resettled Indochinese are located. Federal and state officials should be made aware of the needs of these newest members of our society.

THE HELPING PROFESSIONAL'S ROLE

The helping professional working with the Indochinese refugee must have an in-depth cultural sensitivity not only to characteristics of Southeast Asians but also to the refugee status itself. Therapy will be irrelevant and possible detrimental if these considerations are not seriously taken into account.

Preferably, well-trained Indochinese mental health professionals and para-professionals should assist the refugee. However, as they are rarely available, American counselors assisting Indochinese refugees should be sensitive not only to the culture and to refugee status, but to many discrepancies between Eastern and Western thought. The cross-cultural counselor should be open and willing to look at emotional problems in a holistic fashion and possible employ traditional Asian cultural means of helping his or her client. Often difficulties with Khmer refugees can best be dealt with through a Buddhist monk or through prescribed ritualistic actions. Duncan and Kang (1984) found simple Khmer ceremonies were helpful with unaccompanied refugee Khmer minors coming to this country; disturbing dreams and visits by hostile spirits were alleviated. Helman (1984) noted that in societies where ill health and other forms of misfortune are blamed on social causes (witchcraft, sorcery, or evil eye), or on supernatural causes (gods, spirits, or ancestral ghosts), sacred folk healers are particularly helpful. Westermeyer and Wintrob (1979) stated that mental disorder among Laotians is largely concerned with behavior viewed as desirable or undesirable in Laotian society. Williams and Westermeyer (1983) described an incident whereby a Southeast Asian refugee woman attempted suicide because her daughter had been disrespectful in allowing a Hmong boy to carry her books home from school.

The culturally-trained therapist working with Indochinese refugees should, if at all possible, use culturally relevant techniques and/or employ Buddhist monks, respected leaders in the ethnic community, elders, and those in the Indochinese community who may be able to ascertain if the presenting problem can be dealt with through traditional methods. If working with an ethnic healer or elder is impossible, the counselor working with the Indochinese refugee has many important considerations to bear in mind. Research indicates that therapeutic interventions with Indochinese refugees should focus on the present and the immediate future rather than on the past. Kinzie, Fredrickson, Ben, Fleck, and Karls (1984) found discussing past events with the refugee leaves them feeling worse, not better. Similarly, Boehnhein, Kinzie, Rath, and Fleck (1985) found that among survivors of Cambodian concentration camps detailed inquiry often intensified symptoms. They concluded that therapy should support avoidance of past events and encourage coping with current problems.

As has been mentioned, the Indochinese refugee is uncomfortable talking about feelings, particularly to a stranger. Our American concept of counseling and mental health is unheard of by the refugee. Aside from concentrating on the present, the counselor should be goal-directed and concrete in his or her counseling interventions. In addition, since problems or crises are often the result of inadequate knowledge of our culture, frequently all that is needed is to teach the refugee what is "proper" or "improper" behavior in our culture.

In working with Indochinese refugee clients, the following suggestions are offered to American counselors:

1. Be thoroughly knowledgable about the Indochinese refugee population. Know their culture, history, and current circumstances. This understanding will be your greatest asset as a counselor

2. Concentrate on the present and future with the client. Avoid questions about their past.

3. Work toward a goal with the client. This fits into the Indochinese model of patient/counselor. Muecke (1983), Tung (1985), and Kinzie (1981) all pointed to the fact that use of medicine suggests to the Indochinese refugee patient something is being done. Similarly, working toward a goal gives the Indochinese client the feeling that the counselor is in control, as the client prefers.

4. Use ethnic leaders, monks, elders, or folk healers and employ traditional healing techniques with counseling interventions. Often a simple ritualistic ceremony may alleviate the suffering of visits from spirits and the like that are not within our own cultural realm of understanding.

5. Keep in mind that a problem or symptom may be the simple result of anxiety due to a misunderstanding or inadequate knowledge of the Indochinese refugee about our society/culture. Teach or model American behaviors to the refugee.

CONCLUDING REMARKS

Working as an American counselor with Indochinese refugees resettled in America is a challenging undertaking. The differences in culture, perspective, and the counseling process itself are all remarkably disparate. Although vast differences exist between cultures, the cross-cultural counselor is behooved to remember, in the words of Harry Stack Sullivan, "We are all more alike than different." Being sensitive to the Indochinese refugees' overwhelming concerns while at the same time acknowledging their incredible strength and endurance is one way the counselor can encourage and support the refugee. Above all, a sincere belief that the refugee can build a new and fulfilling life in this country is the key to a positive counseling encounter with the newest members of our society.

REFERENCES

Boehnhein, J.D., Kinzie, S.D., Rath, B.E, & Fleck, J. (1985). One year follow-up study of post-traumatic stress disorder among survivors of Cambodian concentration camps. *American Journal of Psychiatry, 141,* 645-650.

Doerner, W.R. (1985, July 8). "To America with skills: A wave of arrivals from the Far East enriches the country's talent pool." *Time,* 84-85.

Duncan J., & Kang, J. (1984). Use of traditional Cambodian culture as mental health program to help children cope with separation and loss. Paper presented at the Unaccompanied Minors Conference, Washington, D.C.

Helman, C. (1984). *Culture, health and illness.* Bristol: Wright Publishing.

Higgibotham, H.N. (1980). Culture and the role of client expectancy in psychotherapy. In Hammet and Brislin (Eds.), *Research in Culture and Learning: Language and Conceptual Studies.* Honolulu: East-West Center.

Kelly, G. (1977). *From Vietnam to America: A chronicle of the Vietnamese immigration to the U.S.* Boulder, CO: Westview Press.

Kinzie, J.D. (1981). Evaluation and psychotherapy of Indochinese refugee patients. *American Journal of Psychotherapy, 35,* 251-261.

Kinzie, J.D., Fredrickson, R.H., Ben, R., Fleck, J. & Karls, W. (1984). Post traumatic stress disorder among survivors of Cambodian concentration camps. *American Journal of Psychiatry, 141,* 645-650.

McLeod, B. (1986, July). The oriental express: Asian-American immigrants are seen as a 'model' minority on a fast track to success. Their own view is less idyllic. *Psychology Today*, 48-52.

Muecke, M.A. (1983). Caring for Southeast Asian refugee patients in the U.S.A. *American Journal of Public Health, 73*, 431-438.

Padilla, A. M., Ruiz, R. A., and Alvarez, R. (1975). Community mental health services for the Spanish-speaking/surnamed population. *American Psychologist, 30*, 892-905.

Robinson, C. (1980). Special report: Physical and emotional health care needs of Indochinese refugees. Washington, DC: Indochina Resource Action Center.

Tung, T.M. (1985). Psychiatric care for Southeast Asians: How different is different. In T.C. Owan (Ed.), *Southeast Asian mental health: Treatment, prevention, services, training and research.* National Institute of Mental Health.

Westermeyer, J., & Wintrob, R. (1979). "Folk" explanations of mental illness in rural Laos. *American Journal of Psychiatry, 136*, 901-905.

Williams, C.L. & Westermeyer, J. (1983). Psychiatric problems among adolescent Southeast Asian refugees: A descriptive study. *The Journal of Nervous and Mental Disease, 171*, 79-84.

Wong, H.Z. (1985). Training for mental health service providers to Southeast Asian refugees: Models, strategies, and curricula. In T.C. Owan (Ed.), *Southeast Asian mental health: Treatment, prevention, services, training and research.* National Institute of Mental Health.

12

ASIAN-AMERICANS

DIANE M. SUE, Ph.D.
School Psychologist
Everett School District
Washington

and

DAVID SUE, Ph.D.
Director
Counseling Program
Western Washington University

DIANE M. SUE, Ph.D.

Diane Sue, who is a school psychologist for the Everett School District in the state of Washington, received her doctorate in Educational Psychology from the University of Michigan, Ann Arbor. Dr. Sue's special interests include minority populations, consultation, and classroom management strategies.

DAVID SUE, Ph.D.

David Sue, Ph.D., is currently Director of the Counseling Program at Western Washington University. He received his undergraduate degree at the University of Oregon and completed his doctorate at Washington State University in 1973. Dr. Sue has research and clinical interests in Asian-Americans, behavior therapy, and human sexuality. Dr. Sue frequently collaborates with his brothers, Derald and Stan, on articles concerning Asian-Americans.

ASIAN-AMERICANS
AWARENESS INDEX

Directions: Mark each answer true, false, or don't know. Compare your answers with the scoring guide at the end of the test.

T F 1. Most Japanese voiced strong objections to the United States government to their forced evacuation to detention camps during World War II.

T F 2. The incidence of poverty among elderly Chinese is much higher than that for elderly black and Spanish-speaking populations.

T F 3. College enrollment rates for Chinese and Japanese between the ages of 18-24 is quite high, but the percentage of these individuals who actually complete college is surprisingly small.

T F 4. Most studies indicate the Chinese and Japanese groups have highly similar values and family structure.

T F 5. Asian-Americans appear to have as varied a choice of careers as their caucasian counterparts.

T F 6. Most Asian-American clients feel more comfortable in a structured counseling environment than one that is unstructured.

T F 7. Most second and third generation Chinese and Japanese children in the United States use English as the primary language in their homes.

T F 8. Asian-American clients often terminate prematurely from therapy.

Scoring Guide for Awareness Index

1. T	4. T	7. F
2. T	5. F	8. T
3. F	6. T	

PERCEPTIONS, SENSITIVITY, FEELINGS

The following poems were written by fifth and sixth grade children from Franklin School in Berkeley, California as part of a class project. They illustrate the perceptions, sensitivity, and feelings of being a member of a minority group in American. (D.W. Sue, 1973, pp. 397-399.)

I'm an Asian and I'm proud of it. I'm a person although some people don't look upon me as one. They call me names and think it's funny! Sure I get called names. Do you think I like it? After all, how would you feel if someone called you a "Ching, chong Chinaman" or a "Nip"? They can't even tell us apart.

They say things about our culture like, "They write so funny." Even our language they make fun of by going Ching, cho chu.

I'm an Asian. I've got dignity but the thing I don't have is friendship.

Robert Chung

Asians are silent people
Never speaking of distress
Bearing much in their heart
The burden of the silent one.

Standing up to their rights
Trying to prove loyal by working hard.
America, a place of hopes...
For white people only!

Leah Appel

I am an Asian. Asians are proud people and I am proud to be Asian. Many people call me Caucasian, especially blacks. I have been called names, as many people have. Asians have been placed in concentration camps, discriminated and bombed. Yet at this moment, they are fighting and dying for their country in Vietnam.

People who don't know the Asian history say things like "All Chinese are laundry men" and "All Japanese are gardeners." Of course, I know it was the only menial labor available when the immigrants first came to America.

I hate that song with, "Japanese eyes slant down and Chinese eyes slant up." Last year I was the only Asian in my class. As an insult they called people "Chinese spies." It is enough to make you sick.

But, I am proud to be Asian and I want all to know.
Naomi Nishimura

Yellow is the sun coming
up in the morning And the sun coming down
in the evening
Yellow is a house being painted
Yellow is the color of some pencils
Yellow is the sunset,
Yellow is the sunrise.
Yellow is the color of some paper.
It's the peeling of a
grapefruit or lemon,
Yellow is the shine
of a light.
Yellow is a banana.
Yellow is a color that
is very bright to
everyone.
Yellow is me!

Jon Mishima

Material written by children on pp. 242-3 is reproduced from Derald Wing Sue, "Asians are....," The Personnel and Guidance Journal, Vol. 51, No. 6, Feb 1973, pp. 397-399 with permission from American Personnel and Guidance Association.

POPULATION

Approximately 3.7 million Asian-Americans are in the United States, accounting for approximately 1.6% of the total population (U.S. Census, 1980). Asian-Americans continue to be one of the fastest growing minority groups. Difficulties arise in an attempt to characterize Asian-Americans because this population is comprised of so many different groups. At least 29 distinct subgroups are within the Asian-American population, each with unique values, customs, religion, and language (Yoshioka, Tashima, Chew, & Murase, 1981). Compounding the problem are the differences that exist within specific Asian-American groups in terms of acculturation, primary language, and generational status in the United States.

The Asian-American population consists both of recent immigrants, many of whom are of refugee status, and individuals who have been in the United States for many decades. Tremendous diversity exists among the Asian-American population with respect to cultural assimilation, knowledge of the English language, socioeconomic status, and educational background. The unique needs of Southeast Asian refugees are addressed in Chapter 11.

CHINESE AND JAPANESE AMERICANS

The diversity of Asian-Americans groups, each with different cultural norms and values, prevents adequate representation of each of the groups in this chapter. The focus of the present chapter, therefore, will be primarily on the Chinese and Japanese groups, which currently comprise two of the largest Asian-American populations in the United States and which have the earliest history of entry into this country. According to the 1980 census, the Chinese are the largest Asian-American subgroup, with a population of 806,207, of which 65% live in California, New York, or Hawaii. The Japanese are the second largest subgroup, comprising .3% of the U.S. population; the majority of Janapese live in Hawaii or California.

The rate of current immigration is much higher among the Chinese than the Japanese. Between 1970 and 1980, in states with more than 15,000 Asian residents, the Chinese population increased by 73% compared to an increase of only 18% in the Japanese population (U.S. Census, 1980). Whereas the majority of Chinese-Americans are of immigrant status, the Japanese-American population is increasingly characterized as American born.

Brief History of Chinese and Japanese in America

Asian-American groups immigrated to the United States for much the same reasons as other immigrant groups—the pursuit of financial security and an improved standard of living. The first Asian group to immigrate heavily to the United States was the Chinese in the 1840s. The immigration was triggered by the discovery of gold in California coupled with a disastrous crop failure in China. In contrast to other immigrant groups, the Chinese were "sojourners"—individuals who did not seek to settle permanently but who desired an opportunity to earn some money and return to China. The Chinese immigrants, who were primarily males, worked as laborers in gold mines and on railroads or were employed at other less desirable jobs such as laundry work. They were subjected to massive discrimination and prejudice soon after arriving. These attitudes resulted in the Exclusion Act of 1882 which prevented the legal immigration of Chinese from 1882 until 1944, when the act was repealed. This ban resulted in the separation of husbands from their wives for decades and a highly unequal sex ratio. In 1890, over 100,000 Chinese males and only 3,868 Chinese women were in the United States (Wong, 1973). Not until the 1960s was a closer balance attained. Today the elderly males still form a higher percentage than their female counterparts (Office of Special Concerns, 1974; U.S. Census, 1980).

Currently, the Chinese are considered a successful minority. However, they form a bimodal distribution with one mode composed of a highly successful group and the second mode encompassing much less successful individuals. More than 40% of the Chinese-Americans earn an annual income of less than $4,000, which is a higher percentage of poverty than the average for the United States (Office of Special Concerns, 1974). Recent immigrants who gain employment in low paying and unskilled work will increase the percentage of poor Chinese. The immigrants migrate to New York City and the larger cities in California, aggravating the ghetto-like conditions in Chinatowns.

Immigration of the Japanese in large numbers began in the 1890s from Hawaii and Japan. They also were lured by the promise of better conditions and wealth in the United States and filled the demand for an inexpensive source of labor to replace Chinese. Many Japanese males came to the Unites States to live and later sent away for picture brides from Japan. As laborers, they worked on railroads and in canneries. Because the great majority were from the farming class, many turned to farming and worked on unwanted lands or found work as agricultural laborers. Although the Japanese were considered more desirable than the Chinese because they brought their families, prejudice and discrimination quickly followed. In 1906, the San Francisco Board of Education issued an order segregating Japanese from White school children (Masuda, 1973). The Gentlemen's Agreement limited immigration and the Alien Land Act of 1920 (which was directed primarily against the Japanese) prevented them from purchasing land. An editorial in the **San Francisco Chronicle** in 1920 reflected the attitude of white Americans at the time (Ogawa, 1973):

> The Japanese boys are taught by their elders to look upon...American girls with a view to future sex relations...What answer will the fathers and mothers of America make...? The proposed assimilation of the two races is unthinkable. It is morally undefensible and biologically impossible. American womanhood is far too sacred to be subjected to such degeneracy. An American who would not die fighting rather than yield to that infamy does not deserve the name...(p. 7).

Feelings against the Japanese culminated in the location of over 110,000 persons of Japanese ancestry into detention camps during World War II. Effects of these camps resulted in financial ruin for many Japanese families, disrupted the family structure, and served to break up Japantowns (Kitano, 1969). Currently, the Japanese are considered a model minority; however, they tend to be underemployed (Office of Special Concerns, 1974).

SPECIAL PROBLEMS

As a group, Asian-Americans have not received widespread attention from educators, counselors, or state and federal officials. The prevailing view that Asian-Americans are model minorities and problem free has resulted in limited financial and moral support. Although special concerns sessions were held for Blacks, Spanish speaking, and Native Americans at the White House Conference on Aging in 1971, Asian-Americans were not included until a request was made by Asian-American groups (Asian-American Elderly, 1972). This exclusion occurred in spite of statistics from the Office of Special Concerns (1974) that the incidence of poverty among elderly Chinese is much higher than that for elderly Black and Spanish-speaking populations. Similarly, Asian-Americans were originally not included in the National Institute for Mental Health Center for Minority Group Programs since problems among this population were unknown (Brown & Ochberg, 1973). Asian-Americans frequently are not categorized as minorities and are often not eligible for affirmative action programs. One Asian-American applying for admission to graduate school was told that in order to qualify as a minority group member he would have to furnish information indicating that he came from a disadvantaged background. Members of other minority groups were not required to furnish this information (Sue, Sue, & Sue, 1975).

Counselors and educators tend to feel that Asian-Americans experience few adjustment difficulties, a view which has been supported by the popular press. In a **Psychology Today** article, "The Oriental Express" (McLeod, 1986) was pointed out the "success" of the 700,000 Indochinese refugees who have settled in the United States since 1975; the majority were either employed or attending school. Approximately 27% of children of boat people attending school in the U.S. have an "A" average. The article also pointed out, however, that 40% of those who had white collar or professional jobs were underemployed. This success myth masks the discrimination and prejudice that Asian-Americans still face (Governor's Asian American Advisory Council, 1973) and has resulted in a lack of financial and government interest. Reflecting the lack of attention placed on Asian-Americans is the finding by Yee (1973), who examined 300 social studies textbooks for elementary and secondary schools. Approximately 75% of these books made no mention of Chinese at all, and the rest provided minimal coverage involving Chinatowns, the development of silk, and Oriental customs.

Although the model minority image has persisted for almost two decades, more recent press coverage has begun to highlight

Asian-American concerns, including subtle forms of discrimination in education and employment settings (Hassan, 1987). In a 1980 U.S. Commission on Civil Rights report was concluded that, although some Asian-Americans are highly successful, the diversity of the population must be acknowledged. Further, the report confirmed that Asian-Americans earn far less than White Americans with equivalent educational levels and that discriminatory employment practices continue.

Housing

Problems among Asian-Americans are not highly visible because many of them occur in Chinatowns. Twenty percent of all Chinese housing is overcrowded. This percentage is 33% in New York City. San Francisco's Chinatown spans 42 square blocks and contains 885 persons an acre, which is ten times the national average (Yee, 1970; Loo & Ong, 1984). Exacerbating the problem is the continued influx of Asian immigrants to communities already overcrowded.

In urban areas, overcrowded living conditions, unemployment, economic exploitation, youth gangs and related criminal behavior, and limited access to health care are daily realities. These stresses may be compounded by concern over immigration status.

In the literature about the Chinese, a frequent misconception involves the mistaken belief that the Chinese (both in the United States and abroad) prefer crowded living conditions and live under these conditions with no ill effects. An interview study undertaken in San Francisco's Chinatown by Loo and Ong (1984) strongly challenges these beliefs. The vast majority (99%) of respondents indicated negative attitudes towards overcrowding in the home and in the neighborhood. Not only were these attitudes consistently expressed, respondents were also able to articulate stressors associated with crowded living conditions including psychological stresses ("makes me feel short-tempered"; "I get in a bad mood"; "Crowding kills your personality"; "It makes me yell at my kids"; "distrust of others"; "I become unreasonable"), and environmental or health risks ("no fresh air," "unsanitary," "too much noise") (Loo and Ong, 1984, p. 72).

Those working with individuals who live under extremely crowded conditions need to realize that frequently few, if any, housing alternatives exist. We need to remember that such living conditions are often the result of social, economic, and linguistic disadvantages experienced by the client, and that a client's sense of "helplessness" may be quite real.

Testing and Education

For many Asian-Americans, entering school with strange and confusing surroundings can be a frightening experience. A lack of facility with English provides an additional disadvantage. Information from the Office of Special Concerns (1974) indicated that 62% of the Japanese in the United States for three or more generations speak predominantly Japanese as children. Among Chinese children under the age of fourteen, 96% of those who are foreign-born speak Chinese and 70% of the second generation children speak Chinese in their homes. Facility with English will continue to be a problem for future generations of Asian-Americans. Because of this difficulty, Asian-Americans may be at a disadvantage with respect to tests such as the **Graduate Record Examination** and the **Miller Analogies Test** which depend heavily on familiarity with English. Watanabe (1973) reported that at the University of California at Berkeley more than one-half of the students of Asian descent failed to demonstrate competence in college-level reading and composition, a failure rate twice that of the general campus population.

Another educational concern has emerged recently related to alleged discrimination in college admission procedures (Hassan, 1987). Asian-American groups have recently challenged admission practices at competitive schools, contending that Asian-American applicants have the lowest acceptance rate of any group, despite the fact that their grades and overall academic standing are higher than the majority of applicant subgroups (Ho & Chin, 1983).

Personal Stress and Conflict

Constant exposure to the values and norms of the host culture, as well as the lack of information on the culture of Asian-Americans in schools and society, may produce stress and conflict. Japanese-Americans have been found to be more tense and apprehensive than their Caucasian counterparts (Meredith & Meredith, 1966). Both Chinese and Japanese students are characterized as internalizing blame and experiencing feelings of isolation, anxiety, and nervousness (Ayabe, 1971; Fenz & Arkoff, 1962; Sue & Kirk, 1973). Chinese-American college students also display a higher fear of negative evaluation and lower assertiveness than Caucasian college students (Sue, Ino, & Sue 1983). Self-esteem problems have been found in Asian elementary students. They were twice as likely as Whites to endorse a statement that "good luck is more important for success than hard work," an indication that they had less sense of control over their environment (Coleman, Campbell, Hobson, McPartland, Mood, Weinfeld, & York, 1972).

PERSONAL AND COUNSELING NEEDS OF ASIAN-AMERICANS

Traditional cultural values have a significant impact on the psychological characteristics of Asian-Americans, particularly those individuals who are the least acculturated. Value conflicts, loneliness, passivity, conformance, deference and reserve are found with greater frequency in Asian students than in Caucasian student groups (Ayabe, 1971; Meredith & Meredith, 1966; Sue & Frank, 1973). Although traits such as passivity, deference, and reserve might be interpreted negatively from a Western cultural perspective, these traits are strongly supported by Asian values. Although indicators show increasing assimilation and changes in social roles within Asian populations (Fong, 1973; Levine & Montero, 1973), Asian-Americans will continue to show unique personality and interest patterns for generations to come. A critical issue for mental health professionals is for them to have an understanding of these cultural values since they relate to rapport building, symptom expression, and comfort with various thera-peutic techniques. Additionally, appropriate conceptualization of the presenting problem frequently necessitates a solid grasp of cultural values and interpersonal dynamics within a specific cultural group.

Values

Chinese and Japanese groups share many similar values. In both cultures, the families are patriarchal with the father in authority. Parent to child communications are formal and flow downward. Relationships between family members as well as role expectations are well defined and each member's position is highly interdependent. Good behaviors such as filial piety (respect, obligation, and obedience to one's parents), achievement, and obedience are defined clearly, and an individual's behavior reflects upon the entire family. Control of the children is maintained by fostering feelings of shame and guilt. These values account for the importance of structure and deference in Asian-Americans.

In working with an Asian-American client, often the counselor will discover that the client has conflicts between traditional and Western values. Traditional values support obedience to parental desires (as it relates to occupational goals, choice of friendships, leisure time activities, etc.), whereas Western values support individual freedom of choice in these pursuits. Asian-American clients may be in a situation where familial *expectations* are for the financial support for aging parents, including the expectation that an aging parent be taken into one's home. Conflicts may arise when the client does not have the financial means for such support or when the more acculturated client has conflicts between Western goals of personal fulfillment and traditional values of family responsibility. The obligation often is felt most strongly by the eldest son. S. Sue and Morishima (1982) presented the case of Mae C., who had immigrated from Hong Kong several years earlier:

> At the advice of a close friend, Mae C. decided to seek services at a mental health center. She was extremely distraught and tearful as she related her dilemma. Since arriving in the United States, Mae met and married her husband, who was also a recent immigrant from Hong Kong. Their marriage was apparently going well until her husband succeeded in bringing over his parents from Hong Kong. While not enthusiastic about having her parents-in-law live with her, Mae realized her husband wanted to help them and that both she and her husband were obligated to help their parents.

> After the parents arrived, Mae found that she was expected to serve them. For example, the mother-in-law would expect Mae to cook and serve dinner, to wash all the clothes, and to do other chores. At the same time she would constantly complain that Mae did not cook dinner the right way, that the house was always messy, and that Mae should wash certain clothes separately. Mae would occasionally complain to her husband about his parents. The husband would excuse his parents demands by indicating, "They are my parents and they're getting old." In general, he avoided any potential conflict; if he took sides, he supported his parents. (pp. 76-77)

This case illustrates the impact that cultural values may have on counseling needs and the necessity of understanding the significance of these values for all involved.

Independence and Self-Reliance

Chinese and Japanese children feel a much greater sense of obligation towards the family and parents than do Caucasians. As Hsu (1953, p. 72) observed, "The most important thing to Americans is what parents should do for the children; to Chinese, what children should do for their parents." In Chinese stories, personal sacrifices for the sake of filial piety are rewarded while in stories such as Cinderella and Hansel and Gretel to which Americans are exposed, the children defeat evil adults. Family expectations of unquestioning obedience often produce problems when Asian children are exposed to American values of independence and self-reliance. These conflicts may be revealed during counseling sessions:

> John's parents had always had high expectations of him and constantly pressured him to do well in school. They seemed to equate his personal worth with his ability to maintain good grades. This pressure caused him to spend endless hours studying, and generally he remained isolated from social activities. John's more formalized training was in sharp contrast to the informality and spontaneity demanded in Caucasian interpersonal relationships. His circle of friends was small, and he was never really able to enjoy himself with others. John experienced much conflict because he was beginning to resent the demands and the pressure his parents put on him. His deep seated feelings of anger toward his parents resulted in passive aggressive responses such as failure in school and physical symptomology.

As Sue (1981) pointed out, the case of John illustrates possible conflicts faced by Asian students between their loyalty to the family and desires for personal independence. Learned patterns of emotional restraint and formality interfere with social interactions, and feelings of guilt and depression result when failing to live up to parental expectations.

Educational Expectations

The pressure to succeed academically among Asians is very strong. From early childhood, outstanding achievement is emphasized because it is a source of pride for the entire family.

Chinese mothers are more likely than White mothers (41% versus 11%) to rate school achievement as "very important" (Sollenberger, 1968). This finding was surprising since 47% of the mothers and 52% of the fathers in the study sample had received no more than elementary school education and were from the lower socio-economic class. Reflecting the emphasis on education is the finding that college enrollment rates for Chinese and Japanese between the ages of 18 and 24 and the percentage completing college is higher than any other group in the United States. Parental expectations for achievement can be an additional stress factor in young Asian-Americans.

Emotional Restraint

In Chinese and Japanese cultures restraint of emotions is emphasized because emotions are viewed as potentially disruptive forces on the family structure. Because of this restraint, emotional expression is considered a sign of immaturity and is suppressed. Most Americans, however, feel that the expressing of emotions is indicative of individuals who are mature and accepting of themselves. The conflict produced by these differences in values is illustrated in this example of an Asian placed in a group situation.

> The Japanese group member is deterred from directly confronting other group members because he has been taught that it is impolite to put people on the spot... The admission and display of personal inadequacy, even in a counseling group is a sign of familial defect... In most situations the Japanese person tends to be non-expressive. He has been raised [reared] since childhood not to show his emotions. Thus, although he may be moved by what is occurring in the group, he is almost instinctively restrained from revealing his concern, and facial expression remains passive... One Caucasian characterized this behavior as a sign of noncaring, and it brought forth this exclamation from him, "Doesn't this have any effect on you? Don't you care at all?" (Kaneshige, 1973, pp. 408-410)

Kaneshige suggested that in group situations involving Asians extra effort has to be made to produce a non-threatening climate. Confidentiality must be stressed and responses from Asians should be actively elicited while minimizing interruptions by other group members.

Career Choices

Sue and Frank (1973) found that in regard to choice of career fields, Chinese and Japanese students were more likely than the general student body to show interest patterns and career majors in non-social science fields such as engineering, chemistry, biology, and physics. Similar findings were obtained for a sample of Chinese-American students attending a large midwestern university (Sue, Ino, & Sue, 1983). Watanabe (1973) hypothesized that the under-representation of Asians in the social science areas may be due partly to culture since forceful self-expression is not reinforced. However, an element of discrimination and prejudice may exist against Asians in the social science fields. Many well meaning counselors may unintentionally restrict the career choices of Asians in the social sciences because of the stereotypic notions that Asians are good in the physical sciences and poor in people relationship areas. An explanation offered for the higher representation of technical majors among Asian-Americans is that less discrimination and more objective evaluation of skills and abilities will occur in technical areas, where verbal skills or assimilation to Western values are less likely to be assessed. As with any group that has faced restricted career choices, careful exploration of all possible fields must be presented to Asian-American students.

Variations in Acculturation

Mental health professionals must remember that a client may be acculturated in some areas but not in all areas. Acculturation can be assessed on the basis of the number of years an individual has lived in the United States; age at the time of immigration; the political, economic, and educational background of the country of origin; and the individual's professional background (Lee, 1982). In general, the earlier the age at the time of immigration, the longer the length of time in the United States, the higher the level of professional attainment, and the more similarity between the United States and the country of origin, the more we can expect that acculturation has progressed.

Sue and Zane (1987) highlighted the critical importance of awareness of individual differences in the backgrounds of ethnic minority clients and warned that overgeneralization or over-reliance on cultural explanations may hinder a therapeutic relationship as much as failure to acknowledge cultural factors.

Typical Presenting Problems

On the whole, Asian-Americans are less likely to seek mental health counseling than are other groups. Additionally, those who do seek treatment tend to be more significantly disturbed, on the average, than are non-Asians who seek treatment (Sue & Sue, 1987). Additionally, depression is more common among Asian-American groups, particularly Koreans, than among the general population (Kuo, 1984).

From an Asian cultural perspective, emotional difficulties experienced by a family member are seen to reflect negatively upon the entire family unit. For this reason, reluctance may be present on the part of the emotionally-stressed individual or family member to acknowledge the need for mental health counseling until the problem becomes quite severe.

Some recent investigations suggest that Asian-Americans' conceptualization of mental illness may differ from traditional Western views and that this may have an impact on typical presenting problems. Asian-Americans are more likely to feel that mental illness is associated with organic variables and that mental health involves willpower and the avoidance of morbid thoughts (Lum, 1982; Sue, Wagner, Ja, Margullis, & Lew, 1976).

Rather than describing specific emotions, Asian-Americans (including refugees) are likely to talk about somatic complaints such as headaches, insomnia, fatigue, heart palpitations, dizziness, or general aches and pains during therapy sessions (Brown, Stein, Huang, & Harris, 1973; Sue & Sue, 1987; Boken & Campbell, 1984).

IMPLICATIONS OF CULTURAL VALUES ON TRADITIONAL COUNSELING

Many counselors do not understand why Asian-American clients do not actively participate in the counseling process and often label them "repressed" or "resistant" (Sue & Sue, 1972). Such reactions illustrate the problems that exist when the helping professional and the client differ in racial and ethnic backgrounds or when the professional lacks understanding of the client's cultural background or degree of acculturation.

Differences in value orientations and expectations may be responsible for premature termination of therapy among minority group members. Sue and McKinney (1975) found in their study of 17 mental health centers that more than 50% of the Asian-American clients dropped out of therapy after only one session as compared to 29% of Caucasian clients. Sue and Zane (1987) argued that an essential component is for therapists to gain credibility with clients within the first few sessions of treatment. If this does not happen, premature termination may occur.

Conceptualization of the problem, means for problem resolution, and goals for treatment are all critical issues and can all be affected by cultural factors. Credibility may be reduced by failure to acknowledge cultural factors or by overgeneralization of cultural knowledge. The importance of meaningful gain early in the therapeutic process also has been emphasized as a method of increasing credibility and avoiding premature termination (Sue & Zane, 1987).

To obtain an adequate understanding of the effects of cultural values on counseling, one needs to examine some of the characteristics of traditional forms of counseling and contrast them with the values of Asian-Americans. Sue and Sue (1977) identified three types of goals or expectations in counseling that may be sources of conflict with minority group members.

First, most counselors expect their clients to exhibit openness and psychological mindedness. To do so, however, the client must be fluent in English and aware of Western cultural concepts of the counseling process. Because many Asian-Americans come from a bilingual background, they may be disadvantaged in this form of verbal expression. Asian clients also have learned to restrain emotional expression and feel that this repression represents a sign of maturity. Additionally, Asian clients may have an expectation of what should happen in a counseling session, looking at counseling as an advice-giving process rather than an insight-oriented process. These factors can hinder verbal communication, and a counselor who is inexperienced with clients from Asian groups may conclude erroneously that the individual is resistant or repressed.

Second, the process of counseling involves the revelation of intimate details on the part of the client. The cultural upbringing of Chinese and Japanese clients may be in opposition to this goal. Discussion of personal problems is difficult because such disclosure is felt to reflect not only on the individual but also on the whole family. The pressure from the family not to reveal personal matters to strangers is strong. In addition, the Asian client comes to the counseling situation expecting advice or practical solutions rather than insight into the nature of his or her problem. Many Asian-Americans believe that mental health is due to the avoidance of morbid thoughts and that mental illness has an organic basis (Tsai, Teng, & Sue, 1979). Problems may be presented in the form of somatic complaints or educational and occupational difficulties. A focus on personality dynamics at the beginning may be misunderstood and serve to drive the client away. History-taking, without adequate explanation, also may be offensive to the client (Tsue & Schultz, 1985).

Third, the counseling environment is often an ambiguous one for the client. The therapist listens while the client talks about the problem. In many cases, little direction is given. The unstructured nature of the counseling environment adds additional stress to Asian-American clients who prefer concrete, tangible, and structured approaches to problems. The pattern of communication also may be unsettling. Asian-Americans may have been reared in an environment in which communication flows down from an authority figure. The counselor may be expected to initiate and direct the conversation. Placed in a situation where the Asian-American client is asked to initiate conversations, the counselor will likely receive only short phrases or sentences. A counselor may respond negatively to Asian-American clients, not knowing that, for them, silence and deference may be a sign of respect.

These factors indicate the importance of flexibility on the part of the counselor and helping professional in working with Asian-Americans. Because an Asian-American will already feel much ambivalence in seeking therapy, a helping professional needs to use a gradual approach. Confrontation will increase already present feelings of guilt and shame. Instead of immediately focusing on personal matters, the counselor may follow the lead of the client and discuss the presenting problem even if it is considered to be "superficial." Sue and Sue (1972) presented a case in which meaningful material was obtained after the individual completed the **Edwards Personal Preference Schedule.** The presenting problem revolved around vocational counseling. The counselor's impression was that the client was encountering conflict over parental expectations of him as the oldest son. Direct approaches to discuss this problem were not successful. However, a discussion of test results in a non-threatening manner provided the opening.

COUNSELOR: Let's explore the meaning of your scores in greater detail as they relate to future vocations. All right?

CLIENT: Okay.

COUNSELOR: Your high score on achievement indicates that whatever you undertake you would like to excel and do well in. For example, if you enter pharmacology, you'd do well in that field (client nods head). However, your high change score indicated that you like variety and change.... You may tend to get restless at times...maybe feel trapped in activities that bore you.

CLIENT: Yeah.

COUNSELOR: Do you see this score (abasement score)?

CLIENT: Yeah, I blew the scale on that one. What is it?

COUNSELOR: Well, it indicates you tend to be hard on yourself. For example, if you were to do poorly in pharmacy school, you would blame yourself for the failure....

CLIENT: Yeah, yeah...I'm always doing that...I feel that...it's probably exaggerated.

COUNSELOR: Exaggerated?

CLIENT: I mean... being the oldest son.

COUNSELOR What's it like to be the oldest son?

CLIENT: Well...there's a lot of pressure and you feel immobilized. Maybe this score (points to change scale) is why I feel so restless. (Sue & Sue, 1972, pp. 642-643)

This approach led to a discussion of the student's resentment toward his parents for the pressure to succeed and eventually to a successful resolution of the problem. The provision of structure as well as a careful explanation of the counseling process can do much to facilitate mutual understanding. Once rapport and trust have been formed, a counselor will have greater freedom in exploring potential areas of conflict.

If group therapy is used with Asian-American clients, expectations of client behavior should again take into account cultural values (Ho, 1984). A group leader might be viewed as an authority figure who will give direct guidance, and the members will have the greatest comfort with structured, goal-directed work with clear objectives. Again, confrontation techniques are likely to be highly counterproductive. Exposure of family conflicts or an open exchange of ideas and opinions also might be difficult for Asian clients. Ho (1984) also recommended that groups be as homogeneous as possible with respect to language, ethnicity, generational status, and cultural variables within the native country. Cross-sex groupings may be difficult, particularly for clients with minimal acculturation. Adequately preparing each client to participate in a group session (discussing confidentiality, problem-solving, honest interpersonal exploration, and common feelings of first time group members) is also important. Additionally, periodic scheduling of individual conferences with each group member can be beneficial in monitoring comfort level with group processes.

Finally, some words of caution should be presented. Most Asian-Americans are able to handle cultural conflicts. The assumption should not be made that all Asian-Americans experience significant stress related to cultural values. Great variability exists among Asian-Americans in the degree to which they are influenced by cultural expectations. Many Asian-Americans are as assertive as Caucasians. A counselor, educator, or other human service worker should not automatically assume Asian-Americans will have conflicts over emotional or assertive expression. Mental health professions must be careful not to rely on generalizations of Asian-Americans as a group, but must instead seek to understand the specific background of each client. The understanding of Asian values may sensitize individuals to potential conflicts and conflict areas, but counselors will still have to rely on their clinical judgement and knowledge of cultural differences.

REFERENCES

Asian-American Elderly. (1972). *The White House Conference on Aging* (1971). Washington, DC: U.S. Government Printing Office.

Ayabe, H.L. (1971). Deference and ethnic differences in voice levels. *Journal of Social Psychology, 85*, 181-185.

Boken, J.A., & Campbell, W. (1984). Indigenous psychotherapy in the treatment of a Loatian refugee. *Hospital and Community Psychiatry, 35*, 281-282.

Brown, B.S., & Ochberg, F.M. (1973). Key issues in developing a national minority mental health program at NIMH. In C. Willie, B. Kramer, & B.S. Brown (Eds.), *Racism and mental health: Essays*. Pittsburgh: University of Pittsburgh Press.

Brown, T.R., Stein, K.M., Huang, K., & Harris, D.E. (1973). Mental illness and the role of mental health facilities in Chinatown. In S. Sue & W. Wagner (Eds.), *Asian-Americans: Psychological Perspectives* (pp. 212-234). Palo Alto, CA: Science and Behavior Books.

Coleman, J.S., Campbell, E.Q., Hobson, C.J., McPartland, J., Mood, A.M., Weinfield, F.D., & York, R.L. (1972). The locus of control and academic performance among racial groups. In S.S. Gutterman (Ed.), *Black psyche*. Berkeley: The Glenessary Press.

Fenz, W., & Arkoff, A. (1962). Comparative need patterns of five ancestry groups in Hawaii. *Journal of Social Psychology, 58*, 67-89.

Fong, S.L.M. (1973). Assimilation and changing social roles of Chinese-Americans. *Journal of Social Issues, 29*, 115-128.

Governor's Asian American Advisory Council. (1973). *Discrimination Against Asians*. Seattle: State of Washington.

Hassan, T. (1986-87). Asian-American Admissions: Debating Discrimination. *The College Board Review* (No. 142), 18-21; 42-46.

Ho, D., & Chin, M. (1983). *Admissions: Impossible bridge, 51*, 7-8

Ho, M.K. (1984). Social Group Work with Asian/Pacific Americans. *Social Work with Groups, 7*(3), 49-61.

Hsu, F.L.K. (1953). *American and Chinese: Two ways of life*. New York: Abeland-Schuman.

Kaneshige, E. (1973). Cultural factors in group counseling with interaction. *Personnel and Guidance Journal, 51*, 407-412.

Kitano, H.L. (1969). *Japanese Americans: The evolution of a subculture*. Engelwood Cliffs, NJ: Prentice-Hall.

Kuo, W. (1984). Prevalence of depression among Asian-Americans. *Journal of Nervous & Mental Disease, 172,* 449-457.

Lee, F. (1982). A social systems approach to assessment and treatment for Chinese-American families. In M. McGoldrick, et al. (Eds.), *Ethnicity and family therapy.* New York: Guilford Press.

Levine, G.N., & Montero, D.M. (1973). Socioeconomic mobility among three generations of Japanese Americans. *Journal of Social Issues, 29,* 33-48.

Loo, C., & Ong, P. (1984). Crowding perceptions, attitudes and consequences among the Chinese. *Environment and Behavior, 16,* 55-87.

Lum, R.G. (1982). Mental health attitudes & opinions of Chinese. In E.E. Jones & S.J. Korchin (Eds.), *Minority mental health* (pp. 164-190). New York: Praeger.

Masuda, M. (1973). The Japanese. In Governor's Asian-American Advisory Council, *Discrimination Against Asians,* p. 6-9. Seattle, WA: State of Washington.

McLeod, B. (1986). The Oriental Express. *Psychology Today, 20,* 48-52.

Meredith, G.M., & Meredith, C.G.W. (1966). Acculturation and personality among Japanese-American college students in Hawaii. *Journal of Social Psychology, 68,* 175-182.

Office of Special Concerns. (1974). *A study of selected socioeconomic characteristics of ethnic minorities based on the 1970 census, Volume II: Asian-American.* Washington, DC: Department of Health, Education, and Welfare.

Ogawa, D. (1973). The Jap Image. In S. Sue & N. Wagner (Eds.), *Asian-Americans: Psychological perspectives.* Ben Lomand, CA: Science and Behavior Books.

Sollenberger, R.T. (1968). Chinese-American child rearing practices and juvenile delinquency. *Journal of Social Psychology, 74,* 13-23.

Sue, D., Ino, S., & Sue, D.M. (1983). Non-assertiveness of Asian-Americans: An inaccurate assumption? *Journal of Counseling Psychology, 30,* 581-588.

Sue, D.W. (1973). Asians are... *Personnel and Guidance Journal, 51,* 397-399.

Sue, D., & Sue, S. (1987). Cultural factors in the clinical assessment of Asian-Americans. *Journal of Clinical an Consulting Psychology* (in press).

Sue, D.W. (1981). *Counseling the culturally different.* New York: John Wiley & Sons.

Sue, D.W., & Frank, A.C. (1973). Chinese and Janapese American college males. *Journal of Social Issues, 29,* 129-148.

Sue, D.W., & Kirk, B.S. (1973). Differential characteristics of Japanese-American and Chinese-American college students. *Journal of Counseling Psychology, 20,* 142-146.

Sue, D.W., & Sue, S. (1972). Counseling Chinese-Americans. *Personnel and Guidance Journal, 50,* 637-644.

Sue, D.W., & Sue, D. (1977). Barriers to effective cross-cultural counseling. *Journal of Counseling Psychology, 24,* 420-429.

Sue, S., & McKinney, H. (1975). Asian-Americans in the community health care system. *American Journal of Orthopsychiatry, 45,* 111-118.

Sue, S., & Morishima, J.K. (1982). *The mental health of Asian-Americans.* San Francisco: Jossey Bass.

Sue, S., Sue, D.W., & Sue, D. (1975). Asian-Americans as a minority group. *American Psychologist, 30,* 906-910.

Sue, S., Wagner, N., Ja, D., Margullis, C., & Lew, C. (1976). Conception of mental health illness among Asian-American and Caucasian-American Students. *Psychological Reports, 38,* 703-708.

Sue, S., & Zane, N. (1987). The role of culture and cultural techniques in psychotherapy. *American Psychologist, 42,* 37-45.

Tsai, M., Teng, L.N., & Sue, S. (1979). Mental health status of Chinese in the United States. In A. Kleinman & T.Y. Lin (Eds.), *Normal and deviant behavior in Chinese culture.* Hingham, MA: Reidel Publishing.

Tsui, P., & Schultz, G. (1985). Failure of rapport: Why psychotherapeutic engagement fails in the treatment of Asian clients. *American Journal of Orthopsychiatry, 55*(4), 561-569.

U.S. Department of Commerce, Bureau of the Census. (1980). *Census of the population: Supplementary report. Race of the population by states.* Washington, DC: U.S. Government Printing Office.

Watanabe, C. (1973). Self-expression and Asian-American experience. *Personnel and Guidance Journal, 52,* 390-396.

Wong, K.C. (1973). The Chinese. In Governor's Asian-American Advisory Council, *Discrimination against Asians,* pp. 2-5. Seattle: State of Washington.

Yee, A. (1973). Myopic perceptions and textbooks: Chinese Americans' search for identity. *Journal of Social Issues, 29,* 99-113.

Yee, M. (1970, February 23). Chinatown in crisis. *Newsweek,* pp. 57-58.

Yoshioka, R.B., Tashima, N., Chew, M., & Murase, K. (1981). *Mental health services for Pacific/Asian Americans.* San Francisco: Pacific Asian Mental Health Research Project.

13

CUBAN-AMERICANS

GERARDO M. GONZALEZ, Ph.D.
Associate Professor
Department of Counselor Education
University of Florida

GERARDO M. GONZALEZ, Ph.D.

Gerardo M. Gonzalez is Associate Professor of Counselor Education at the University of Florida. He is also the founder and past-president of BACCHUS of the U.S., Inc., a national college and community organization for the prevention of alcohol abuse. Prior to joining the faculty on a full-time basis in 1986, he served as director of the Campus Alcohol and Drug Resource Center and Assistant Dean for Student Services at the University of Florida.

An authority on alcohol and drug abuse prevention, Dr. Gonzalez is an accomplished lecturer and frequently conducts formal presentations on such topics as "Models for Alcohol and Drug Abuse Prevention" and "Substance Abuse Education Programs." His work has been described in numerous scholarly publications including *The Journal of Alcohol and Drug Education, The Journal of Student Personnel,* and the *National Association of Student Personnel Administrators Journal.*

Dr. Gonzalez has been a consultant on alcohol and drug abuse prevention to numerous universities across the country as well as several national and state groups. He is a member of the Florida Joint Executive/Legislative Task Force on Drug Abuse Prevention and was recently appointed by the Secretary of Health and Human Services, Dr. Otis R. Bowen, to serve on the National Advisory Board for the Alcohol, Drug Abuse and Mental Health Administration.

Born on September 24, 1950, in Las Villas, Cuba, Dr. Gonzalez immigrated to the United States with his family in February, 1962, and was later naturalized as an American citizen. A graduate of the University of Florida, Dr. Gonzalez received his B.A. degree in psychology in 1973 and his Ph.D. in counselor education from the same university in 1978.

CUBAN-AMERICANS

AWARENESS INDEX

Directions: Please test your knowledge by responding to the following questions before proceeding to the text in this chapter.
Compare your score with the scoring guide at the end of this Awareness Index.
Select the best response for each item.

1. The first major exodus of Cubans to the United States occurred during:

   a. The Cuban wars of independence
   b. World War II
   c. The Castro revolution

2. In comparison with other Hispanic populations, as well as with the total U.S. population, Cubans are:

   a. The wealthiest group
   b. The most chauvinistic group
   c. The oldest group
   d. The youngest group

3. Cuban women in the United States exhibit a high rate of:

   a. Fertility
   b. Labor force participation
   c. Anemia

4. The majority of Cubans who arrived in the United States after the Castro revolution were professionals, landowners and businessmen in Cuba.

   a. True
   b. False

5. The characteristics of Cubans who arrived in the United States during the 1980 port of Mariel boatlift were significantly different from earlier arrivals.

   a. True
   b. False

6. The majority of Cubans who arrived in the United States after the Castro revolution:

    a. Plan to go back as soon as possible
    b. Left because of economic conditions on the island
    c. Would like to go back for a visit
    d. Plan to acquire U.S. Citizenship

7. An experience common to all Cubans who immigrated to the United States is:

    a. The process of acculturation
    b. Discrimination
    c. Having to learn English

8. The acculturation gap hypothesis refers to:

    a. The distance between Cuba and the U.S.
    b. The difference in perceptions between Cubans and Americans
    c. The different rates at which older and younger immigrants adapt to a new culture

9. Family disruption among Cuban-Americans is often the result of:

    a. Cuban girls wanting to go out without a chaperone
    b. Differential rates of acculturation within the family
    c. Having to live in small houses
    d. Inability to speak English

10. One of the major problems confronting Cuban immigrants arriving in the United States is:

    a. Lack of family to provide support
    b. Discrimination from the Anglo community
    c. Lack of knowledge of the English language
    d. Not having a social security number

11. Older Cuban Americans often experience the results of a cultural tradition of:

    a. Respect within the family
    b. Self-diagnosis and self-prescription for various ailments
    c. Never accepting assistance from government agencies
    d. Never discussing their problems with others

12. Cuban American women often perceive the American way of life as:

   a. Extremely stressful
   b. Too permissive
   c. Free from traditional roles
   d. None of the above

Scoring Guide for Awareness Index

1. a	4. b	7. a	10.c
2. c	5. b	8. c	11.b
3. b	6. d	9. b	12.a

Many people in the United States have a vaguely defined, often erroneous, stereotypic perception of the Cuban-American community. Cubans are a heterogeneous people. Because of its European, African, and Indian roots traditional Cuban culture was described by Diaz (1981) as "ajiaco" (a typical stew of vegetables, roots, and meat). This stew has been further complicated by the pervasive influence of American institutions, language, and culture upon Cuban-American life. As Cubans here struggle to retain some of their mores, values, language, and traditions, Cuban culture in the United States displays elements of Cuban traditional culture that may be disappearing in Cuba itself. These are commonly found in eating patterns, recipes transmitted from older Cubans to the young, and religious events involving small-town patron saints and Afro-Cuban rituals held only secretly in today's Cuba (Sandoval, 1979).

In order to assist and work effectively with Cubans in the United States, this unique culture and its traditions must be understood. In this section a description of the population characteristics, the cultural adjustment problems of immigrants and special acculturation experiences of Cuban families will be discussed. The hope is that a greater understanding of the need for culturally sensitive social and personal interactions will emerge that may be used to assist this diverse, dynamic, and growing ethnic group in America.

Population Characteristics

Cuban migrations to the United States predate this century. By the late 1800s about 100,000 Cubans were concentrated mainly in New York City, Tampa, Key West, and other Florida cities. Fleeing the Cuban wars of independence (1868 to 1895), this first massive wave of immigrants established the tobacco industry in South Florida and largely remained there to become the first large enclave of Cuban-Americans (Diaz, 1981). However, the majority of Cubans residing in the United States today arrived in six stages of migration between 1959 and 1980, following the Cuban revolution.

Between 1959 and 1980 some 600,000 Cubans immigrated to the United States. According to the 1980 U.S. Census of the Population, a total of 803,226 persons were identified as Cuban-Americans based on the respondents who indicated on the census forms that they are of "Cuban origin or descent." Perez (1985) presented an excellent, comprehensive summary of the most significant results of the 1980 U.S. census with respect to the population of Cuban origin residing in the United States. Much of the information on population characteristics presented here is based on these highlights.

Most of the Cuban population in the United States is urbanite. The Cuban population surpasses the total U.S. population, as well as every other Hispanic group, in the proportion that resides in urban areas. The Miami-Fort Lauderdale area (Dade and Broward counties in Florida) accounts for slightly more than 52% of the entire Cuban-origin population in the United States. The Miami-Fort Lauderdale, greater New York, and Los Angeles areas combined contain more than three-fourth of this population. Moreover, the trend is toward an accelerated concentration in Florida. A state-by-state comparison with the 1970 census shows that the proportion of all Cubans declined everywhere in the United States except in Florida, where it greatly increased.

In comparison to other Hispanic populations, as well as to the total U.S. population, Cubans are the oldest group. Middle-aged and elderly persons are over-represented in the Cuban population, a totally atypical characteristic for a population that is largely composed of immigrants that have arrived within the last decade. Whereas 36.2% of the U.S. population was 40 years of age and over in 1980, the corresponding percentage among Cubans was 47.2. The numerical importance of the elderly is apparent in the high proportion of persons who indicated in the census form that they were "other relatives" of the head of the household. The percentage of Cubans 65 years of age and above who identified themselves as "other relatives" is 30.7 as compared to only 8.9 in the total U.S. population. According to Perez (1985) these figures lend support to the argument that the high proportion of elderly persons has led to the relatively widespread existence among Cuban-Americans of the three-generation family.

Another important characteristic of the Cuban population in the United States is the overrepresentation of females. The sex ratio of the Cuban-American population shows only 90.8 males for every 100 females. This compares with 94.5 for the total U.S. and 103.4 for the Mexican population. Although a low sex ratio is typical of an older population, in the case of the Cubans it also reflects the restrictions imposed by the Cuban government on the immigration of men eligible for military conscription. Consequently, the 1980 census shows that among Cubans in the United States is an abnormally large deficit of men between 25 and 40 years of age. This has presented some special problems for divorced women who wish to remarry within the group. In comparison to other Hispanic groups and even with the total U.S. population, Cubans have the highest proportion of women in the divorced category. However, in the Cuban population the high proportion of divorced females does not translate itself into the family characteristics usually associated with a high divorce rate. Perez (1985) pointed out that "in comparison to the other Hispanic groups and with the total U.S. population, the Cuban-origin population has: (1) the highest proportion of children under 18 living with both parents, (2) a relatively low percentage of families headed by females with no husband present, and (3) the lowest incidence of mother-child subfamilies (i.e., mother and child residing within the larger family)" (p. 79). Perez explained these facts by speculating that the divorced Cuban woman returns to her parents' household, but because of low levels of fertility also found in the Cuban population, she is not likely to be accompanied by children.

Cuban women also exhibit a high rate of participation in the labor force. According to the 1980 census, the percentage of all

Cuban females 16 years of age and over in the labor force who were employed full-time all year was 47.1. This compares with 40.1 % of the total U.S. population and 35.0% of the Mexican-American population. Given the tendency of Cuban women to be employed, Cubans lead all other comparison groups (Mexican, Puerto Rican, other Spanish, and total U.S.) in the percentage of families containing two workers. The high incidence of female labor force participation is consistent with low fertility as well as with the three generation household and the relatively high proportion of children three and four years of age enrolled in school. The census data shows that Cubans under 35 years of age have the highest rates of school enrollment of all the populations under consideration. This holds true for each age group from 3 to 34, but is especially true at the pre-school level with 42.2% of all Cuban-origin children 3 and 4 years of age enrolled.

The impact of the high rates of female labor force participation among Cubans is especially evident in the fact that the median income of Cuban married-couple families with children under six is higher than the income of other such families in the U.S. The majority of female Cuban workers are employed in administrative support occupations, including clerical workers, and operators and fabricators in light manufacturing and textiles. Perez (1985) pointed out that apparently working in "la factoria" is indeed an important phenomenom among Cuban women.

The large numbers of elderly and working women, the high levels of school attendance, and the presence of the three-generational family raise some important questions about the future of the Cuban community as it continues to age. For example, Perez (1985) suggested that "A high proportion of persons over 40, combined with low fertility, points to a rapid aging of the population, a process that could severely tax the community resources for dealing with the dependent elderly. This may be a special problem if the younger and more acculturated Cubans prove to be reluctant to establish the type of three-generation households in which they themselves grew up" (p. 16).

CULTURAL ADJUSTMENT PROCESSES

As mentioned earlier, the majority of Cubans in this country arrived in various stages of migration beginning in 1959 after the

Castro revolution. Starting with the professionals, landowners, and businessmen of the early 1960s, successive waves of the migrant flow have brought to the U.S. a virtual cross-section of Cuban society (Bach, Bach, & Triplete, 1981-1982). The largest migration occurred from 1965 to 1973 when more than one-quarter million Cubans were airlifted into the United States. The airlift group was larger than the group of Cuban immigrants who came to the United States between 1959 and 1965 (Azicri, 1981-1982). The airlift brought about a change in the characteristics of the Cuban-American population. While approximately one-third of the early Cuban refugees were professionals and managers, the rate was reduced by one-half in the early '70s and has not shown significant changes during the past decade. However, the image of a Cuban exodus made up of professionals, businessmen, and middle-class families prevailed until 125,000 Cubans migrated to Key West from the port of Mariel near Havana in the summer of 1980. In May 1980 alone, more Cuban refugees arrived in the United States than in all of 1962, the previous record year for Cuban immigration.

If one characteristic distinguishes the Mariel "Freedom Flotilla," the latest influx of Cuban immigrants, from all preceding waves, it is the frustrating ambivalence with which the new exiles have been received in the United States. Part of this ambivalence is due to the changed conditions in the United States which conflicted directly with the open admissions policy of historical precedent. Already beseiged with high unemployment, inflation, and recession, many in the U.S. perceived this dramatic influx as yet another burden (Bach et al., 1981-1982). This perception was not alleviated when the Cuban press claimed the island was ridding itself of "social undesirables." However, an examination of the first 62,000 Mariel arrivals processed in and released directly to the Miami community did not warrant the various perjorative labels ("socially undesirable," "scum," and "deviant") used by the Cuban government to describe this group of immigrants. In fact, the proportion of family groups, women, and persons with relatives already in the United States who were resettled relatively quickly were underestimated. Moreover, the Mariel entrants appeared to be no different than previous Cuban refugees, especially when compared to those who arrived during the airlift period of 1965 to 1973. This contention was supported by Fernandez (1981-1982) who showed that the major differences were race and age. A larger number of the Mariel entrants (approximately 14%) were mulattoes and Blacks, and they were approximately ten years younger than previous refugees.

Insight into the adjustment problems of these refugees was provided by Portes, Clark, & Manning (1985) who studied a sample of 514 adult Cubans who arrived in the United States from the port of Mariel in 1980 and were interviewed in late fall 1983 and spring 1984. A comparison was made between this group and an earlier cohort of Cuban refugees who were followed during the 1970s (Portes et al., 1981-1982). The overwhelming proportion of the 1980 arrivals gave political reasons, such as escape from communism and lack of personal freedom, as their main cause for departure. These reasons are almost identical to those found among Cuban refugees arriving in the 1970s.

As reported by Portes et al. (1985), the modal major problems confronted since arrival by 1980 refugees were unemployment and other economic difficulties among males and inability to speak English among females. In both cases, the distribution of reported difficulties was similar to that among Cuban refugees who arrived ten years earlier. In 1983 as in 1973, language and economic difficulties were by far the principal problems encountered; interestingly, one-fifth to one-fourth of respondents indicated that they had faced no major obstacles upon arrival.

One major difference between the 1980 and 1973 arrivals was the extent of family networks and family support experienced. The 1980 entrants had an average of only three relatives awaiting them in the United States. This number was only one-third of the corresponding figure among 1973 refugees. Moreover, the proportion reporting substantial aid from relatives during the first month in the United States was more than 10 points lower among 1980 entrants than among 1973 refugees. Close to one-half of the 1980 sample depended primarily on public agencies and private charities for their main sources of help.

Both the 1980 and 1973 samples experienced significant declines in professional and managerial employment between Cuba and the United States (Portes et al., 1985). In both cases, after three years of resettlement the numbers of professional or managerial occupations had dropped by seven percent. The most dramatic difference between both samples, however, was found in the degree of labor market participation after arrival in the United States. After three years, the jobless rate of 1980 male entrants more than doubled that of Cuban male refugees during the 1970s; and among Cuban women, this rate reached almost 60%. The unemployment rate for the 1980 entrants reached 27%, a figure three times greater that the 8.4% unemployment rate found among the rest of the Cuban born population in 1980. In addition, the size of the earnings gap between the 1980 and 1973 entrants in constant 1979 dollars was, on an average, $240 more for the 1973 group. One of the most important variables in relation to the likelihood to have found paid work after three years was having and receiving aid from at least one relative in the United States at the time of arrival. Among employed respondents, occupational status was strongly related to education, knowledge of English language, information, and number of kin in the United States.

The final set of questions in the Portes et al. (1985) study dealt with perceptions and attitudes. The overwhelming majority of the respondents from both the 1980 and the 1973 samples reported satisfaction with life in the United States despite the serious difficulties faced. Approximately one-fourth of both samples indicated discrimination in economic opportunities in the United States, and about 40% believed that the American way of life weakened the family. Despite these critical perceptions, over 70% of both samples indicated that they planned to acquire U.S. citizenship in the future, a finding which fits the reported high levels of satisfaction.

The most striking finding with respect to perceptions concerned discrimination by Cubans living in the United States prior to 1980 against Cubans who arrived during the 1980 Mariel flotilla. Three-fourths of the 1980 arrivals indicated that discrimination against this group did in fact exist among "older" Cubans, that is, those living in the United States prior to 1980. Approximately one-half of the 1980 arrivals reported having suffered the consequences of such discrimination at least occasionally. In comparative terms, 1980 arrivals were three times more likely to have experienced the effects of discrimination within their own ethnic community than by Anglos outside of it.

ACCULTURATION PROBLEMS

Acculturation refers to the problem of adjustment—the borrowing, acquiring, and adopting of cultural traits from a host society by people immigrating from another society. According to Szapocznik, Ladner, and Scopetta (1979), clinical experience with the Cuban immigrant community in Dade County, Florida indicated that the acculturation process has often resulted in family disruption. Moreover, since youngsters acculturate more rapidly than their parents, this process often exacerbates intergenerational differences. As an outgrowth of family conflict resulting from different rates of acculturation, these authors found an increased tendency for Cuban youngsters to participate in social support networks influential in the choice of antisocial activities such as drug abuse and other delinquent behavior. While new groups of first-generation Cuban immigrants have continued to arrive in the United States since 1959, about one out of every five Cubans is now a Cuban-American born in the United States (Diaz, 1981). These Cuban-American youth are being brought up in the midst of two different and often conflicting cultures. The result has been a youthful Cuban-American population afflicted with a host of problems related to the process of maturation and acculturation.

One specific area of concern has been the high and rapidly increasing rate of Cuban high-school students who drop out before graduation. In one year the Hispanic high school students (80% of whom are Cubans) enrolled in the Dade County public school system had an 18.76% dropout rate. This rate represented a 27.9% increase from the previous year, while the comparative rate for Blacks dropped 2.2%, and the rate for Whites increased by 3.5%. In reporting these findings, Diaz (1981) commented that "Gradual but steady increases (preceding the Mariel arrivals) in school dropouts, juvenile delinquency, and the number of Cuban families seeking or receiving mental health services in Miami suggest that Cuban families could benefit from increased availability of bilingual, culturally sensitive educational and mental health services" (p. 20).

SPECIAL NEEDS AND APPROACHES

The modern Cuban-American community is a community in evolution. Throughout 20 years of successive migration waves into the United States, Cubans have become a pluralistic group. Now Cuban enclaves are in practically every state of the Union, although most reside in Florida and a few other states (Diaz, 1981). As Cubans settle in the United States, they face the social problems and needs of other minorities, particularly those common to other Hispanic groups, the elderly, low-income working mothers, and adolescents caught between two cultures. The arrival of the latest wave of Mariel immigrants has broadened the need for counseling, employment services, training, and education that are culturally sensitive to the needs of Cuban immigrants. The following sections present some of the special needs of Cuban-Americans in each of these areas and provide examples of approaches which have been found effective in dealing with some of these problems.

Counseling and Family Interventions

Understanding the concept of acculturation is crucial to counseling with Hispanics generally and Cuban-Americans specifically (Ponterotto, 1987; Szapocznik, Scopetta, Kurtines, & Arnalde, 1978). Differential levels of acculturation among migrant families as a group have led to more than the usual levels of intrafamilial conflict and stress. In a study of acculturative differences in self and family role perceptions among Cuban-American college students, Kurtines and Miranda (1980) found strong support for the hypothesis that one of the mechanisms that generates family disruption within migrant groups is the occurrence of intergenerational differences in rates of acculturation. According to the acculturation gap hypothesis, families experiencing the greatest distress are those in which the levels of acculturation within the family unit are most discrepant. Further, the mechanism by which the acculturation gap generates family disruption appears to be intrafamilial role conflict, both within and between family subsystems. Kurtines and Miranda (1980) reported that acculturative change was significantly related to a decline in the high esteem parental roles have traditionally occupied in the Cuban family. Based on their findings, these authors suggested that when counseling migrants, treatment type and modality should be adjusted to deal with disruptive acculturative differences when they occur within families. In such cases, family therapy provides a useful adjunct to individual therapy, and role playing techniques serve as a tool for reducing intrafamilial role conflict.

Perhaps the most extensive work with regard to the effects of acculturation on the Cuban family has been done by Szapocznik and his associates at the Spanish Family Guidance Center in Miami, Florida. Two innovative, culturally sensitive counseling approaches developed and tested there are Bicultural Effectiveness Training (BET) (Szapocznik, Santisteban, Kurtines, Perez-Vidal, & Hervis, 1986) and One-Person Family Therapy (Szapocznik et al., 1983). BET is based on a model of adjustment which says that individuals living in bicultural contexts tend to become maladjusted when they remain or become monocultural. In this model, Cubans who fail to learn how to, or do not want to interact within the Anglo American context tend to underacculturate and experience adjustment problems related to this phenomenom. On the other hand, individuals who reject the skills necessary to interact within the Hispanic American context tend to overacculturate and lack the flexibility necessary to cope with their entire cultural milieu.

The One-Person Family Treatment approach is based on the hypothesis that it is possible to achieve the goals of family therapy (i.e., structural family change and symptom reduction) by working primarily with one person. This hypothesis is based on the notion underlying family therapy which says that changing a part of the system almost inevitably brings about changes in the whole system. In a study of the relative effectiveness of Conjoint Family Therapy (CFT) versus One-Person Family Therapy (OPFT) for a Cuban-American population, Szapocznik et al. (1983) proposed a redefinition of family therapy as "a treatment modality in which the therapist's interventions target on changing family systems, regardless of who is present at a particular therapy session" (p. 890). The results of this comparative study showed that the OPFT treatment group attended significantly more sessions than the CFT group. Szapocznik et al. attributed this to the difficulty of retaining entire families in therapy. However, both modalities were effective in bringing about improvement in family functioning and symptom reduction in the individual participant (IP) at the time of termination. Follow-up analyses provided further evidence of the continued efficacy of both modalities on family functioning and slightly greater efficacy of the one-person modality in symptom reduction in the IP in several areas of functioning. The researchers concluded that OPFT would be preferred over CFT where there is particular difficulty in scheduling the whole family for therapy (as is often the case in working with Hispanic groups), when one family member requires a great deal of strengthening, or when family members are unwilling to participate in the therapy process. Their strongest suggestion, however, was to combine both modalities whenever possible.

One implication of these studies is that Structural Family Therapy can be effective with a Cuban population. Further, the researchers showed that participation by the entire family is not always required for this form of therapy. This is an important finding because Hispanics generally, and Cuban-Americans in particular, tend to underutilize mental health services, and to obtain full family participation is difficult even when some family members are willing to seek therapy. Moreover, since one of the outcomes of the acculturation gap within Cuban families is family stress and disruption, effective forms of family therapy can make an important contribution to the overall adjustment and assimilation of Cuban-Americans to the new culture.

One noteworthy characteristic of Structural Family Therapy with regard to its use with Hispanics is its focus on behavioral goals. Behavioral approaches generally are more effective than intrapsychic therapies with this population (Ponterotto, 1987). This action-oriented, problem solving approach is deemed more appropriate for Cubans who, when compared to Anglo-Americans on a value orientation scale, tended to have a greater present-time orientation and not to endorse idealized humanistic values (Szapocznik et al., 1978). Counseling with the Cuban client should be present oriented. Cubans are usually mobilized for treatment by the onset of a crisis and expect the therapist to provide immediate problem-oriented solutions to the crisis situation. Rather than being motivated to seek treatment by the search for personal and spiritual growth, Cubans are more likely to be motivated to seek treatment by concrete and obtainable objectives.

Vocational Development and Interest Inventories

One of the most pressing problems that Cuban-Americans face in the United States is finding employment in areas where they have a particular skill or personal interest. Portes et al. (1981-1982) showed that the aspirations of newly arrived Cubans for new occupations in the United States were higher than past attainments in Cuba. However, these high aspirations compared quite negatively with subsequent attainments. Almost one-half of the sample studied by Portes and his colleagues worked in the lower blue collar sector after several years in the United States. Little more than one-half the population employed in professional or managerial occupations in Cuba held similar positions in the U.S. Mean occupational prestige as measured by a socioeconomic index was 10 points below that at arrival, indicating significant downward mobility.

One of the major concerns for counselors who work with Cuban-American clients is the selection of appropriate interest inventories for measurement and assistance with career development goals. Very few studies have examined whether vocational development theories and interest inventories normed primarily on White Anglo samples have relevance to Spanish-speaking individuals (Harrington & O'Shea, 1980). The Spanish translations of English tests are not always appropriate. Butcher and Garcia (1978) warned that even when adequate translation is achieved, the assumption can not be made that the same constructs are being measured in a different culture. Being cognizant of these problems, Harrington and O'Shea (1980) conducted a study designed to determine the construct validity of Holland's hexagonal model with Spanish-speaking subgroups and to establish the construct validity of the Spanish form of their own *Career Decision Making* (CDM) instrument.

The subjects for this study were 267 Spanish-speaking persons who resided in the United States and indicated their ethnic background as Mexican-American, Puerto Rican, Cuban, or South American. The intercorrelation matrix of the six CDM scales was compared with that of Holland's *Vocational Preference Inventory.* The results provided confirmation of the Holland hexagonal model in this diverse Spanish-speaking sample. According to the researchers, "This suggests that Spanish-speaking cultures have present work models whereby crafts, scientific, artistic, social, business enterprises, and business detail interests can develop" (p. 249). It also suggested that vocational interests of the Spanish-speaking can be validly measured through the Holland scales. Therefore, the CDM Spanish form provides counselors with a Holland-based tool to explore career choices with the

Spanish-speaking client. Research is needed to see whether the CDM scales can be used to help Cuban immigrants explore various career choices and obtain proper training for their choice of work in the United States.

Bilingual Education
and School Achievement

The majority of Cuban immigrants arriving in the United States indicate that the lack of knowledge of the English language is the principal problem confronting them (Portes et al., 1981-1982). English comprehension among Cuban exiles is surprisingly low even after several years of residence in the United States. Only 24% of Portes' sample were fluent in English, even when a liberal definition was adopted. This finding is not entirely surprising when one considers the existence of a large immigrant community where knowledge of the host country language is not imperative for economic survival. However, the lack of knowledge of the English language does present some rather serious problems for economic advancement and school achievement.

To what extent lack of knowledge of the English language is responsible for the excessive school dropout rates which prevail among Spanish-speaking students in Dade County, Florida is impossible to say. Despite the Supreme Court 1974 decision (*Lau v. Nichols*) which indicated that without help, students who do not speak the school language are effectively foreclosed from any meaningful education. However, numbers of Hispanic students enrolled in bilingual education are still low (Wagenheim, 1981). This problem was confounded for Cuban-Americans when a referendum was adopted in November, 1980 prohibiting Dade County from officially using any language other than English.

Since the Supreme Court did not prescribe any specific remedy to the language problem of Spanish-speaking students in American schools, many different approaches to bilingual education have been developed, but most of these can be divided into two broad categories: transitional and maintenance. Under the transitional approach the student's native language is used as a medium of instruction only until the student can function in an English language classroom. Under the maintenance approach, both the student's native language and English are taught under the transitional approach. Students are expected to stay in these transitional programs for one to three years, until they can be "mainstreamed" into regular classrooms. Unfortunately, since the language most often spoken at home and outside the classroom is Spanish, many of these students never become sufficiently fluent in English to properly compete with their Anglo counterparts in the schools. The results are lower school achievement and increased dropout rates.

Greater sensitivity and special programs are needed to help Cuban-American students cope with the pressures of a home and peer environment that promotes adherence to the native culture and language, and a school environment that demands optimal performance in the English language. The same is true for workers out of school who wish to receive special training or instruction for career advancement. Both of these groups need special English instruction presented in a culturally sensitive way. To be most effective this instruction must be presented by appropriate role models who can clearly communicate an appreciation for the cultural pressures experienced by Cubans while at the same time making clear the practical benefits of fluency in the English language.

Life Enhancement Counseling
With Older Cuban-Americans

As noted earlier, Cubans in the United States are a population older than the mean. The need is growing for social services which are sensitive to two sets of characteristics unique to this population: (1) cultural background and (2) advanced age. The concept of matching services, particularly counseling modalities, to client characteristics has been well established in the mental health field. Recognition of the need for counseling approaches designed specifically for the elderly Cuban-American population led Szapocznik, Santisteban, Kurtines, Hervis, and Spencer (1982) to deveop a *life enhancement counseling model* that is culturally sensitive to the basic values of this group. this model makes therapeutic use of specific characteristics of elders, such as the tendency to reminisce, and employs an ecological approach to allow the therapist access to the elder's social environment. The overall goal of this form of therapy is to enhance the meaningfulness of life for elders. It conceptualizes many of the psychological difficulties and "disorders" of elders as potentially reversible rather than inevitable consequences of the aging process. The life enhancement counseling model was evaluated by Szapocznik, Santisteban, Hervis, and Spencer (1981) for its effect in the treatment of depression among Cuban-American elders and was found to be effective both when used alone and in combination with pharmacotherapy. However, clients who received both medication and life enhancement counseling tended to improve more than those who received either form of therapy alone.

Validation of the efficacy of life enhancement therapy as an effective treatment model has important implications for the treatment needs of this population. Cubans in general have a strong tradition of self-diagnosis and self-prescription. This tradition has been traced to the historical development of the pharmacist as a quasi-medical practitioner in Cuba (Page, 1982). What began as a one-stop form of caregiving by physicians who diagnosed, treated, and dispensed medicines in the same place, later gave rise to the expectation that pharmacists would do the same. This expectation continues and is very much alive within the Cuban-American community today. The one-stop pharmacist-practitioner represents a convenient means for the self-diagnoser to obtain reassurance that the identified malady and chosen course of treatment are correct, according to an "authority." Thus, the potential over-reliance on legal drugs, which are often obtained without a doctor's prescription, should be taken into account when counseling with older Cuban-Americans. Very early in the development of the counseling relationship the client should be encouraged to obtain a complete medical examination that includes an assessment of drugs being consumed. Based on the results of this examination, the counselor can then develop a treatment plan that may include physician supervised pharmacotherapy in conjunction with life enhancement therapy, or life enhancement therapy alone as an alternative to self medication.

Changing Roles of
Cuban-American Women

The strong Cuban tradition of self-diagnosis and self prescription combines with the acculturation pressures of immigration to the United States has had an important effect on another major group of Cuban-Americans: women. Historically, the role of women in traditional pre-Castro Cuban society has been that of housekeeper and mother (Boone, 1980). However, the need for economic survival upon arrival in the United States made it necessary for increasing numbers of Cuban women to join the labor force. Employment in the U.S. labor force has been tantamount to a loss of prestige because the role of nonworking housewife traditionally carried prestige in the upper social strata in°pre-revolutionary Cuba (Gonzalez & Page, 1981). Furthermore, their participation in the labor force has often led to the double burden of employment and domestic responsibilities for the Cuban woman. One outcome of this discrepancy between the traditional maternal role and the present day worker/housekeeper dual role has been a significant increase in acculturation-related stress and prescription drug use.

Using a research strategy entailing contacting a group of 100 Cuban women who participated in a network or set of networks of social relations, Gonzalez and Page (1981) identified exile uncertainty and acculturation problems as the two most important sources of stress-related drug use among Cuban-American women in Miami. All of the respondents in this study agreed that Cuban women drastically increased their use of tranquilizers and sedatives after immigrating. Apparently the Cuban tradition of self-medication and the use of various herbs to calm the nerves in concert with psychoactive chemicals available from pharmacists, friends, and relatives in the Cuban-American community increased use of these substances.

Gonzalez and Page (1981) offered the following before and after perspective on generalized acculturation stress from a 65 year-old woman:

> Before Castro, I had no reason to suffer from nerves; we lived a very tranquil life. We were a very united family, and we all got along together. All of the siblings, in-laws, everybody got along well. It was a normal life. I didn't need to eat my meals in a hurry to get to work on time. So, I suppose that if I had stayed in Cuba and if Fidel hadn't been in power I could have enjoyed a much calmer life. (p. 49)

The increased stress and drug use related to the change in lifestyle among Cuban women in the United States is not limited to the older segment of the population. Page (1982) offered yet another example of the effects of acculturation stress in the following passage from a Cuban woman:

> Well, I will tell you, I never knew what a sedative [calmante] was [in Cuba]...The way things are here with the use of pills is terrible. Of course, the pharmacies [in Cuba] sold them, but then everybody had their pills at home, but you took them once in a great while, when your head hurt or your wisdom teeth ached. But I see so many young girls here taking Valium and sleeping pills and their nerves are shattered. But I don't remember seeing young girls taking such things in Cuba, and I left when I was 43 years old...It's the environment, the standard of living we live in that bothers people here. (p.68)

Clearly, Cuban women perceive the American way of life as extremely stressful. In counseling Cuban women, an important procedure is to acknowledge the stressful nature of adaption to a new way of life. The counselor should express an understanding of and an appreciation for the anxiety of migration, acculturation, loss of country of origin, and the demands of changing sex roles. The primary avenue for engagement of the Cuban female client may well be through focusing on the difficulties they experience here, and the differences from their life in Cuba. However, once the client has been engaged and a therapeutic relationship has been established, the treatment must be decidedly present time oriented. As with other Cuban groups, Cuban women are likely to be mobilized into treatment by the onset of a crisis and expect the counselor to provide immediate problem-oriented solutions to the crisis situation. The culturally sensitive counselor is cognizant of how to use crises to promote growth and alter self-destructive lifestyles. If the use of drugs has become the primary means of dealing with stress generally, most likely drugs will be seen as a means to deal with the present crisis. The counselor must be ready to take charge of the counselor-client relationship and suggest behaviors to restructure the interactions of the client with her environment. Many traditional Anglo-American counseling interventions are based on a model of a growth-oriented, self-actualizing individual who is ready to take control of his or her own destiny. In contrast, the counselor must relate to the Cuban client hierarchically, recognizing that the counselor's role is perceived by the client as a position of authority (Szapocznik, Scopetta, & Aranalde, 1978). Alternative ways of coping must be suggested which are concrete and obtainable.

Whenever possible, Cuban women suffering from acculturation stress and related depression also should be involved in group counseling with peers. Cubans generally have high levels of need for social approval (Tholen, 1974). The warm, culturally familiar atmosphere of the group, with peers and possibly a counselor who speaks their language, helps the Cuban client to feel accepted and less depressed. The group activities should focus on the here and now and provide concrete advice and help in dealing with acculturation stress or other problems. When environmental pressures or tensions are the source of the Cuban client's dysfunction, as is often the case with Cuban women, the counseling interventions need to help the client develop the skills necessary to restructure the interactions of the client with her environment. Because of the Cuban client's tendency to perceive self as unable to control or modify environmental circumstances, reinforcement and feedback from group members can be an important source of support in learning these new skills.

SUMMARY AND CONCLUSIONS

Cubans in the United States are a diverse group. Most have arrived here in successive immigration waves following Castro's revolution and takeover of power in Cuba in 1959. While some of the initial waves of Cuban immigrants were over-represented by professionals and upper middle class persons, later arrivals closely paralleled the demographics found in the Cuban population at large. Counselors, teachers, and others who work with this population need to dispel the myth that Cubans are a privileged, affluent minority with no special needs. The fact is that Cuban-Americans experience many of the problems associated with immigration and social deprivation found among other Hispanic groups.

All Cubans in the United States have in common the experience of acculturation pressures as they try to adapt to a new way of life. Ever since Homer's description of the wonderings of Ulysses and his weeping and rolling on the floor at the thought of home, many writers and investigators have been aware of the relationship between the process of cultural adjustment among immigrant groups and the presence of acculturative stress (Santisteban, 1980). Cuban-American immigrants are no exception, particularly in regard to the impact on the family, to parental roles, and to family organization. Discrepancies in the rate of acculturation within families have been found to have strong causative effects on family dysfunctions. Cuban parents often hold idealized values of the Cuban culture which emphasize moral and social conservatism and strong religious beliefs. However, their children have generally developed a greater affinity for American values and are thus faced with the demands of the parents and other relatives on the one hand, and the expectations of their peer group on the other. These two forces often represent conflicting values and behavioral expectations resulting in high levels of dysfunction including juvenile delinquency, drug use, and school dropout problems among Cuban adolescents. A concerted effort must be made to understand the special cultural pressures that impact on the Cuban adolescent and to develop culturally sensitive strategies specifically designed to prevent and treat these dysfunctions.

While the existence of an ethnic subculture or reference group with whom the individual can identify tends to be a positive factor in the process of cultural adjustment, the emergence of a "self-sufficient" Cuban community in American cities with large Cuban populations has made command of the English language unnecessary for everyday survival. However, when the issue of career or educational success is considered, fluency in the English language is needed to establish a proper balance between cultural identity and acclimation to the host country. Cuban children and adults alike must be provided with opportunities to learn the English language in an environment that respects the Cuban community traditions and native language. Faced with the difficult pressures of acculturation and adaption, a Cuban-American often develops the false belief that knowledge of the English language is not necessary for social and economic success. Such a view places severe constraints on the individual's capacity to function effectively in a bicultural community.

In terms of sex roles and function, different value orientations between males and females have combined with environmental and economic pressures to produce uncharacteristically high levels of psychological stress among Cuban-American women. Moreover, the Cuban tradition of self-diagnosis and prescription has led to informal channels of legal drug distribution and consumption as a means to deal with the stress produced by the changing roles of Cuban-American women. The Cuban value structure must be understood in order to develop effective helping interventions to assist Cuban women in finding more constructive ways to deal with acculturation stress. Assumptions made by traditional Anglo-American counseling approaches are not comparable to the attitudes and expectations of the Cuban client. Therefore, counselors must become comfortable with the more directed hierarchical types of specific goal-oriented approaches that Cuban clients expect.

The Older Cuban-American population, like other older Americans, is concerned with the problem of failing health, but they are also experiencing the diminishing traditional importance of their position in the family. As younger Cubans become more acculturated and socially mobile, the traditional function of the extended family as a source of support and acceptance for older Cubans is eroding. In addition, the rapidly growing numbers of older Cubans in America and the diminishing numbers of younger family members who are available for their care present a serious challenge to community agencies charged with the responsibility for services to this population.

In this paper several examples of approaches developed to respond to the various needs of Cuban-Americans were discussed. These examples were selected because of their cultural sensitivity, creative approach, research basis, potential for replicability, and implication for further development and study. They do not represent an exhaustive review of effective approaches. Many other educational, therapeutic, and community responses must be explored and developed in order to meet the needs of the growing Cuban-Americans population. However, the basic premise underlying any type of intervention that may be developed for Cuban-Americans is that they must be sensitive to the particular needs, expectations, and values of this culture-rich, complex, and diverse population.

REFERENCES

Azicri, M. (1981-1982). The politics of exile: Trends and dynamics of political change among Cuban-Americans. *Cuban Studies, 11 & 12,* 56-70.

Bach, R.L., Bach, J.B., & Triplete, T. (1981-1982). Flotilla "entrants": Latest and most controversial. *Cuban Studies, 11 & 12,* 29-48.

Boone, M.S. (1980). The uses of traditional concepts in the development of new urban roles: Cuban women in the United States. In E. Bourguigan, *A world of women: Antropological studies of women in the societies of the world.* New York: J.F. Bergin Publishers.

Butcher, J., & Garcia, R. (1978). Cross-national application of psychological tests. *Personnel and Guidance Journal, 56,* 472-475.

Diaz, G.M. (1981). The changing Cuban community. In *Hispanics and grant-makers: A special report of Foundation News* (pp. 18-23). Washington, DC: Council on Foundations.

Fernandez, G.A. (1981-1982). Comment—The flotilla entrants. Are they different? *Cuban Studies, 11 & 12,* 49-54.

Gonzalez, D.H., & Page, J.B. (1981). Cuban women, sex role conflict and the use of prescription drugs. *Journal of Psychoactive Drugs, 13,* 47-51.

Harrington, T.F., & O'Shea, A.J. (1980). Applicability of the Holland (1973) model of vocational development with Spanish-speaking clients. *Journal of Counseling Psychology, 27,* 246-251.

Kurtines, W.M., & Miranda, L (1980). Differences in self and family role perception among acculturating Cuban-American college students: Implications for the etiology of family disruption among migrant groups. *International Journal of Intercultural Relations, 4,* 167-184.

Page, J.B., (1982). A brief history of mind-altering drug use in prerevolutionary Cuba. *Cuban Studies, 12,* 55-71.

Perez, L., (1985). The Cuban population of the United States: The results of the 1980 U.S. Census of the Population. *Cuban Studies, 15,* 1-16.

Ponterotto, J.G., (1987). Counseling Mexican Americans: A multimodal approach. *Journal of Counseling and Development, 65,* 308-311.

Portes, A., Clark, J.M., & Lopez, M.M. (1981-1982). Six years later, the process of incorporation of Cuban exiles in the United States: 1973-1979. *Cuban Studies, 11 & 12,* 1-28.

Portes, A., Clark, J.M., & Manning, R.D. (1985). After Mariel: A survey of the resettlement experiences of 1980 Cuban refugees in Miami. *Cuban Studies, 15,* 37-58.

Sandoval, M.C. (1979). Santeria as a mental health case system: An historical overview. *Social Science and Medicine, 13B,* 137-151.

Santisteban, D. (1980). *Acculturation/assimilation and psychological stress: A review of the literature,* Unpublished manuscript, University of Miami, Spanish Family Guidance Center, Miami.

Szapocznik, J., Kurtines, W.M., Foote, F.H., Perez-Vidal, A., & Hervis, O. (1983). Conjoint versus one-person family therapy: Some evidence for the effectiveness of conducting family therapy through one person. *Journal of Consulting and Clinical Psychology, 51,* 889-899.

Szapocznik, J., Ladner, R.A., & Scopetta, M.A. (1979). Youth drug abuse and subjective distress in a Hispanic population. In G.M. Beschner & A.S. Friedman (Eds.), *Youth Drug Abuse.* Lexington, MA: Heath and Company.

Szapocznik, J., Santisteban, D., Hervis, O., & Spencer, F. (1981). Treatment of depression among Cuban-American elders: Some validation evidence for a life enhancement counseling approach. *Journal of Consulting and Clinical Psychology, 49,* 752-754.

Szapocznik, J., Santisteban, D., Kurtines, W.M., Hervis, O.E., & Spencer, F. (1982). Life enhancement counseling: A psychosocial model of services for Hispanic elders. In E. E. Jones & S.J. Korchin (Eds.), *Minority mental health.* New York: Holt, Rinehart & Winston.

Szapocznik, J., Santisteban, D., Kurtines, W.M., Perez-Vidal, A., & Hervis O. (1986). Bicultural effectiveness training: A treatment intervention for enhancing inter-cultural adjustment in Cuban families. *Hispanic Journal of Behavioral Sciences, 6,* 317-344.

Szapocznik, J., Scopetta, M.H., Kurtines, W.M., & Arnalde, M.A. (1978). Theory and measurement of acculturation. *Interamerican Journal of Psychology, 12,* 113-130.

Szapocznik, J., Scopetta, M.A., & Arnalde, M. (1978). Cuban value structure: Treatment implications. *Journal of Consulting and Clinical Psychology, 46,* 961-970.

Tholen, J.F. (1974). *An interactive approach to the study of outcome in group counseling: Matching conceptual level with degree of structure.* Unpublished master's thesis, University of Miami.

Wagenheim, K. (1981). The Hispanic phenomenon. In *Hispanics and grantmakers: A special report of Foundation News* (pp.49-53). Washington, DC: Council on Foundations.

14

MEXICAN-AMERICANS

DONALD L. AVILA, Ed.D.
Professor of Educational Psychology
Foundations of Education Department
University of Florida

and

ANTONIO L. AVILA, Ph.D.
School Psychologist
Alachua County School System
Gainesville, Florida

DONALD L. AVILA, Ed.D.

The senior author is a professor of Educational Psychology in the Foundations of Education Department at the University of Florida where he teaches personality theory. His area of specialization is self-concept theory.

ANTONIO L. AVILA, Ph.D.

The junior author is a practicing school psychologist in Gainesville, Florida, where he is employed by the Alachua County School System.

MEXICAN-AMERICANS

AWARENESS INDEX

Directions: Mark each answer true, false, or don't know. Compare your answers with the scoring guide at the end of the test.

T F   1. Mexican-Americans have a lower educational level and illiteracy rate than blacks.

T F   2. Mexican Nationals and Mexican-Americans feel that they have many problems in common.

T F   3. Many Mexican-Americans long to return to the "Old Country".

T F   4. There was a good deal of intimate fraternization between the Spanish and the natives of the lands they conquered in North America.

T F   5. The speaking of Spanish is often banned in our public schools.

T F   6. When counseling Mexican-Americans, it is best to spend a fairly large amount of time exploring each individual's personal history.

T F   7. Group counseling is effective with Mexican-Americans.

T F   8. One of the most important aspects of counseling Mexican-Americans is helping them learn new values.

T F   9. Standardized tests are useful when counseling Mexican-Americans for individual guidance but not for comparisons with members of other ethnic groups.

T F 10. **Mestizo** is the Spanish word for **alien.**

T F 11. Mexicans often try to "pass" for some other nationality.

Scoring Guide for Awareness Index

1. T	4. T	7. T	10. F
2. F	5. T	8. F	11. T
3. F	6. F	9. T	

A LITTLE HISTORY

The best place to start anything is at the beginning, and the Mexican-American begins with one of the most incredible stories in the history of the world—the conquest of Mexico.

On February 19, 1519, Hernando Cortes, eight hundred troops, fourteen cannons and sixteen horses landed on the Yucatan Peninsula of Mexico (Prescott, 1934). In less than three years this handful of men conquered an entire empire numbering millions of people and established not only a new nation, but also a new breed of human beings.

How was this feat possible? How could a relatively few individuals have such a tremendous impact on history? Several factors contributed, but three were major ones. The first, understandable; the other two, uncanny.

The first circumstance that allowed this small band to accomplish what seems like an impossible task is not unusual—a state of affairs that has caused many empires to fall. At the time of Cortes' arrival, Mexico consisted of many separate tribes under the loose control of the Aztec Empire. Although considered a unified people, great disharmony existed among the separate tribes. Many of them had been conquered by the Aztecs and, like many of the peoples conquered by Rome, still resented their conquerers. Consequently, when Cortes came to the Mexican shores, he was able to recruit fairly large numbers of natives to his cause.

A second key to the success of the conquistador involved the experience of the natives. Although the Aztecs were civilized in many ways, in others they were barbaric and crude. The native armies consisted of foot soldiers armed with clubs, knives, and swords. They had never heard gun powder ignite nor seen horses. Rumors of these new weapons made them reluctant to fight. When they did engage in battle with the Spanish, the explosions of rifle and cannon and the awesome sight of huge animals and their riders terrified many natives, causing them to flee in fear.

Judging the impact of the third and perhaps strongest factor in Cortes' success is difficult, but the impact was considerable. The Aztec religion held that a white, bearded god once ruled Mexico and would one day return. Clearly, many of the natives thought Cortes was that god, and they either failed to resist the Spaniard or joined his cause because of this belief. The Aztec Emperor himself, his judgment clouded by the uncertainty of Cortes' divinity, made many blunders that contributed to the empire's downfall. He neither wanted to give his nation to plunderers nor offend a god. Consequently, a nation was conquered by little more than a group of bandits.

The establishment of a new nation and a new breed of people was much more straightforward and natural. Having subdued the natives, Cortes' men began to fraternize with them, and that fraternization created a new being—the Mestizos. Mexico City became the first Mestizo city in history. The current ancestral heritage of Mexico is reported to be 55% Mestizo, 29% Indian, and 15% European.

Now the Mexican-American story begins. Three major causes contributed to the migration of the Mexican to what is now the southwestern and far western portions of the United States. First, the Spanish search for booty, conversion, and expansion did not end in Mexico. While acquiring Mexico and most of Central America, the Spaniards sent bands of priests, soldiers, and unidentifiable scoundrels north for farther conquest. The people living in these lands were mostly small tribes of rather primitive and unaggressive Indians and offered little resistance. As usual, these adventurers began settling the land by converting, plundering, and again breeding with the locals (Longstreet, 1977).

Later, in what might be called the second phase of Mexicanization, these Mestizos decided that independence from Spain was in order. But freedom was not easy. Years of war, oppression, and poverty followed the decision to free themselves from Spain and establish an independent nation. Thus, because of the warfare and poverty, thousands left their native land and headed north in search of greener pastures.

What then is the modern Mexican-American ancestry? That's not an easy question. Today to trace one's ancestry in any true linear fashion is nearly impossible and as for a "pure" strain of any ancestry—biological, religious, political, or otherwise—in this melting-pot nation of ours is very unlikely. Surely, the Mexican-American is no exception.

While Mexican-Americans are mostly of Mestizo ancestry (Aztec and Spanish), other strains have resulted from Mexicans combining with Mexican Indian, American Indian, and northern Europeans. These people eventually occupied most of the west and southwestern United States. Without question their history has been that of a people seeking new and better lives, some coming from Mexico to settle new lands, but most fleeing revolution and poverty. While conditions in Mexico are constantly improving, that migration and hopeful search has not ended.

The Mexican-American experience has been disappointing. Dreams of a better life have been realized by a relative few. In the beginning they were treated and exploited as slaves. Later they were accepted as a necessary evil, segregated into ghettos or barrios and no less exploited. They have always been looked at as a cheap source of labor and been regarded by the majority with all the cruelty of rampant prejudice and discrimination. Some changes have occurred, but Mexican-Americans still face the same problems that have plagued them from the beginning.

MINORITIES—BLAH, BLAH, BLAH

When a person decides to analyze minority groups, the first thing that sets in, if you are not a member of such a group, is boredom. Boredom, because so much of the information reads alike. To paraphrase, if you have looked at one of them, you've looked at 'em all. And, in a very real way this is true; unless, of course, you are looking at privileged minorities like the rich and famous. But oppressed, dispossessed, poor minorities are the same in many ways. They all fit the cycle of poverty, and they are all the victims of prejudice and discrimination. Thus the general descriptions and statistics are the same over and over again.

The authors want least of all to bore the reader. Therefore, we shall, here and now, quickly dispense with the description and statistics. Like every minority the Mexican-American is

1. the victim of prejudice and discrimination,

2. alienated from the greater society,

3. segregated and isolated, and

4. generally poor.

What else is new? Not much. The facts of the matter are as follows (Carter, 1979; Hernandez, 1973):

1. Approximately 12 million Mexican-Americans reside in the United States.

2. One-third live in poverty and are disproportionably represented in the low income manual labor occupations.

3. They obtain, on the average, 7.1 years of education.

4. They have a lower educational level than Blacks or Whites and a greater school drop-out rate than either.

5. They have the highest illiteracy rate of any group in the U.S.

6. By the 12th grade, 40% have dropped out of school.

7. Only 1% go to college.

8. Many are segregated in schools that are almost all Mexican-American.

9. Many are 2, 3, or even 5 years behind in school.

Sound familiar? Of course, All statistics on oppressed minorities sound like a broken record.

BUT—DIFFERENCES DO EXIST

Now that we have taken care of the statistics, let's go to the focus of this article. That focus is understanding. The writers believe that one of the most important characteristics a counselor must have if he or she is to be successful is empathetic understanding of the client. If the counselor does not understand the unique qualities of the client, he or she cannot help that client. The major purpose of this chapter, then, is to give the reader a better idea of what being a member of the Mexican-American minority is like.

What are some of the factors that make this minority different from others?

Language

Language, of course, is the most obvious problem for the Mexican-American. However, the problem is not the same for all. Some Mexican-Americans speak virtually no English; some speak no Spanish; and others speak every possible state between these extremes. All are, however, members of the same minority group and subject to the same experiences, especially those experiences of a prejudicial nature. The less English spoken, however, the worse the problem.

Little, if anything, is more frightening or will give a person more of a sense of helplessness than will being surrounded by people speaking a language one does not understand. Thousands of Mexican-Americans of all ages are in this predicament. Older individuals often find protection by surrounding themselves with other Spanish speaking people, but children are sometimes thrust into the greater society without tools to express even their most basic needs. Youngsters consequently withdraw, become quiet, and hope that they at least do not get in harm's way. Imagine yourself as being a nine or ten year old child in a room with twenty or thirty other people and not being able to comprehend a word that is spoken. Of course, those around you are confused and unable to communicate also and behave in ways that are not conducive to growth. They reject, ignore, or aggravate you, the exotic child. In any case, what results is a frightened, confused, isolated, and lonely you—a small child. As time passes, children in conditions similar to this often become more withdrawn and isolated, developing various defenses for protection or reacting with open aggression and hostility.

Migrant Status

Unlike most other minorities, a tremendously dispropor-tionate number of Mexican-Americans is in the migrant labor force. What does this mean? In terms of physical health alone (Hernandez, 1973) the picture is not a pretty one:

1. The infant mortality rate for migrants is 12% higher than the national average.

2. The rate of death from influenza is 200%, from tuberculosis 260%, and from accidents 300% higher than the national average.

3. The life expectancy of the migrant worker is 49 years.

The psycho-social picture is no better. Migrant means moving-constant moving. Many Mexican-Americans remain in one place for only three or four months. They have no roots, no home, no place to belong. Each time they follow the crops they are thrown into a totally new situation with no psychological anchors to grasp. when they arrive at their destination, conditions are disgusting and they are totally exploited. Little is as depressing as the sight of migrant camps and the abuse to which the migrant is too often subjected. Worst of all, they are in a cycle that offers little hope of being broken. The process keeps adults from being able to improve their skills or positions and the children are offered small hope of breaking the mold.

Viva Mexico

Mexican-Americans are in a unique situation because they are so close to the country with which they are identified. This causes the larger society to misunderstand the real nature of the Mexican-American and confuse two groups of people which are in some respects very different. Mexican-Americans are not simply dis-placed Mexican nationals. The problems of Mexicans and the problems of Mexican-Americans are not the same. While many

Mexican-Americans can and do take pride in their heritage, it is as Americans and not as Mexican nationals.

Back to Africa movements have failed because Blacks in this country are native Americans, not Africans. They do not go back to Africa because Africa is not their country. For the same reason, many Mexican-Americans have little or no desire to see, hear, or talk about the "old" country. When Mexican nationals and Mexican-Americans encounter one another, often no sense of loyalty or brotherhood is felt. In fact, they may well have little in common. Mexicans from Mexico have their problems and Mexicans, who are American and a distinctly different group, have theirs. On occasion one may even detect a degree of hostility between the Mexican nationals and the Mexican-Americans, as though the Nationals regard the Mexican-Americans as being a bit beneath them and perhaps consider them as "having deserted the ship." By the same token, those Mexicans who migrated to the U.S. did so because they were unhappy and were escaping a past they did not want following them. Therefore, they can be very uncomfortable when the past interjects itself into their present lives in the form of a Mexican national. The authors, although of Mexican-American heritage, have not particularly identified themselves with Mexico. They have visited there, but when they did the visits were clearly perceived as trips to a foreign country.

This schism will be widened even further by sweeping legislation that has recently been passed in the U.S. affecting the status of illegal aliens in this country. Among other things, the new immigration bill allows millions of these individuals to become American citizens. For most Mexicans this event will most likely separate them permanently, both physically and psychologically, from the "old country."

Who Am I?

The more a person resembles an Indian, the more prejudice and discrimination he/she will encounter. Mexican-Americans who do not have these features experience much less discrimination than those who do and have found it much easier to gain access to and integration into the larger society. Those Mexican-Americans who most closely resemble the North American Indian suffer the same kind of nightmarish experiences as the American Indian and American Black, while those who do not have these features may go through life relatively untouched by prejudice and discrimination. These conditions have to do with how easily one is identified with a minority and how much different that minority is from the majority. Blacks, as a total group, have suffered the most in this country because they have the most easily identifiable physical characteristic separating them from the majority of Americans— the color of their skin. Mexican-Americans who have distinctively Indian features know exactly the kind of prejudicial hell that the Blacks have experienced because Mexican-Americans have experienced and continue to experience the same. The authors have often heard the expression, "Niggers and Spics! They are just alike. Dumb, dirty, lazy, and smelly." The referents were usually talking about Mexican-Americans who "look" Mexican. Hollywood has always know about and taken advantage of this situation. For years Mexicans have been playing Indians and Indians have been playing Mexicans. Yet, not one of either group has ever become a superstar except perhaps Anthony Quinn—but after all, he only looks a tiny bit Indian.

The Mexican-American who does not have the Indian features of his or her brothers and sisters can, with a little trickery, self and social denial, and maybe some transportation, escape nearly all the hazards of prejudice and discrimination. For you see, Mexican is not necessarily Mexican all the time.

When one of the authors was a young boy, he had occasion to mail a package on which was printed the family name, Avila. The postal clerk read the name and brightly asked, "Is that your name?" The author answered that it was; the clerk then asked in a very friendly manner if the name was Spanish. The author in his, then, boyish naivete said, "No, it's Mexican." At that, something happened which the author did not understand until sometime later after he had seen it happen many times. The clerk's entire demeanor changed. He said, "Oh," and was no longer cheery and friendly, but cold and distant. The business was conducted with no further verbal exchanges. The author discovered that people of Mexican and Spanish descent were not the same, and that Spanish was somehow better than Mexican. He also discovered that by simply saying he was Spanish he could be treated much better and have many more doors open for him. (He didn't do this very often though, because when he said he was Mexican and there were no flinches or character changes, he know he was meeting a potential friend. There were times, however, when it was necessary to do so in order to avoid the possible loss of something or someone important to him.)

Thus, "Spanish" people are welcome in many places across this land where Mexicans are not. And many Mexican-Americans have played this game throughout their lives to avoid discrimination. Some, just to be sure, have gone so far as to deny both Mexican and Spanish heritage, passing themselves off as Italian, Jewish, or some other nationality for which they thought they could be mistakenly identified.

One aspect of this game that would be comical, if it were not so sad, is what the authors call the "Castilian Hussle." Some Mexican Nationals as well as Mexican-Americans believe that throughout the history of Mexico a strain of Mexicans dating from the time of Cortes has been able to keep their ancestors pure and untainted by the blood of the natives of the countries they conquered. These true believers refer to themselves as Castilians, and even if they were born in Mexico they will say, "Yes, I am from Mexico, but I am not Mexican; I am Castilian Spanish." And it works!, which probably tells us more about the people it works on, than those who play the game.

The authors' intention is not to make fun of anyone, but to emphasize the desperation that oppressed people can feel and the lengths to which they must go in order to escape injustice. But doing so is sad, because the kind of self-denial we have been discussing must leave terrible psychic scars upon those forced to engage in the process.

In any event, while the Mexican-American is like all other minorities, he or she is different, too.

WHAT'S ALL THAT CRAP ABOUT...

Intelligence

To the authors, one of the most insensitive, damaging and inconceivable pastimes in which academicians engage is the attempt to compare the intelligence of minority groups with that of the majority, particularly if the minority group involved has experienced the consequences of extreme prejudice and discrimination. Individuals who persist in suggesting that the native intelligence of the majority can be compared with that of a minority simply do not have a basic understanding of intelligence measurements and their limitations.

Our most sophisticated intelligence measurements are not culture free and our so-called culture free measurements are notoriously foul with regard to validity and reliability. ***Intelligence tests do not measure basic capacity.*** They measure a person's total life experience and cultural milieu. The closer one's life experience is related to the structure and content of an intelligence test, the higher he or she will score; the less related, the lower the score. Intelligence tests in their present form, rather than measuring basic potential, more accurately compare how closely one group's socialization process resembles another group's.

Individuals born into a lower socioeconomic class, shut out of the society, suffering mental and physical deprivations, and having different cultural values are most certainly going to score lower on intelligence measurements constructed by members of groups not fitting this sociocultural mode. Furthermore, until better measurements are developed or a universal indicator of basic intelligence is found, any attempt to compare one group's intelligence with another's is futile, and studying the current research on this topic will tell the reader little about the ability of Mexican-Americans or any other minority group.

Self-Concept

The self-concept is one of the most important aspects of behavior. It must be at least mentioned when speaking of any human being. Yet, little time will be spent on the topic because in relation to minorities so little is known about it. The research available on the self-concept of minorities is totally conflicting. Some of these data reveal no difference between the self-concept of minority and majority members; some say that majority members have a higher self-concept than minorities; and some say that minorities have a higher self-concept than majorities. It is confusing just to say it.

The self-concept is probably the most important factor in anyone's life and understanding the self-concept of their clients may be counselors' most important task. A study of literature, however, will not help the counselor much in trying to do so.

The conflicting data most likely arise from two factors. One is the nature of the groups being sampled and the other is the nature of the instrument used. Minorities cannot be treated as a total group in self-concept studies. If they are, those data are bound to be spurious. Study after study has demonstrated that social class is a much greater group differentiator than is minority status. In other words, members of the same social class are more alike and more different from other social classes than are different racial, religious, or national members when compared with one another. Therefore, when one compares a minority group with a majority group, especially when one group has a much larger percentage of its members in lower socioeconomic classes, a more positive response will be obtained from the group with the greater representation from the higher socioeconomic classes. And, when examining the converse, the situation where one might be studying a sample of minority members who are mostly in the higher socioeconomic classes, a better self-concept may be obtained than a normally distributed population. They, because of their association with an oppressed minority, have had to have extraordinary ability and personal strength to get where they are.

Furthermore, instruments being used may be totally inadequate for reflecting the true picture of a particular minority group, especially if class representation is biased. Self-concept instruments are based on middle-class majority values. Examining the self-concepts of groups not representing these values may completely distort the resultant data.

Mexican-Americans, in particular, not only have class and social values that differ from but also are in direct contradiction to the values of the middle-class majority. The Mexican-American has many conflicts with the institutions of the larger society, i.e., educational, legal, and social; but these conflicts do not mean that they do not have a great deal of self-respect and confidence in themselves. These positive feelings simply may not be related to the kinds of items one finds on the typical self-concept scale. The young Mexican-American male may not feel too competent with regard to reading, "ritin," "rithmetic," and social skills, but he may feel and experience a great deal of confidence and self-respect from being a member in one of the toughest gangs in a Los Angeles barrio. Let it be enough to say that if teachers or counselors approach the Mexican-American expecting a shy, self-depreciating, inadequate individual with no self-respect, the professionals are in trouble; at best they will be fooled, at worst they may be igniting an explosive situation.

The authors suggest that Mexican-Americans and all minority groups probably have as good a self-concept and as much self-respect as any member of a majority, which is why many minority groups are refusing to be oppressed any longer.

CASE EXAMPLES

Let's briefly examine some of the experiences typical of those the Mexican-American encounters in the growth and socialization process. The following are real life anecdotes common to the Mexican-American experience.

John

John's real name is Juan, but the school has changed it in order to accelerate the acculturation process. John's father has managed to escape the backbreaking work of the migrant laborer and find a menial, but less demanding job in the city. Unfortunately, only a few other Mexican-American families reside in the area. John and the rest of his family can speak only enough English to satisfy their basic needs.

John is dutifully placed in the local school in the grade appropriate to his cohorts. After two or three days we find his teacher speaking to one of her co-workers:

"May, does anyone on the staff speak Spanish?"

"Not that I know of, why?"

"Well, I have this little Mexican boy in class and he doesn't understand a word I say. I'm at my wit's end. I can't find any teacher or student who speaks Spanish.

"What are you going to do?"

"I don't know."

"Well, if I think of anything, I'll let you know."

We run into the two colleagues several days later. May speaks first:

"How are things working out with that little Mexican kid, Julie?"

"Oh, I don't know. The principal is looking into some possibilities for help, but he says we don't really have a program for kids like that. He's a quiet kid, and mostly just sits. He does like to draw, so I let him do that a lot. If he doesn't cause any trouble, I guess I will just let him be and maybe the problem will take care of itself. It is tough, though. The other kids won't play with him because they can't understand him either. They think he's weird. So do I."

Mike

Mike finally sorted it all out to his own satisfaction, but it wasn't easy. Decisions made by others and things happening over which he had no control complicated his life and confused him. He was the product of a mixed marriage, his mother being Mexican-American and his father a typical American mixture of ancestry.

Mike's parents gave him an Anglo name because they believed he would have an easier time of it. They also refused to teach him Spanish. They were afraid he would develop an accent, and they knew children with accents were treated badly in schools. These two decisions, alone, caused Mike trouble throughout his life. His maternal grandparents and assorted aunts and uncles could not speak English; therefore, the only way he was ever able to communicate with them was non-verbally or by having his mother sit beside him and translate the conversations. Not once in his life had he ever spoken directly to his own grandparents or other relatives.

These things also made it difficult for Mike to relate to his peers. Living in a multicultural neighborhood, none of the other children was sure what he was or where he belonged, and neither was he. The Blacks knew he wasn't one of theirs but the Mexicans and "Whites" weren't sure whether he was one of theirs or not. "What kinda Mexican can't speak Spanish?", and "What kinda American has a Mexican name and mother?"

As a child, Mike adjusted to this particular problem by being meaner and tougher than all the other kids so that he could go where he pleased. In the type of neighborhood in which he lived, that made him a leader. Sometimes he roamed with the Mexican kids and sometimes with the non-Mexican kids, but it was a hard way to go.

Confusion really set in as he would often hear his relatives on his father's side speak about those "dirty Mexicans" and "smelly niggers." He knew he wasn't Black, but weren't he and his mother Mexican He would often try to get one of his relatives to explain what they meant, if it meant that they didn't like him and his mother, but he wouldn't get much satisfaction. He would usually get a response like, "Aw, you and your Mom ain't like that. You're not greasers; you're different." This worked out well, however, for he came to the conclusion the whole world was a little crazy and grew up almost totally free of prejudice.

Mike's mother probably was right, and his life may have been much more difficult had he been more easily identifiable as a Mexican-American. But he suffered many adjustment problems as he grew up because of the confusion over his identity, and on many occasions wished he could speak his mother's native tongue. He tried in later years to learn Spanish but was unable to do so. Since he had three college degrees, it didn't seem likely that this was due to a lack of intelligence. He concluded, therefore, that not only did he not learn Spanish as a child, but also at some level of awareness he must have developed a mental block to its acquisition.

By his wits and some luck, Mike made it well enough, but he has many scars left from making it as a minority group member; and the making it, itself, was a difficult process. There is no telling what he might have become or have contributed had he not been burdened by the evils of prejudice.

Gloria

Maria had just arrived at her friend's house in answer to a tearful phone call from Gloria in which the latter had said she and her boyfriend had broken up.

"What happened," asked Maria.

"It was his parents. He didn't even have the guts to tell me himself. His mother called and told me that she and her husband did not think that different races and religions mix and that they just thought it better if their son did not go around with a Mexican Catholic."

Maria sighed and said, "Oh shit."

"What is it, Maria, this thing about being Mexican? Why does it seem to make everything so hard?"

"I do not know."

"Does it last forever?"

"I think so, Gloria; I think it does."

Friends

Five boys were sitting in a restaurant having lunch. They looked like a group of typical anglo-Saxon, middle-class American teenagers. One, however, was not. He was a Mexican-American. His name was Henry.

Four members of the group, including Henry, had been friends for some time, and the other three knew Henry was of Mexican descent. The fifth boy was a relatively new member of the group, and the heritage of the others had not crossed his mind.

As they sat, a couple entered the restaurant. The man could have been of Indian or Mexican descent because he had very black, long, straight hair and the physiognomy spoken of earlier that is typical of American Indians and many Mexican-Americans. The lady had blonde hair and fair skin.

"God damn! Will you look at that. Nothing pisses me off more."

The other four boys looked up at the fifth, and Henry asked, "What?"

"Seeing a beautiful white woman hunched all up against a greasy spic."

The other four boys froze. Henry's three friends had seen him tear into many another boy for much less. Fortunately, though young, Henry was maturing and beginning to learn the futility of trying to beat prejudice out of people. He let it pass, but you can be assured that the other three friends soon clarified an issue for the fourth, and such an incident, in this group, did not happen again.

A CULTURAL HERITAGE

Aside from the dual-headed monster of prejudice and discrimination, two things seem to be the major complications of the problems in the Mexican-American experience. The first is a cultural heritage that often contradicts that of the majority. The second is the attitude of majority group members.

Some Mexican-American values are in direct conflict with those of the majority and place the minority group member at a disadvantage when trying to survive.

First, the nature of the Mexican-American cultural heritage is socialistic. The family is of primary importance and takes precedent over any outside concerns, be they school, work, or social matters. The family members develop a sense of cooperation rather than competition. Many Mexican-Americans, therefore, enter the competitive society of the majority favoring group rather that individual success.

Second, the Mexican-American culture, like all Latin cultures, is highly authoritarian. The children are taught to give unquestioning obedience to the head of the family and to be strongly dependent on that authority for decision making. Thus, partly because of their training to be obedient, partly because they are taught to be polite, and partly as a defensive coping behavior, Mexican-Americans may be quiet and submissive.

Third, many Mexican-Americans have a present orientation that does not stress preparation for the future nor place importance on the acquisition of material goods.

Fourth, the Mexican-American may have a code of honor that emphasizes the "macho" image, where one suffers frustration and disappointment in silence, avoids losing face, and adjusts to problems rather than solves them. Finally, the status of women is clearly inferior.

Without question, in our present day American society, any child—brown, black, or white—who is not adamantly achievement and competition oriented, is unquestioning of authority, submissive, uninterested in material things, more loyal to a group than to themselves, and consider females to be inferior is in trouble.

But, let persons engaged in helping professions be forewarned. These characteristics are deeply engrained and at the core of the Mexican-American character. They are not aspects of the latin persona to be challenged, attacked, or degraded. To do so is to guarantee that one will not see a helpee again.

The best entry into the Mexican-American's confidence is to take the attitude, "I accept you as you are and want only to help you acquire skills that will better enable you to reach your potential." Then if further counseling and guidance temper some of their beliefs, so be it.

Situational Factors

Aside from long-term factors of cultural heritage that conflict with the potential development of the Mexican-American, situational factors make integration difficult. Certain behaviors have grown out of the Mexican-American attempt to adjust to the majority society or failure to do so.

Many Mexican-American parents feel unable to give their children the necessary skills to cope with the larger community.

They actually feel inferior to the Anglo members of the society and avoid them, not from lack of concern, but out of this fear. Mothers and fathers will not question their employers and will not go to school or may not even answer the door when some perceived authority comes calling. Not uncooperativeness but rather fear of making a fool of themselves or embarrassing their children causes this behavior.

Related to this sense of inadequacy is the fact that parents are sometimes hesitant or refrain altogether from helping their children with school work. They are concerned that they will not know how to help or might do more harm than good if they interfere with their child's studies.

Another consequence of situational factors is that parents, knowing their values conflict with the majority, refrain from trying to instill them in their children. They hope their children will somehow assimilate the values of the majority, making a better adjustment than they themselves did. This, of course, is no answer. What usually happens is that children reach adolescence without a clear set of values, are more confused, and have more trouble coping. Because of all the conflicts, the Mexican-American family is replete with all the problems related to domestic disharmony—delinquency, hostility, academic difficulty, and the like.

SOCIAL ATTITUDES AND ACTION

The other factor mainly responsible for the failure of our society to adequately integrate the Mexican-American is the attitude and actions of the larger society toward this minority. The most tragic and inexcusable circumstance in the greater society is that where large numbers of Mexican-Americans are found something very much like a caste system exists. This is similar to the situation of Blacks, but needs to be emphasized because many do not realize that the Mexican-American experience is often no less oppressive or restrictive than that of Blacks. As always, the system results in geographical isolation, job and pay discrimination, restriction of personal interactions, and all of the other deprivations associated with racial or religious prejudice.

Our schools, institutions which should be most responsive to the integration of our minorities, perpetrate some of the worst injustices. When studies have been made, the following attitudes have been found to exist among non-Mexican public school personnel toward Mexican-American (Carter, 1970; Hernandez, 1973):

1. inferior,
2. lazy,
3. unable to learn,
4. happy with their lot,
5. peculiar,
6. hopeless, and
7. dangerous.

Some of the school practices found to exist are (Carter, 1970; Hernandez, 1973):

1. teachers ignoring students;
2. schools making no allowance for the schedule of migrant workers;
3. universities not preparing teachers to deal with any minority;
4. schools assigning teachers, who do not speak Spanish, to predominantly Mexican-American classes or schools;
5. banning of the Spanish language or reference to anything Mexican; and
6. prohibiting students from speaking Spanish.

RECOMMENDATIONS

The failure of our society to fully integrate the Mexican-American as a first-class citizen is long standing and inexcusable. This integration is not going to be accomplished by the publication of a single chapter in one book. Hopefully, though, from this reading the counselor will be better able to contribute to that integration in a more effective way. Toward this end we offer some recommendations. The reader may consider them to be no more than common sense. But, we humans are often guilty of not using common sense enough and are more likely to do so if we receive little reminders now and then of just what that commodity is.

Before we enumerate these recommendations we would like to point out what as counselors we are definitely *not* trying to do. Too often the Mexican-American is looked upon as a foreigner who has to be acculturated; that is, taught the characteristics and values of the larger society, usually at the expense of his or her own cultural heritage. Mexican-Americans are not foreigners. They are Americans who have historical roots different from, but not inferior to those of other Americans. Our purpose is not to make them like all other Americans, but to give them the skills and knowledge that enable them to succeed, as they share with us those positive things from their culture. Our task is to **integrate,** not acculturate the Mexican-American.

Acculturation is an insult. It says that one set of principles, values, beliefs, and behaviors is right while another is wrong. An attempt to acculturate almost always results in an approach where the majority member says, "What you are is bad, and what you have is useless. Leave all that behind, and let me show you the way."

The quickest way to failure is to begin our first interaction with other persons by telling them that what they are is bad, wrong, inept, or immoral. If we do so, not only are we doomed to failure, but also we are usually dead wrong! Most often our own house is not in such great order that we can offer it up as a perfect model at the expense of another life style.

In light of this purpose, recommendations of the authors and of Carter (1970) and Hernandez (1973) when working with Mexican-Americans or any minority are as follows:

1. Always accept clients exactly as they are, accepting their values, beliefs, and behaviors, and go from there. Take the position that what they are is good and that your function is to add to what they are, not to subtract or distract from it. Project an attitude that says, "What you are is good. What I want to do is lend you some things of mine that I think will make life easier for you and give you a better potential for success."

   If you can't honestly and sincerely do this, we suggest you do not be a counselor for the counselee. You're wasting time, or worse.

2. Although you are working with a Mexican-American, recognize and treat that person as an individual. The purpose of this article has been to give the reader some insight into Mexican-Americans, not to suggest that they are all alike. They are not. They are like every other group; their members differ from each other in as many ways as they differ from another group. Ascertain those differences before you go blundering in and making a fool of yourself with some kind of generalization.

   A word about the term "Chicano" may be in order. It is currently the "in" word and many writers use it to designate the Mexican-American. Militant and poor Mexican-Americans also are using it as a designation of pride or unity. It has not always been so. The exact origin of the term is not known, and it has no exact meaning. To many, especially older members of the minority, it represents a picture of the poor, uneducated, exploited field hand. To many Mexican-Americans it historically has and still does have the same distasteful meaning as the word "nigger" or "spic." These individuals would consider it an insult to be addressed in that way. That is why these authors have used the term Mexican-American. To our knowledge no one is offended by that designation. The term is discussed here in order to emphasize the importance of knowing the individual to whom you are speaking.

3. If you have group counseling skills, use group counseling with the Mexican-American because of their orientation to group cohesiveness. Also, at times a helpful procedure is to have groups that are homogeneous so as to achieve better self-understanding and at other times for better minority-majority group interaction and understanding have heterogeneous groups.

4. Initiate programs early and work on them over an extended period of time. Such programs are of an invitational nature, but counselors have found that starting early has a snowballing effect and accomplishes much more than waiting until specific problems arise. Some examples of such programs are as follows:

a. occupational exploration groups,

b. sensitivity groups,

c. college orientation programs which include bringing to the group Mexican-Americans who are successfully pursuing college programs,

d. role model groups which invite successful Mexican-Americans from all walks of life to discuss their lives and work with the members, and

e. cultural exploration groups.

5. Whenever possible, integrate the values and beliefs of the Mexican-American into your counseling with them by showing the use and place of such values and beliefs.

6. Recognize that the teaching of skills is usually more useful than the teaching of values. Mexican-Americans have most likely already been exposed to any value that might be introduced to them. What they need most are better, more effective skills.

7. Initiate a counseling program early; do not delay the beginning; begin immediately and make subsequent appointments soon and frequently.

8. When counseling is initiated, get to the problems. Do not delay with the accumulation of long case histories or explorations of the past.

9. Be flexible. This client is not likely to be susceptible to "pure line" counseling theory. Get a feel for the client; then select what you believe will be the best process approach to use, whether that be client-centered, behavioristic, rational, or combination.

10. Use standardized tests for individual guidance, not for comparative purposes.

11. Focus on one objective at a time rather than taking a shotgun approach. Sometimes this gives a particular client a better sense of success and more confidence in the counselor.

12. Be a leader in initiating programs in your community, agency, or school that respond to the special needs and problems of this group. Help to accept and utilize the cultural heritage of the Mexican-American.

13. Don't judge your Mexican-American clients by your own value system. Find out as much as you can about their culture and make your judgments from that frame of reference.

14. Involve the Mexican-American community. The greater the involvement, the more successful a program will be. Every attempt should be made to utilize the total available Mexican-American population in what you are doing. You will be most successful if you will

    a. involve parents;

    b. form community groups to achieve

        1) language improvement,
        2) community counseling,
        3) sensitivity to certain issues or concerns, or
        4) community orientation to the agencies and facilities available;

    c. engage in public relations;

    d. encourage the employment of Mexican-Americans in the schools, businesses, and community agencies; and

    e. utilize in your program as many successful Mexican-Americans as you can find.

In working with our Mexican-American population a special urgency exists because this minority group is increasing faster than other minorities. For example, the estimate is that the

Hispanic population of which Mexican-Americans are by far the greatest number, will be the largest minority in the U.S. by 1990 (Long, 1982). Furthermore, because of the new immigration bill mentioned earlier, larger numbers will become American citizens than ever before; and as a result of certain stipulations of the bill that require greater services and protection to aliens, tremendous increases in monies and resources will be needed to provide for their needs. Of special importance, then, is the preparation of professionals to work with this growing minority. Cultural sensitivity is a beginning whereby the counselor can enhance effectiveness in addressing the pressing needs of Mexican-Americans.

REFERENCES

Carter, T.P. (1970). *Mexican-Americans in schools: A history of educational neglect.* New York: College Entrance Examination Board.

Long, S.M. (1982). An American profile: Trends and issues in the 80s. *Educational Leadership, 39,* 460-464.

Hernandez, N.G. (1973). Variables affecting achievement of middle school Mexican-American students. *Review of Educational Research. 43,* 1-39.

Longstreet, S. (1977). *All star cast: An anecdotal history of Los Angeles.* New York: Thomas Y. Crowell. pp 15-18.

Prescott, W.H. (1934). *The conquest of Mexico.* Garden City, N Y: International Collectors Library American Headquarters.

15

PREPARATION for HELPING PROFESSIONALS WORKING with DIVERSE POPULATIONS

LARRY C. LOESCH, Ph.D.
Professor and Graduate Coordinator
Department of Counselor Education
University of Florida
Gainesville, Florida

LARRY C. LOESCH, Ph.D.

Larry C. Loesch, Ph.D., is currently a Professor and Graduate Coordinator in the Department of Counselor Education at the University of Florida, Gainesville, Florida. He received both his undergraduate and graduate degrees from Kent State University. He has been at the University of Florida since completion of his doctoral program in June of 1973. Dr. Loesch has had over fifty articles published in professional journals, including more than a dozen specifically relating to the professional preparation of counselors. His recently co-authored book, **Counseling as a Profession,** was released in 1987 by Accelerated Development Publishers. He served from 1984 through 1986 as a member of the Council for the Accreditation of Counseling and Related Educational Programs. Dr. Loesch also is actively involved in several counseling and educational organizations. He is the current Examinations Coordinator for the National Board for Certified Counselors. He and his wife, Barbara, have four daughters.

PREPARATION FOR HELPING PROFESSIONALS WORKING WITH DIVERSE POPULATIONS

Diverse populations are by definition unique: they differ significantly in one or more regards from "typical" client groups. What follows is that in order for helping activities to be effective with persons from diverse populations, those activities also must be unique. Therefore, to speak of the "basic facets," or commonalities, in the professional preparation of persons who intend to work with special groups is to raise an inherent contradiction. Fortunately, however, this situation is not without resolution.

If a certain perspective is maintained, then commonalities can be discussed. This perspective holds that the implementation of a preparation method is unique with regard to diverse populations rather than to the method itself. *What is needed is not unique training methods but rather unique applications of existing training methods.* Thus, many of the preparation methods for assisting "typical" populations also are effective for training in helping diverse populations if the methods can be adapted successfully. Therefore *emphasis in training is shifted from a focus on the nature of the activity to a focus on the method of implementation.* By the same token *the preparation method selection process may be shifted from evaluation of the relative merits of various methods to evaluation of the ease with which any chosen method may be implemented with a given diverse population.*

This situation, however, should not be construed to mean that innovative preparation methods are not needed or do not exist. On the contrary, innovative methods are an excellent complement to the implementation of established methods. The point is that, as with the preparation for helping any client group, a solid foundation must be built before the garnishments are added (Dash, 1975).

Preparation methods offered in this chapter fall in the proven or established category because space does not permit allusion to all possible methods. In reading the following discussion a helpful procedure may be to keep a particular special population in mind in order to consider the question, "How do the points or suggestions made apply to that diverse population?" Hopefully, this consideration will provide the reader a more practical frame of reference.

POTENTIAL COUNSELING FUNCTIONS

The professional preparation of helping professionals who intend to counsel, or otherwise work with, persons from diverse populations must necessarily take into account potential professional functions (McDavis & Parker, 1977). In other words, for what are these helping professionals being prepared? A multitude of specific answers could be provided, but practical constraints again only allow for discussion of several major functions.

For current purposes, a convenient categorization of functions is that provided by the Council for the Accreditation of Counseling and Related Educational Programs (CACREP) in their Standards for the Preparation of Counselors and Other Personnel Services Specialists (CACREP, 1986). These standards identify six major counselor functions: individual and group counseling, vocational counseling, assessment, consultation, and research. In order to be as comprehensive as possible, two additional functions also will be considered: special types of counseling (e.g., marriage, family, life style, leisure, and so forth) and teaching.

1. INDIVIDUAL COUNSELING

The helping professional's functioning in individual counseling is typically dictated by a preferred orientation, degree of "directiveness," or both. Therein lies the crux of the issues of individual counseling with persons from diverse populations. The question is not whether individual counseling is an appropriate function with persons from diverse populations, but rather which approach is potentially the most effective. For example, the suggestion has been made in other chapters that more structured individual counseling approaches are more effective with Asian-Americans (see Chapter 12) and Blacks (see Chapter 7). Selection of the "right" counseling approach is a tenuous proposition at best; no proven guidelines are readily available. However, regardless of the approach taken, consideration of the client's cultural context is essential (Ivey, 1987).

2. GROUP COUNSELING

Like individual counseling, group counseling has been viewed as a typical or common helping professional function. It has the advantages of maximizing the helping professional's use of time and providing clients with simultaneous multiple interactions and perspectives. It has the disadvantages of reducing the amount of individual "client-counselor" interaction and a somewhat reduced degree of confidentiality. Theoretically, any concern which might be covered in individual counseling also might be covered within the group counseling context.

The helping professional's functioning in the group context is dictated by preferences for various possible orientations, and thus preferences also are an issue here. In addition, the group context brings into consideration the natures of the interactions among the group members. Persons from some special populations are much more willing to interact under such circumstances than are other groups. Accordingly, the social interaction characteristics of a special population are an important issue in the group counseling process (Kaneshige, 1973).

3. VOCATIONAL COUNSELING

The key issues in vocational counseling with persons from diverse populations center on the unique characteristics of those persons (Griffith, 1980; Lewis, 1969; Locke, 1969). To what extent do these unique characteristics affect the nature of the vocational counseling offered? How do they affect the vocational development of these persons? What about their ability to capitalize on vocational opportunities? Questions such as these will be faced by any helping professional working with persons from diverse populations.

4. ASSESSMENT

More than any other function, assessment has been, and remains, at the center of controversy within the helping professions (Samuda, 1975). Assessment procedures range from unobtrusive measures to performance or behavioral criteria. Yet, regardless of the procedures employed, some evaluation is made.

Bias is the term applied when the comparison process is deemed "unfair." Typically, bias in assessments with persons from diverse populations centers on socio-linguistic differences, which in extreme cases may invalidate the assessments. This does not necessarily mean that assessments should not be made with such persons. Rather, it suggests that assessments (and subsequent evaluations) should be made carefully.

5. CONSULTATION

The function of the helping professional as a consultant is a relatively new and emerging one. Perhaps more than any other function, consultation activities allow helping professionals to influence very large numbers of persons (Dinkmeyer & Carlson, 1977). The major concerns in the consultation function relate to the fact that the helping professional is "one step removed" from the people to be affected by the consultation activity and that the consultant may assume several roles (Moracco, 1977). The consultant helps one or more persons help still other persons in the diverse population. This distance between source and impact raises significant questions about which (consultation) tactics have the greatest potential for success. Should the consultant assume an "educative" (i.e., teaching), "counseling," "advice-giving," or "source of information" role for the consultee? The unique characteristics of the diverse population, as well as those of the intermediary, further compound the situation. For example, are socio-political ramifications to the consultants actions present? What is a "perfectly logical," reasonable, and effective course of action for one group may have deleterious effects for another. Therefore, careful examination of all facets of a consultation situation is essential.

6. RESEARCH

The research function in the helping professions is another one which has been a source of controversy, though certainly not to the extent of assessment. The need for research in and on counseling is generally acknowledged and widely espoused (Sweeney, 1979). However, only a minute proportion of helping professionals actually ever engage in research projects. Relatedly, only a small portion of the research is specifically concerned with applications or implications for diverse populations.

The major issue in research concerning counseling with persons from diverse populations traditionally has been the lack of significant numbers of persons from which to derive data. Relatively large samples of subjects are difficult to obtain because large groups of persons from diverse populations often are not available in readily accessible geographic areas. More recently some special population groups have resisted participation in research endeavors because of concern about the validities of previous research done with or applied to them. These situations necessitate caution and sensitivity from helping professionals engaging in research activities.

7. SPECIAL TYPES OF COUNSELING

The rapid growth of the helping professions and the increasing recognition of their positive values in our society have allowed for the development of many new functions. Among the more recent innovations (at least in terms of relatively widespread practice) are such things as marriage and/or family counseling, bereavement counseling, life style counseling, leisure counseling, midlife and pre-retirement counseling, assertiveness training, stress management, and health counseling. While services such as these have expanded the member helping professions, their implementation with persons from diverse populations has been somewhat slower (Draguns, 1981; Pedersen, Lonner, & Draguns, 1976). This latency is probably in fact a positive phenomenon. Thorough understanding of the pertinent characteristics (e.g., familial dynamics, typical leisure patterns and values, or religious tenets about grieving) of the diverse population and establishment of empirical support for the effectiveness of particular techniques with particular diverse populations should be established before these special types of counseling are implemented. Fortunately, in view of the rapidly expanding knowledge base in the counseling professions, probably this implementation lag is only a temporary phenomenon.

8. TEACHING

The teaching function is not one normally associated with the "counseling" connotation of the helping professions. Yet much of what helping professionals do is teaching in its most rudimentary form (Rustad, 1975). In concert with the reasoning throughout this chapter, the teaching methods used with persons from diverse populations must be uniquely adapted or implemented. Some of the more common teaching activities that can be readily adapted in this regard include use of literature (e.g., pamphlets, articles, or books), role-playing, visual media (e.g., videotapes or films), and experiential activities (e.g., field-trips or attendance at social functions). Similarly, assessing, gaining and evaluating cultural knowledge, investigating ethnic literature, and using specific behaviors to increase sensitivity to ethnic minorities, also are applicable to direct service work with persons from diverse populations (Parker, Vally, & Geary, 1986).

EVALUATING FUNCTIONS FOR USE

The eight functions described are all potentially useful for working with persons from diverse populations. The word **potential** must be emphasized because each of the functions will not necessarily be helpful for all the diverse population groups. Indeed, some of the preceding chapters have provided specific examples of functions which would have little or no utilitarian value to helping professionals for work with some persons. Further, specific recommendations about specific functions for specific groups would be too numerous and lengthy to be much practical help. Accordingly, a more fundamental approach is in order.

The appropriateness (and therefore potential for success) of any of these eight functions for a given diverse population may be easily evaluated by considering three basic questions.

1. **Is it feasible to use the function with the person(s) in question?** If the function is "completely out of the

question" for the person(s), the evaluation process obviously stops here. However, an affirmative response raises another question.

2. **Is the use of the function necessary?** Feasibility in and of itself is insufficient justification for the application of a function. A definable need must be established. Again, a negative response stops the evaluation process, while an affirmative response raises another question.

3. **Is the use of the function worth the effort?** A particular function may be feasible, desirable, and necessary, but its implementation "costs" may far exceed the potential benefits to be derived. To engage in a function under such conditions is to be highly inefficient. A negative response to this question implies either termination of the evaluation or re-evaluation of the answer to the second question; perhaps an alternative approach is more appropriate. Of course an affirmative response suggests that the function should be implemented.

Effective preparation programs will provide helping professionals with the skills and knowledge necessary to provide sound answers to these questions. This then is a good time to consider the components of an effective preparation program.

COMPONENTS OF A TRAINING PROGRAM

Preservice and inservice training programs for helping professionals intending to work with persons from diverse populations must encompass a wide variety of dimensions and experiences. In order to acknowledge the complex interrelations among these dimensions and experiences, a training program may be more appropriately described in terms of its major, basic components. For our purposes, four such components will be addressed: knowledge acquisition, attitude awareness, experiential interaction, and skill development. Obviously these components are related integrally in actual practice, but they are separated here for discussion clarity.

1. KNOWLEDGE ACQUISITION

A strong cognitive base is an acknowledged foundation for any aspect of the helping professions (Calia, 1974; Parker, Valley, & Geary, 1986). Indeed, for this particular type of preparation program, a significant portion of the trainees' time will be spent in attempting to answer the question, "What makes a diverse population special?"

One of the primary things a helping professional needs to know is the cultural and/or sociological characteristics of the diverse population (McDavis & Parker, 1977; Parker, 1987). What, if anything, is unique about them in terms of their appearance, dress, or other aspects of self presentation? Where do they live? What are the identifying characteristics of their lifestyles? Are common personality traits present? Do they have socioeconomic, political, or religious similarities? In general, the helping professional needs to learn how the diverse population is similar to, or different from, other groups in regard to identifiable cultural or sociological characteristics.

In a like manner, a helping professional needs to be informed about the normative behaviors, both verbal and nonverbal, within the diverse populations. Do they have unique speech patterns? Do they have a specific vocabulary? Do they use unique gestures, facial expressions, or body movements? In essence, the helping professional needs to know what is acceptable behavior within the diverse population and how such behavior differs from other groups.

A helping professional also must know which behaviors are idiosyncratic within the diverse population. That is, are some behaviors sometimes evident within the diverse population which are not modal within that group but also are not necessarily characteristic of other groups? Knowledge of these and modal behaviors will afford the helping professional insight into "socially acceptable" behavioral interactions within the diverse population.

If helping professionals are to be able to interact effectively with persons from diverse populations, the professional also must be familiar with the socio-political functioning within that population. That is, they must know who the leaders are and what types of persons earn the greatest respect. More importantly, they must understand the reasons why those persons are influential.

With regard to direct contact helping functions (e.g., individual counseling), helping professionals must be knowledgeable of preferred modes of interaction (Christensen, 1984; Pedersen, Holwill, & Shapiro, 1978). What helping techniques have been proven to be effective? Which have been ineffective? Which have been as yet untried or evaluated for effectiveness?

Finally, the helping professional who works with persons from special populations needs a thorough knowledge of professional ethics as well as the "informal" ethics within the diverse population. Do these sets of ethics ever come into conflict? In what ways, or areas, are they similar? This type of knowledge will, to a great extent, enable helping professionals to avoid situations which are both personally and professionally difficult or compromising.

A strong cognitive base may be described as a necessary but not sufficient condition for effective helping. Accordingly, this foundation must be complemented by the second major component in the preparation process.

2. ATTITUDE AWARENESS

Attitude awareness has been deemed especially important for working with persons from diverse populations (Gump, 1974; Neimeyer & Fukuyama, 1984). This includes personal attitude awareness as well as awareness of the diverse population person, and this emphasis is typically based on the assumption of attitudinal differences between helping professionals and persons from diverse populations. If such differences exist, they may interfere with the helping process. Of course this assumption may be invalidated to some extent if the helping professional is a member of the diverse population.

Given the need for professional preparation in terms of attitude awareness, the question then becomes of which attitudes should the helping professional be aware? For the purposes here, five types of attitudes will be considered within this preparation component.

Professional's Attitude About Self. The first type of attitude of which the helping professional should be aware is attitude about self (Banikiotes, 1975; Fuhrmann, 1978). A helping professional's self (attitude) awareness has been shown to be directly related to helping effectiveness. Those helping professionals who are able to assess and evaluate accurately their own attitudes generally are more effective in helping others because they are aware how their self-attitudes affect their counseling activities (Neimeyer & Fukuyama, 1984).

Professionals' Attitudes about Diverse Populations. Helping professionals' attitudes about diverse populations are a second important type. Helping professionals must be aware of their own biases, positive or negative, if they are to be able to work with persons from diverse populations effectively (Hulnick, 1977; Parker, Bingham, & Fukuyama, 1985). This type of attitude awareness enables the helping professional to be "authentic," a characteristic generally understood to be necessary for competent helping interaction. Further, it enables professionals to compare their attitudes about the diverse population with their attitudes about themselves. This comparison then provides a framework from which to approach their helping activities, or if the differences are too great, to move toward referrals.

Diverse Populations' Attitude about Helping Professionals. A third type of attitude often overlooked, but which may be crucial to the helping process, is the diverse populations' attitude about helping professionals. Perceptions of the worth and value of the helping process (as typically conceived) vary greatly across diverse populations. Some groups readily enter into the helping process while others do so only if forced. Preparation in the awareness of such attitudes is essential, particularly for the initial stages of the helping process.

Society's Attitude About the Diverse Population. A fourth type of attitude of which helping professionals should be aware is society's attitude about the diverse population. Particularly important in this regard are stereotypes (Paradis, 1981). Which characteristics of the diverse population are typically stereotyped? What validity, if any, is in the stereotypes? How do such stereotypes relate to, or affect, people's behaviors? Which of society's attitudes about the diverse population are evolving or changing? What characteristics of the diverse population seem to be the basis of stereotypes? The answers to questions such as these allow the helping professional to have a perspective on the society in which the special population exists. This perspective should in turn enable the helping professional to understand some of the "realities" of people in the special population, thus facilitating the helping process.

Diverse Population Members' Attitude About Themselves. The last type of attitude to be considered is the diverse population members' attitude about themselves. What do they perceive as their positive and negative characteristics? What are their self-perceived strengths, weaknesses, assets, and liabilities? What is the nature of their collective self-concepts? And perhaps most important, how do these attitudes interact with the others previously mentioned?

Development of Valid Attitude Awareness. The establishment of a comprehensive cognitive base and the development of valid attitude awareness are absolutely essential for the effective preparation of helping professionals who intend to work with diverse populations. However, their worth will be diminished if they are not grounded in reality for the trainee. Thus they serve as the lead into the third preparation component.

3. EXPERIENTIAL INTERACTION

An effective preparation program will provide helping professionals with a diverse set of experiences with diverse populations (Paradis, 1981; Parker, Valley, & Geary, 1986; Woods, 1977). These experiences are important because they allow helping professionals to validate their own knowledge base and attitude awareness. They also aid the helping professional to gain appreciation for the lifestyles of the diverse population. On a different tact, they have the subtle benefit of allowing the people from diverse populations to interact with potential helping professionals. Thus experiential activities play a significant role in the preparation process by benefiting both trainees and helping professionals.

The most obvious type of experiential activity to be incorporated into a training program is direct interaction with the diverse population, under supervision (MacGuffie & Henderson,

1977; Parker, Valley, & Geary, 1986). Beyond "laboratory" types of experiences, helping professionals also should be provided with opportunities for less formal interactions, including visiting homes, social gathering places, or work locations typical of the population. Helping professionals should note the environment, social and familial atmospheres, and behaviors in order to solidify their conceptualizations of the lifestyles of the diverse population.

A related set of experiences should allow helping professionals to interact formally and informally with persons from diverse populations (Parker, Valley, & Geary, 1986). Formal activities might include such things as participating in vocational activities or formal social meetings. Informal activities might include such things as casual conversations, participation in leisure activities, or going to informal social events. The intention of these types of experiences is to allow the helping professional to become aware of and practice ways of establishing rapport with persons from diverse populations.

Another set of experiences which helping professionals should have is experiences with other groups who have reason to interact with persons from the diverse population. These experiences should be similar to those described previously, particularly in the areas of formal and informal interactions. These types of experiences will provide helping professionals with two additional first hand perspectives. The first concerns how the diverse population is perceived by members of the other group. The second concerns how persons from the diverse population are likely to be received by members of the other group. Again, such experiences will enable the helping professional to gain an appreciation and understanding of the life circumstances of the diverse population.

While experiences such as these generally add significantly to the preparation of helping professionals, some caution should be noted. In any preparation program only a relatively limited number of experiences with any given diverse population will be possible because of time and/or resource constraints (Lloyd, 1987). Accordingly, these experiences should be carefully selected and developed so that maximum benefit may be achieved (Hood & Arceneaux, 1987). At the same time, helping professionals should be cautioned against overgeneralizing from very small samples. That is, they must realize that such experiences may have only limited representative value across the diverse population. If helping professionals do not realistically evaluate the nature of their experiences, the experiences may do more harm than good.

Strong cognitive and experiential bases and attitude awareness do much to aid helping professionals in their professional interactions with persons from diverse populations. Yet knowledge, perspective, and social interaction skills are not enough. A professional must by definition have specific, identifiable skills. The provision of these skills constitutes the fourth preparation component.

4. SKILL DEVELOPMENT

A major portion of the professional literature in the helping professions has been devoted to the theoretical development, practical application, and subsequent evaluation of a variety of helping skills (Burke, 1978). These processes have led to the identification of a large number of such skills. However, they also have fostered considerable debate as to what constitutes basic helping skills, particularly for use with persons from diverse populations (Ivey, 1987). At best, the resolution of these debates seems to be that the basic skills are what any particular author believes them to be. The ones to be presented are no exception.

In regard to helping persons from diverse populations, to adopt a perspective similar to the one recommended for helping functions seems imperative. That is, skills themselves are not unique but rather the ways they are used with particular individuals. Accordingly, each of the following types of skills should be considered in regard to their potential for use with persons from various diverse populations.

Active Listening. Active listening (facilitative responding) skills have been cited by numerous authors as being at the heart of helping. However, to assume that active listening, from within the context of a nondirective approach, will be effective with all persons from diverse populations would be wrong (Holiman & Lauver, 1987). Indeed, some research shows that for persons from some diverse populations a highly directive approach may be necessary. Consequently, helping professionals should receive training in some of the directive helping approaches. Also these helping professionals should receive approach discrimination training so that they will be able to use an appropriate approach with any given diverse populations.

Individual and Group Appraisal. Individual and group appraisal (i.e., measurement and evaluation) skills also are among the commonly cited basic helping skills. However, as mentioned previously, considerable debate has occurred as to the validities of appraisals made on persons from diverse populations. This debate suggests that helping professionals should receive two related but distinct types of preparation in appraisal. The first type is preparation for the more common methods of appraisal, typically referred to as standardized testing. This training is important because helping professionals will (1) sometimes use standardized testing procedures since such procedures will in fact be the most appropriate, and (2) need to know whether standardized testing procedures are the most appropriate or if some other procedures should be used. The second type of preparation is for the less common methods of appraisal: unobtrusive measures, behavioral observations, self reports, structured interviews, and the like. For many diverse populations this latter type of appraisal may be the only possibility. However, failure to provide effective training in both types would seriously limit the trainee's eventual professional effectiveness.

Vocabulary Adjustment. A third basic skill in which helping professionals should be trained is vocabulary adjustment. Diverse populations, like any other societal group, have elements of speech which have interpretable meaning only in the context of the diverse population group (Parker, Bingham, & Fukuyama, 1985). Helping professionals must be aware of these dialectic patterns and subtleties if they are to interact effectively. This is not to suggest, however, that helping professionals must learn to use a new language. Rather, it means that they should gain an understanding and appreciation for differences in communication patterns and modes among people with different life circumstances. Likewise, nonverbal communication behaviors and their associated interpretations often differ dramatically across societal subgroups. Helping professionals must gain an understanding and appreciation of the differences in both verbal patterns and nonverbal behavior interpretations if they are to achieve acceptance from persons from diverse populations and work effectively with them.

Confrontation. The last of the so-called basic skills to be considered is confrontation. The process of confrontation within the helping process is indeed a difficult one for several reasons. First, it at least temporarily puts the helping professional and the person being helped in an adversary position. Second, it often raises feelings of defensiveness and withdrawal in the person being helped. Third, some helping professionals interpret confrontation as license to be aggressive and punitive. And fourth, because of these other reasons, confrontation is a common reason for premature termination of a helping relationship. Thus the use of confrontation is potentially "dangerous" in, or to, any helping relationship. This potential is increased with persons from diverse populations because of the greater possibility for communication misinterpretation. However, confrontation is often the most powerful method of bringing about "psychological movement" within a helping relationship. Accordingly, helping professionals should have careful and thorough training in the use of confrontation.

Effective Preparation. Effective training in these basic skills should allow helping professionals to be at least minimally competent in their helping efforts with persons from diverse populations. One must remember, however, that these are only basic skills. Other skills, including those specific to particular diverse populations, also should be included in the preparation process. Unfortunately, space does not permit discussion of these other skills, save acknowledgment of their importance to a fully and completely trained helping professional.

PREPARATION IMPLEMENTATION

The professional preparation of the helping professional intending to work with persons from diverse populations must be a lifelong and extensive process if it is to be effective. Yet the process does not have to be a difficult one if careful attention is given to planning and implementation.

Activities for Cognitive Base Preparation

The first stage of the preparation process should provide a broad base of cognitive knowledge about diverse populations.

Obviously a careful reading of this book is a first step toward establishing such a base (Paradis, 1981; Parker, Valley, & Geary, 1986). The following are some related activities which might be used to supplement this reading and lead toward the same goal.

1. Reread any two chapters of this book and develop a list of similarities and differences between the two diverse populations described.

2. Select any chapter (i.e., diverse population) and create an annotated bibliography of at least seven references appropriate for that chapter.

3. Select any particular point made by an author and write a paper, complete with references, arguing the opposite point of view. For example, you might argue that intelligence tests are not unfair to Mexican-American children because these children must exist and function within the majority society.

4. Select any chapter of interest and then create five multiple-choice, factual questions not covered in either the pre or post tests.

5. Identify ten sources of information (e.g., books, journal articles, or other media) about a particular diverse population which are not cited in this book.

6. Assume that you have the opportunity to interview some persons from a diverse population of interest to you. Develop a set of at least ten questions which will enable you to obtain factual information from the persons you will interview.

7. Assume that you have been asked to describe a given diverse population to a class of fifth graders. Prepare a ten minute presentation you could use to fulfill this request.

8. Select any chapter of this book and attempt to recreate the outline the author(s) used to write it. Then identify other pertinent topics which might have been included.

9. Identify a particular diverse population. Then write a paper, complete with references, defending the use of a particular helping orientation with persons from that diverse population.

10. Examine the reference lists from any two chapters of this book. Then identify the references from one chapter which might apply (approximately) equally to the other chapter; repeat for the second chapter.

Activities such as these should provide a strong cognitive base which should in turn serve as the foundation for subsequent activities.

Activities for Attitude Awareness Preparation

The second stage of the preparation process should focus on attitude awareness. Activities such as the following may be helpful in bringing about such awareness.

1. Identify any particular diverse population and then create a list of at least ten stereotypes you think people hold about that population (exclude stereotypes presented in the pertinent chapter of this book).

2. Assume that you have the opportunity to interview some persons from a particular diverse population and that you would like to know what they are really like. Create a list of questions that you would ask each person.

3. Assume that you are an arbitrator between a group of persons from a diverse population and a group of persons from the White, middle-class majority. Compose a "treaty" to settle the differences between the two groups.

4. Assume you have the power to enact legislation which would benefit a particular diverse population. List and explain the laws you would enact.

5. Assign each person in a group to be representative of a different diverse population and then conduct a mock

United Nations activity by having the representative create a plan for the world wide enrichment of the human condition.

6. Select any particular diverse population and then ask children from different grade levels (e.g., third, seventh, and twelfth) to describe a person from that population. Compare and contrast the responses.

7. Select any two diverse populations and interview at least five persons from each as to their attitudes about the other population.

8. Select any diverse population and interview at least five persons from that population about their attitudes about the helping professions. Include a question concerning how they feel about being interviewed.

9. Create a self attitude awareness activity which would be effective for use with a given diverse population group.

Other activities intended to enhance attitude awareness may be found in the references of some of the chapters in this book.

Experiential Activities as Preparation

Experiential activities constitute the next step in the helping professional preparation process. The following activities exemplify some possible experiential activities which are well-suited for training purposes.

1. Visit, individually or with others, a restaurant which caters primarily to persons from a particular diverse population.

2. Attend a religious ceremony (e.g., church service) which is intended primarily for members of a particular diverse population.

3. Interview an identified political leader of a particular diverse population. Incorporate questions about current issues and problems as well as future political actions for the population.

4. Observe a group of children from a particular diverse population while at play. Note consistent behavioral patterns and interaction styles.

5. Interview at least five persons from each of three different diverse populations as to their favorite leisure activities. Compare and contrast their responses.

6. Interview a helping professional from a particular diverse population. Inquire as to the professional problems and issues that person most frequently encounters in professional activities.

Supervised Practice as Preparation

The final stage in the preparation process is supervised practice in helping relationships with persons from diverse populations. The following activities might serve as initial activities in this regard. Note that these activities should be used only after the participants have successfully completed the first three recommended stages.

1. Have one person role play the part of a helping professional and another the part of a person from a diverse population. Have a third person serve as an observer. Role play a helping session for approximately five minutes. Then stop and critique the activity. Change roles in the triad and repeat two more times.

2. Have one person role play the part of a helping professional and several other persons role play the parts of people from a given diverse population. Simulate a group helping session for approximately 20 minutes. Then critique the simulation. Change roles (i.e., of the helping professional) and repeat as time allows.

3. Prepare a critique, individually or with others of an audio or video tape of a session between a helping professional and a person from a particular diverse population.

4. Solicit volunteers from various diverse populations. Role play the part of a helping professional working with them.

These culminating activities should allow helping professionals to put into practice all that they have learned from their previous learning experiences.

Continuous Preparation

Successful completion of each of these preparation stages should result in a helping professional with adequate competencies to undertake unsupervised professional interactions. For many professionals this preservice or inservice training terminates the preparation process. Truly competent professionals, however, continue the preparation process across their professional lifespans through additional training.

This additional training of helping professionals should be a continuation of all aspects of the preservice preparation program (George, 1974). Unfortunately, however, such training typically focuses only on the development of new skills at best and on relearning of old skills at least. To expand continually a helping professional's repertoire of skills is a noble effort, but to develop these skills on a foundation of knowledge which is continually becoming outdated is to diminish greatly their potential utilitarian values. Thus additional training should provide for extension and improvement in all the preparation areas: cognitive knowledge, attitude awareness, experiential interaction, and skill development. To do less is to foster imbalanced professional growth.

CONCLUSION

The professional preparation of helping professionals intending to work with persons from diverse populations presents both unique problems and unique opportunities. It necessitates that helping professionals be prepared to work with persons from any population as well as those from diverse populations; by no means a simple task. On the other hand, something is very special about working with people who have needs, concerns, and problems that are different from those of the majority of society. In this light, also something is very special about preparing helping professionals with the necessary unique skills. On balance, the merits of the rewards far outweigh the disadvantages of the effort involved.

REFERENCES

Banikiotes, P.G. (1975). Personal growth and professional training. *Counselor Education and Supervision, 15*(2), 149-151.

Burke, J.B. (1978). A comment on skill training: Cautions and recommendations. *Counselor Education and Supervision, 17*(3), 230-232.

Calia, V.F. (1974). Systematic human relations training: Appraisal and status. *Counselor Education and Supervision 14*(2), 85-94.

Christensen, C.P. (1984). Effects of cross-cultural training on helper response. *Counselor Education and Supervision, 23*(4), 310-320.

Council for the Accreditation of Counseling and Related Educational Programs. (1986). *Accreditation procedures manual and application for counseling and related educational programs.* Washington, DC: Author.

Dash, E.G. (1975). Counselor competency and the revised ACES standards. *Counselor Education and Supervision, 14*(3), 221-227.

Dinkmeyer, D., & Carlson, J. (1977). Consulting: Training counselors to work with teachers, parents, and administrators. *Counselor Education and Supervision, 16*(3), 172-177.

Draguns, J.G. (1981). Cross-cultural counseling and psycho-therapy: History, issues, and current status. In A.J. Marcella & P.P. Pedersen (Eds.), *Cross-cultural counseling and psychotherapy.* Elmsford, NY: Pergamon.

Fuhrmann, B.S. (1978). Self evaluation: An approach for training counselors. *Counselor Education and Supervision, 17*(4), 315-317.

George, R.L. (1974). Inservice training for counselors: Teaching old dogs new tricks. *Counselor Education and Supervision, 13*(4), 314-315.

Griffith, A.R. (1980). Justification for a Black career development. *Counselor Education and Supervision, 19*(4), 301-310.

Gump, L.R. (1974). Counselor self-awareness and counseling effectiveness. *Counselor Education and Supervision, 13*(4), 263-266.

Holiman, M., & Lauver, P.J. (1987). The counselor culture and client-centered practice. *Counselor Education and Supervision, 26*(3), 184-191.

Hood, A.B., & Arceneaux, C. (1987). Multicultural counseling: Will what you don't know help you? *Counselor Education and Supervision, 26*(3), 173-175.

Hulnick, H.R. (1977). Counselor: Know thyself. *Counselor Education and Supervision, 17*(1), 69-72.

Ivey, A. (1987). Cultural intentionality: The core of effective helping. *Counselor Education and Supervision, 26*(3), 168-172.

Kaneshige, E. (1973). Cultural factors in group counseling and interaction. *Personnel and Guidance Journal, 51,* 407-412.

Lewis, S.O. (1969). (I) Racism encountered in counseling. *Counselor Education and Supervision, 9*(1), 56-58.

Lloyd, A.P. (1987). Multicultural counseling: Does it belong in a counselor education program? *Counselor Education and Supervision, 26*(3), 164-167.

Locke, D.W. (1969). (II) Racism encountered in counseling. *Counselor Education and Supervision, 9*(1), 56-58.

MacGuffie, R.A., & Henderson, H. (1977). A practicum-internship model for counselor training. *Counselor Education and Supervision, 16*(3), 233-236.

McDavis, R.J., & Parker, W.M. (1977). A course on counseling ethnic minorities: A model. *Counselor Education and Supervision, 17*(2), 146-149.

Moracco, J.C. (1977). Counselor as consultant: Some implications for counselor education. *Counselor Education and Supervision, 17*(1), 73-75.

Neimeyer, G.J., & Fukuyama, M. (1984). Exploring the content and structure of cross-cultural attitudes. *Counselor Education and Supervision, 23*(3), 214-224.

Paradis, F.E. (1981). Themes in the training of culturally effective psychotherapists. *Counselor Education and Supervision, 21*(2), 136-152.

Parker, W.M. (1987). Flexibility: A primer for multicultural counseling. *Counselor Education and Supervision, 26*(3), 176-180.

Parker, W.M., Bingham, R.P., & Fukuyama, M. (1985). Improving cross-cultural effectiveness of counselor trainees. *Counselor Education and Supervision, 24*(4), 349-352.

Parker, W.M. Valley, M.M., & Geary, C.A. (1986). Acquiring cultural knowledge for counselors in training: A multifacited approach. *Counselor Education and Supervision, 26*(1), 61-71.

Pedersen, P., Holwill, C.F., & Shapiro, J. (1978). A cross-cultural procedure for classes in counselor education. *Counselor Education and Supervision, 17*(3), 233-236.

Pedersen, P., Lonner, W., & Draguns, J. (Eds.). (1976). *Counseling across cultures.* Honolulu: University of Hawaii.

Rustad, K. (1975). Promoting psychological growth in a high school classroom. *Counselor Education and Supervision, 14*(4), 277-285.

Samuda, R.J. (1975). Psychological testing of American minorities. New York: Dodd, Mead and Company.

Sweeney, T.J. (1979). Trends that will influence counselor preparation in the 1980's. *Counselor Education and Supervision, 18*(3), 181-189.

Woods, E. (1977). Counseling minority students: A program model. *Personnel and Guidance Journal, 55,* 416-418.

INDEX

INDEX

G

H

O

Oberstone, A.K. 72, 87
Ochberg, F.M. 247, 260
Office of Special Concerns 245, 246, 247, 249, 261
Ogawa, D. 246, 261
Older Americans Act 194, 206-7
Older persons
    See persons, older
One-Person Family Therapy 276
Ong, P. 248, 261
O'Shaughnessy, M. 21, 27
O'Shea, A.J. 278, 287
Owan, T.C. 237

P

Padesky, C. 77, 88
Padilla, A.M. 232, 237
Page, J.B. 282, 287
Paguio, L.P. 98, 105
Paradis, F.E. 328, 329, 334, 340
Paraplegic 172
    counseling 177-8
    normalization 176-9
    personality 175
    poem 176
Parent, single 89-104
    career needs 99
    finanaces 99
    helping professional's role 101-4
    intimacy 98-9
    numbers 82-3
    population 92-3
    problems 93-100
    public policy 100
    single parent family 96-7
    special services 100
    standard of living 93
Parker, W. M. 25, 27, 127-8, 320, 324, 326, 328, 329, 330, 332, 334, 340
Pedersen, P. 19, 25, 27, 323, 327, 339, 340
Penn, W. 45, 51
Peplau, L.A. 77, 88
Perceptions
    Asian-Americans 242-3
    communication 21

prejudice 21
    stereotyping 21
Perez, L. 268, 269, 287
Perez-Vidal, A. 276, 288
Persons
    needs of older minority 206
Persons, older 189-216
    ability to learn 199
    aging 194-7
    cases 192-3
    counseling 211-2, 215-6
    counseling needs 201-6
    definition 193-4
    demographic characteristics 195
    disengagement 198
    employment 196
    formal education 196
    health 196-7
    helping professional's roles 209-11
    inflexibility 199
    marital status 195-6
    race 195-6
    role performance 209-11
    senility 199-200
    serenity 201
    services 206-9
    sex 195-6
    sexual activity 200-1
    stereotypes 197-201
    support system 213-4
    unproductiveness 198
Persons, southeast Asian 219-36
    See Asian persons, southeast 219-36
Persons with disability
    advocacy 185
    assumptions, basic 182-3
    body requirements 184
    cases 177-9
    counseling 177-8
    current problems 173-6
    daily functions to address 183
    educational programs 179-81
    feelings 175
    helping professional's role 182-4
    mobility 183
    normalization 176-9
    personal disposition 184
    personality 175

S

Saddock, B.J. 87
Saghir, M.T. 69, 88
Sakheim, D.K. 70, 88
Samuda, R.J. 322, 340
Sandoval, M.C. 269, 287
Santisteban, D. 276, 280, 281, 284, 287, 288
Santrock, J.W. 97, 105
Schaie, K. 199, 217
Schutz, A. 22, 27
Schwartz, P. 66, 85
Scopetta, M.A. 274, 275, 277, 283, 288
Seating
    sense of space 20
Seaver, J.E. 110, 126
Sees koffee 41
Self-concept
    Amish 55-6
    Mexican-Americans 301-3
Self-reliance
    Asian-Americans 252
Seneca Indians 110
Senile 199-200
Senility
    persons, older 199-200
Senior Action in a Gay Environment (SAGE) 73
Sensitivity
    Asian-Americans 242-3
Serenity
    persons, older 201
Services
    older persons 206-9
    persons with disability 184-6
Sexual activity
    persons, older 201
Shanley, P. 66
Shapiro, J. 327, 340
Sheen, P. 98, 105
Shelton, B. 203, 206, 217
Silverstein, C. 75, 83, 88
Singlehood
    stigma 93-4
Skill development
    active listening 331-2
    confrontation 333
    effective preparation 333
        for counselors 331-3
        group appraisal 332
        individual appraisal 332
        vocabulary adjustment 332
Sloan, I. 132, 149
Smith, D. 72, 88
Smith, E.L. 54, 59
Smith, K. 72, 86
Smyth, A.H. 125, 126
Soddy, K. 23, 27
Sollenberger, R.T. 253, 261
Spees, E. 65, 88
Spencer, F. 280, 281, 288
Stein, K.M. 255, 260
Stereotypes
    older persons 197-201
Stereotyping
    perceptions 21
Stonewall bar 82
Street Tranvestite Action Revolutionaries (STAR) 82
Stress
    Asian-Americans 249-50
Strodtbeck, F. 17, 20, 27
Stuffle, C.R. 54, 59
Sturgis, T. 74, 85
Sue, D.M. 134, 135, 149, 150, 239-40, 247, 250, 254, 255, 256, 261, 262
Sue, D.W. 25, 27, 242, 243, 247, 250, 252, 253, 255, 256, 258, 261, 262
Sue, S. 247, 251, 254, 255, 256, 257, 258, 260, 261, 262
Sukoneck, H 72, 87
Support systems
    See systems, support
Sweeney, T.J. 323, 340
Systems, support 213-4
    educational 213
    health 214
    services 214
    social 213-4
Szapocznik, J. 274, 275, 276, 277, 280, 281, 283, 288
Szasz, T.S. 186, 187

T

Taft, R. 22, 27
Tashima, N. 244, 262
Teaching
    counseling 324

ABOUT
THE
AUTHORS

NICHOLAS A. VACC, Ed.D.

Dr. Nicholas A. Vacc is a Professor, and a Chairperson of the Department of Counseling and Specialized Educational Development at the University of North Carolina, Greensboro. He received his degrees from Western Reserve University, Syracuse University, and State University of New York. Prior employment includes being a teacher, school psychologist, VA Counselor, Director of Counseling, and University Professor. For four years, Dr. Vacc served on the Chautauqua County Mental Health Board and was chairman of the Subcommittee on Mental Retardation. He was a member of the Board of Visitors of the J.N. Adam Developmental Center, a state residential unit for the developmentally disabled. In addition, he has served as a consultant to programs and agencies serving special populations. Dr. Vacc has a special interest in research with emotionally handicapped children. He is actively involved in the American Association for Counseling and Development and the Council for Exceptional Children.

JOE WITTMER, Ph.D.

Joe Wittmer, reared in the Old Order horse-and-buggy Amish faith in Indiana until age 16, holds a Ph.D. from Indiana State University in Psychological Services. Prior to earning the Ph.D. in 1968, he was a teacher-counselor and guidance director in Fort Wayne, Indiana, schools. Dr. Wittmer also worked in the National Teacher Corps Program in the slums of Gary, Indiana, for two years. He is currently Professor and Chairperson, in the Department of Counselor Education at the University of Florida.

Dr. Wittmer's professional interests include writing and consultation in interpersonal communication. He has co-authored three books and has published more than eighty-five articles in refereed journals.

Dr. Wittmer has been vice-chairperson of the National Committee for Amish Religious Freedom since 1970 and has been actively involved in litigation activities concerning their religious freedom.

Susan B. DeVaney, M.Ed.

Susan DeVaney received her masters degree in counseling from the University of North Carolina at Greensboro where she is a doctoral candidate, teaching assistant, and student supervisor in the Department of Counseling and Specialized Educational Development. A former public school teacher and business partner, her special interests include exercise psychology and career development. A single parent, she shares custody of her two teenaged sons with their father.